Praise for *Pray For Them: The True Story of a Racist White Christian Called to Black Seminary*

"Absolutely brilliant... excruciatingly honest."

-Indies Today

"Truly thought-provoking and brutally forthright... I highly recommend this book."

-The International Review of Books

"Hard-hitting... refreshingly honest... unique and intentional."

-BookLife

"I would never read a book like this. But, because my wife wrote it, I sort of had to. I could not put it down."

-Trisha Fenimore's husband

Pray For Them

PRAY

FOR

THEM

"IT'S SO HARD
NOT TO BECOME THE THING
WE GREW UP SEEING"

THE TRUE STORY of
A RACIST WHITE CHRISTIAN
CALLED TO BLACK SEMINARY

TRISHA
FENIMORE

PUBLISHED BY
PAPER THOUGHTS PUBLISHING
NEW YORK, USA

Scripture taken from the New King James Version®. Copyright © 1982 by Thomas Nelson. Used by permission. All rights reserved.

Excerpt from Oprah's Master Class printed with permission of Harpo, Inc.

This book is a memoir. It reflects the author's present recollections of experiences over time. Some names and characteristics have been changed, some events have been compressed, some timelines have been shifted, some characters have been amalgamated, and some dialogue has been recreated.

The conversations contained in this book all come from the author's recollections and are not written to represent word-for-word transcripts (which would, of course, be impossible to recreate by anybody). Rather, the author has retold the conversations in a way which evokes the feeling and meaning of what was said. In all instances, the essence of the dialogue is accurate.

paperthoughtspublishing.com

ISBN: 979-8-9868599-1-0

Title: Pray For Them

Cover design: Ömer Faruk Yıldız

This book is dedicated to
the real life
"Reverend Doctor Shepherd"

I threw my shoulder into telling this story,
just like you taught me.

AUTHOR'S WARNING

They say if you throw a frog into a pot of boiling water, it will leap out.

But— according to whoever "they" are— if you throw that same frog into a pot of room-temperature water, and then gradually raise the water's temperature over time, the frog doesn't even notice and gets boiled all the same.

PART I is where I get boiled.

The severity of the stories— like the water temperature of our ill-fated amphibious friend— increases gradually over such a stretch that it's hard for the one swimming around in it to notice.

PART I will make you uncomfortable. If you're a good person, PART I will probably make you *very* uncomfortable. That's okay. (After all, you're watching someone get boiled.)

If you cannot stomach reading the stories in PART I any further, I suppose you can skip ahead to PART II, where the story picks up on the day I realized I had become racist.

But be warned: each story in PART I is addressed later in the book. Without reading it in its entirety, you will not truly experience my story. It would be my preference that you read all of PART I. But, if you cannot, I understand.

After all, it's hard watching someone get boiled.

CONTENTS

PART I: LEARNING RACISM

"He wears a mask, and his face grows to fit it."
George Orwell, *Shooting an Elephant*

Fall 1993
In honor of the NYPD banning chokeholds
November that same year

The first time I heard that word, I was six.

My grandmother was eighty-four years old at the time and the sweetest person I'd met in my entire— albeit short— life.

She never reached even five feet tall and despite suffering horrific loss, like losing a son in a car accident and, later, her husband to suicide, I had never seen or heard her be unkind to anybody before or after the incident I am about to tell you.

Unlike the house I grew up in, her home was a cheerful place, filled with weighty, ornate glass dishes on wooden coffee tables, wildly patterned orange and green armchairs, and an endless supply of costume jewelry with which she tirelessly allowed me to play dress up.

I loved being around her. She was gentle, funny, and kind.

"Grandma GiGi," as we called her, was born just after 1900 and always had peanut M&Ms in a pink and clear plastic bubblegum dispenser on the white laminate table in her small (evidently appropriately) all-white kitchen.

Every time I was over to see her, she would cook me a meal in which every food group was represented at least once. Then, for the duration of the visit, we would snack on things like Chex Mix, yogurt-covered raisins, Cracker Jack, and yes, the peanut M&Ms. She called the ever-rotating assortment of snacks "fiddle-faddle," and we would enjoy the treats while we played games like Gin Rummy, Go Fish, and Old Maid. She would always let me win.

I loved every moment of my time with her.

For as many evenings as I'd spent laughing in her balmy home, I only remember two nights in particular. The first was the night of the citywide power outage, where she and I sat in a pitch black house together for over an hour. The second was *this* night...

My parents were at a sporting event of my older sister's and they had dropped me off at Grandma GiGi's, which was usually how it went.

The constantly-sweatered old woman and I were trying to determine who would go first in the game "Uno." As I placed my little, pale fist next to her wrinkled and veiny one, she began to point alternatively from mine to hers, while reciting what began as a familiar rhyme:

"Eenie, meenie, miny, mo," she sang in a low tone.

I watched her crooked finger continue to point.

*"Catch a **that word** by the toe..."*

My tiny fist seized.

"If he hollers..."

She sang, still pointing back and forth with a nude-painted fingernail.

"...*let him go.*"

I felt the inside of my small body tense further.

"*Eenie...*"

"*Meenie...*"

"*Miny...*"

"*Mo.*"

I forget whose fist she landed on.

But I'll never forget the way I felt.

I had never heard that word before, yet as soon as the sound of it hit my innocent ears, I knew it was bad.

I could just... *tell.*

My blonde eyebrows furrowed, confused, as we leaned in and began playing our game. But I said nothing.

At least until the next morning...

"Hey Mom, what's a **that word**?"

I watched my mother's body jolt over the kitchen sink, as she dropped the syrup-coated porcelain plate from her hands. A clatter rang out as it landed on the other dirty plates beneath her.

4

She turned to me with even wider eyes than usual.

All I could hear was the sound of running water while she stared at me.

"*What* did you just say?" she finally sought to clarify.

"Uh... umm," I stammered, "a... a **that**... **word**... I, uh..."

I told her, slowly and nervously, what had happened the night before, feeling as though I was finally confessing to the police about a crime I'd witnessed and, in some weird way, even helped commit. Every moment which had passed since hearing that word made me feel more and more to blame for it.

> Though, to be fair, when your parents fight miserably, yet boast that they are "staying together for the kids," guilt is not a far-off emotion at any given point.

My mother stepped away from the running water at the sink and whipped her tan kitchen towel over her right shoulder, the way she always did as she whisked from one task to the next. I watched her shoulder-length blonde hair blow back from the momentum of this particular whip.

She walked over to me, as I was still seated at the breakfast table, and knelt down on our hardwood floor to my level, looking seriously into the pale eyes I inherited from her.

The water continued to run.

I felt her hands lay themselves gently on my narrow white shoulders, as she carefully explained that *that* word was a very bad word... a very *mean* word used to describe black people, and that we *never* say it.

I asked her why Grandma GiGi did.

She rolled her eyes theatrically and jutted out her chin with visible anger toward the old woman whom she already had a considerable amount of resentment toward.

She took a heavy breath and raised herself back up again to stand.

"Grandma GiGi was born in a different time," she told me plainly, "and they had different ways of behaving back then."

I didn't understand. But, again, I said nothing.

I simply nodded as though I did, then watched her lift the damp towel off her shoulder and return to the waiting dishes in the sink.

Later that night, I would hear her and my father arguing about how he needs to speak to his mother before I'd be allowed to go see Grandma GiGi again.

He told her it was unnecessary. She yelled back, asking if he was crazy.

I didn't mean to start any trouble.

Late Winter 1995
In memory of Jonny Gammage
Pittsburgh, PA

It was nearly Christmas, and Nickelodeon had been airing toy commercials on loop without mercy for the last few months.

My tender eight-year-old heart yearned to be only two things when I grew up: a mommy and the next Mariah Carey.

Since my own mother had recently— and rather ruthlessly— informed me that I didn't have the singing ability to become the next Mariah Carey, I ached for almost every new babydoll advertised between episodes of All That and Doug.

Maybe eight years old is too old for babydolls, I would occasionally worry.

But I didn't have my dream of becoming Mariah Carey to fall back on anymore, so Newborn Nancy would have to do...

One thing I always noticed back then was that all babydoll commercials were the same.

They always showed a blonde-haired, blue-eyed, peach-faced babydoll being happily cradled and fed by seemingly the same young, generic, brunette white girl.

7

Then it would show the young girl skipping about, as she rolled the doll around in the $12.99 add-on stroller.

And then, at the *very* end, in what always looked like an odd split-screen comparison, as well as mere afterthought, the doll commercial would flash the blonde-haired doll with her ripe pink cheeks on one side of the screen, contrasted with a dark-haired, dark-skinned, dark-eyed babydoll on the other.

They both wore the same pale pink cotton outfits and pink satin ribbons in their hair. And they both posed with the same pink binkies and bottles.

Both just sat there while we stared at them.

My young eyes always drew toward the dark babydoll: the stranger.

Who was that doll? We hadn't met her during the commercial...

"Mom, I want the dark one," I pointed to the living room TV one afternoon, hoping my mother had not yet completed all of our Christmas shopping.

She looked up from the mail she had been opening at the kitchen counter.

"Not the blonde one," I volunteered, eagerly.

I watched my mother blink hard.

"No."

Her gaze returned to the envelope she was wrestling with, as my tiny jaw dropped.

"Wha... *why?*"

"You want the *black* babydoll?" she set down the envelope and looked up incredulously on what had been a run-of-the-mill Saturday until this, evidently, treasonous moment.

I nodded so hard my little cheeks jiggled.

Up to that point, the only black person ever invited into our home was Oprah Winfrey on weekday afternoons.

"Why?" she asked with genuine bewilderment.

"Because all my babydolls look the same," I chirped, ignorantly believing I was making progress with her, "I want one that looks different."

"No," she immediately restated, returning her focus sharply to the mail.

"But *why?*"

She didn't even look back up.

"Because I said so."

My blonde pigtails dropped, along with my heart.

That was the end of the conversation.

That line was *always* the end of the conversation.

When Christmas morning finally arrived, I unwrapped yet another blonde-haired, blue-eyed, peach-faced babydoll, and I wondered which lucky mommy received the black babydoll I had wanted, but was not allowed to have.

The second time I heard that word, I was in fourth grade.

I was in one of only a handful of geography lessons I would ever receive during my rural, public school education.

My teacher had a clear slide of Africa pulled up on the projector. Every nation's borders were outlined, and each country was labeled.

I stared at the shape of the far-off land, painfully picking at the skin around my fingernails and trying to sound out the foreign names in my head before Mrs. Cooper told us their correct pronunciations.

"And this one is camer-OON," she pointed to the word with the lid of her yellow Sharpie marker.

She moved the Sharpie, as her cheap bracelets jangled noisily.

"And ny-JEER-ee-yah," she pointed to the other outline and its name.

Then the shadow of her marker slid up.

"And this one..."

"IS **THAT WORD**!" Reed Jacobs shouted wildly from the back row.

11

White was the face of every child in the room, but not from horror at Reed's outburst.

Instead, there was an eruption of children snickering and feverish whispering.

Reed was easily the skinniest kid in our class. From the rumors I had heard, he had terrible ADHD and, depending on the time of day, was either completely catatonic or sliding around the room on his knees, shouting wildly, while Mrs. Cooper tried fruitlessly to command order.

I remember my jaw dropping and turning to my then-best friend Hayley, who mirrored my expression back to me.

After all, we never *ever* say *that* word.

Mrs. Cooper said nothing, as the entertained whispers and giggles around the classroom continued, except: "Reed, it's pronounced ny-JEER."

Reed shot a shit-eating grin to us, his audience.

"LOOKS LIKE **THAT WORD** TO ME!"

Mrs. Cooper rolled her tired eyes and, while doing so, glanced up at the black and white clock above the classroom door.

Class continued as usual, and I lost count of how many times I heard the word after that.

The next year in school, I became an atheist.

I had recently been declared "gifted" and enrolled in a program for select students from the three local elementary schools who were considered, by their teachers, to possess above average intelligence and may benefit from extra challenge.

We would arrive at the junior high once a week, by bus from our respective elementary schools.

I was one of only four girls in the group of sixteen children.

And the entire group was white, except for Tiya Bhatt, who was both Indian *and* a girl.

None of those proportions struck me as odd at the time, even though I knew the *other* two elementary schools had black children and obviously all three were about half female.

As it happened, all four of the girls came from *my* elementary school. One was a girl that the other three of us didn't speak to much, one was me, one was Tiya, who had recently told us what being a vegetarian was like, and the fourth was my good friend, Brooke.

13

One day, while we worked on algebraic word problems, Brooke told me that her family didn't pray or go to church.

I asked why.

"We're atheists," she informed me, "We don't believe in God."

I'll admit, I was jealous.

If I didn't believe in God, that would mean I'd never have to go to church again.

Church was always the worst part of my week.

My family would bicker relentlessly the whole ride there, always arguing about who was most responsible for us being late *that* week, and then we'd sheepishly sneak into empty back pews during the First or Second Reading, depending on just *how* late we were.

Once seated, we were told by my mother to sit up straight and "pay attention."

It was there I began the habit of picking at the skin around my cuticles when I grew bored and restless in the hard, wooden pews. My fingers would often bleed as a result, and then my lone focus would be to stop the bleeding before it was time for everybody to shake hands... which was, frankly, always a more interesting task than listening to the Gospel.

On the way home, my father would always remark to us how attractive the reader Isabelle was or, if another person was reading that day, how much he missed seeing Isabelle up at the podium.

Church was hell.

Plus, the Sunday School teachers never seemed to like me much.

I was always asking pesky questions, like "Why?" And they could never give me any firm answers, other than the canned response: "You just have to have *faith*."

No church and no Sunday School sounded like Heaven to me.

When I went home that night, I asked my mother as she cleaned the dinner plates if people who didn't believe in God were allowed to go Heaven.

Staring down at the plate she was scrubbing, she asked me why, and I told her about my close friend's family.

To her credit, she did not traumatize me with doctrine detailing Brooke and her loved ones burning in eternal hellfire. Instead she told me that God judges people based on their hearts, and if Brooke had a good heart, she would make it into Heaven. And so would her family.

Being as smart as all my teachers told me I was and believing I could maintain a good enough heart on my own (how hard could *that* be?), I decided then I had no further use for the concept of God, which, frankly, never made much sense to me anyway.

I guess I'm an atheist now, too, I remember thinking.

The next day, I returned to my usual fifth grade class and when we all recited the Pledge of Allegiance, I said every word except two: "under God."

I would continue that ritual of omission each morning throughout my entire remaining public school career.

Early Winter 1999
In memory of Amadou Diallo
New York City, NY

The following year, my family took a trip to New York City.

My rural Midwestern eyes had never seen anything like it and as soon as they did, I knew I was destined to end up there.

I could just... *tell.*

I don't remember much from that trip.

I remember taking a picture with my sister in the lobby of the Empire State Building, but not going to the top because my father said it was too expensive.

I remember walking through Times Square, amazed by the bright lights and how different everybody looked from each other.

And I remember that every time we loaded into a subway car filled with varying shades of brown faces, my mother would silently turn her engagement ring to hide the otherwise out-facing diamond in her palm.

I don't remember much from that trip.

But I remember that.

Spring 2000
In memory of Malcolm Ferguson,
who had been arrested the week prior to his own
death while protesting the acquittal of the four police
officers responsible for the death of Amadou Diallo,
who the last chapter was dedicated to
New York City, NY

I loved going to Jenna's house.

Her older brother, Steve, was a senior in high school and the most handsome guy I had ever laid eyes on.

He had dark brown hair and piercing hazel eyes.

Anytime he'd walk through the room, I was captivated.

I don't think he ever even knew my name.

One day, Jenna and I were watching TV in their living room after school, while Steve ate a sandwich at the kitchen table in the next room.

Since the living room and kitchen were joined, I was basically sitting in the same room as him for the first time.

"Did you hear about that girl in the high school?" Jenna queried, snapping me from my dreamy— and quite unsubtle— gaze toward an ambivalent Steve, "The cheerleader?"

"Huh?" I turned my adolescent eyes toward her, "No."

An uncensored episode of Taxicab Confessions played in the background since Jenna's parents paid extra for HBO. Her parents were rarely home, which always made going to her house feel taboo.

"She's pregnant by one of the black boys."

I blinked a few times at her.

"She's white," Jenna clarified to me.

I blinked again.

"Oh," my voice answered in a surprised tone.

"Good," Steve muttered from fifteen feet away, still chewing his ham sandwich.

Jenna and I looked up at him.

"What?" she asked her older brother.

"Good," he repeated firmly, finally looking up at us.

The look in his eyes was very different from the gaze I so-often fantasized about him giving me.

"I thought you would be against that because he's black and she's white."

He stared at his sister with a small smirk.

"Water down the black genes with white. The more that happens, the less full black there is."

"That's stupid," she retorted quickly, "because then the less full white there is."

"White isn't the side causing all the problems, Jenna," he nearly yelled, "Black needs diluting. I don't care how it happens."

We stared at him.

He went back to eating his sandwich, and a man with a thick New York accent admitted in the background that he was "high as hell" and on his way to work, as a Rescue Squad member for the NYPD.

Fall 2000
In memory of Alfred Sanders
Minneapolis, MN

In seventh grade, I liked a black boy.

The junior high merged our city's three elementary schools, and for the first time, I was attending school with black kids.

Up to then, I had been at the "rich" elementary school, which was all-white, except for Tiya and her younger sister.

In the short time I'd been at the new school, I developed a crush on a boy named Terrell Jackson.

He was funny, silly, and happy.

He had an older brother and a single mom, and every time he walked into a room, he could somehow make everyone in it laugh.

He was a walking firecracker, always confident and able to make me smile on even my toughest day.

A week earlier, at Alex Fallon's thirteenth birthday party, Terrell and I held hands.

I remember a few kids stared, as he and I sat on top of a plastic folding table, fingers laced in the dark, strobe-lit room of the Kiwanis Club.

We sat there for nearly two hours, simply holding hands.

I'll never forget how dark his hand looked holding my pale one.

He showed me his keychains, and I occasionally commented on whether or not I liked the song that was playing.

My heart raced the whole time.

Half of me was nervous about what the chaperones and other kids were thinking— if word would get back to my parents— and the other half was growing anxious about my deepening feelings toward him.

Throughout our entire junior high and eventually high school careers, Alex would become known for throwing the best parties in town.

It's funny, though...

I don't remember anything about any of his locally-famous birthday parties aside from that two-hour stretch at his thirteenth, where Terrell and I held hands in relative silence near the sporadically foggy dance floor.

One week after Alex's thirteenth birthday party, on a snowy Saturday, I sat in the passenger's seat of my mother's Mazda Tribute, while the two of us drove up to the mall.

My mother was a teacher in the neighboring school district and had just asked me, seemingly in passing, who I had a crush on at school.

I blushed nervously.

Looking over with eager eyes, I naively confided to her how fast my heart beat around Terrell. I told her how happy I felt every time I was around him.

I shared with her how disappointed I was that he and I only had one period together, but added optimistically: "At least it's study hall, so we can sometimes talk."

My mother looked away from the road and over at me, staring in earnest for a moment, then proceeded to speak in a low, serious tone.

I could tell her words were measured, although in hindsight, I'm not sure with which unit she had been measuring.

"Trisha," she began in a foreboding tone, "I understand how exciting it can be to have a crush on somebody new."

I smiled excitedly, feeling the familiar rush of relief we all experience when we confide in somebody about our crushes.

But she continued.

"Have you told anyone else about this crush of yours?"

"Not yet," I answered, as my eyes briefly gazed past her to the snowflakes quietly landing then melting on the glass of the driver's side window.

She nodded, while staring out seriously at the nearly empty road.

The feeling in the car began to shift, and I suddenly became very uncomfortable.

"Look at the high school..." she finally spoke.

And I listened to her, while Faith Hill sang quietly in the background.

"There are always a few girls who become pregnant each year, and their *whole* lives are ruined."

I continued to listen.

"And in many of those cases, the father is black."

My fingers began picking at the skin around my other fingers.

"I'm not saying you shouldn't be friends with Terrell," my mother graciously extended to me, "but, if I could make a suggestion, I would keep it at just that. You don't want your life ruined like those girls in the high school, especially like that cheerleader recently, who had to quit cheerleading."

I, a first-year cheerleader, nodded at the windshield, suddenly very fearful.

"And I would *certainly* never tell anyone else about this," she paused, "especially not your father."

I listened to her that day and stopped talking to Terrell altogether.

> Years later, at my high school graduation, it was with a hollow sort of sadness, as I watched Terrell walk up to collect his diploma, that I realized he had never impregnated— or even dated— anybody at all.

> And, like so many before and after me, I wondered what might have been...

Late Winter 2000
In memory of Prince Jones Jr.
Fairfax County, VA

"My dad asked me to watch porn with him again last night," Candice wrinkled her nose to the semi-circle of six other white girls.

"WHAT?" I turned toward her, horrified.

My look of revulsion faded when her brown eyes darted angrily at me.

"Sorry," I looked down, "I ain't mean nothin' by it."

The white girls from the poor side of town were the earliest bloomers in our newly-blended class and, thus, the most popular.

Being so flat-chested I was nearly concave, I had been trying to speak like they did, in the hope that some of their popularity would mercifully rub off on me.

> In elementary school, I used to lecture other children on the playground how "ain't" wasn't a real word, echoing my mother's teachings to me, and now I was using it daily in an attempt to fit in. Desperate people do desperate things.

Candice rolled her heavily-lined eyes at me, and the other cool girls dismissively shook their heads, as she continued her jarring story.

"I walked in last night and he was on the couch, watchin' it again," she recounted, shrugging as though such a thing were a normal occurrence in her household, "He asked if I wanted to sit beside him and watch it. I said 'no' and just went upstairs."

She rolled her exhausted young eyes again, this time in reference to her pedophile father instead of me, but seemingly with equal disdain for us both.

> I had, also, started to wear my eyeliner like her and the other cool girls, but my own father told me I looked "like a skank" and grounded me until I stopped. This only inspired me to bring the eyeliner to school *with me,* then wash it off before I went home, but I digress...

"I heard him and my mom havin' sex in the shower later that night. They're always so loud. It's nasty."

A few others in the group nodded sympathetically, including Crystal who, also, showed signs of sexual abuse by her father, but never vocalized anything like Candice did. At least, not to me.

"After they was finished, he walked out in his towel and yelled at me that he ain't want me hangin' out with the **that word** boys in the neighborhood anymore," Candice recalled, side-eyeing the group, "He don't know me and André been hangin' out, and I ain't gonna stop."

Crystal chimed in.

"My dad said I gotta stop hangin' out with Tyrone, but I'm not gonna either."

The two nodded in solidarity with one another.

As I looked around the semi-circle, I remember thinking: *Maybe Candice and Crystal are so repulsed by their white criminal fathers, they simply want the opposite and are trying to find it in the black guys their fathers forbid them from seeing.*

Spring 2001
In honor of Officer Robert Byrd
Washington, D.C.

The day we watched "Amistad" in History class was awkward.

Mr. Killner was the only black teacher in the whole school, and he insisted on the importance of the film.

I always liked Mr. Killner. On the very first day of his class, he told us how there were only "some coins and a few History books" in his desk. He told us he didn't care if we sat in his chair just so long as we didn't steal the books.

"If you take my quarters," he added with a sly smile, "it's cool. I'll just assume you need them more than I do."

He always seemed so happy. But this day in class was different...

There were four black kids in the class, one of whom was only half-black.

The hard plastic chair beneath me was even more uncomfortable than usual and seemed to have come alive, I heard it shift so many times.

I assumed it was awkward for the black kids by their sad, tense silence and dejected facial expressions.

And I *know* it was awkward for the white kids because it was certainly awkward for me.

29

I looked around the room at all the other white students.

None of us really knew what to say, but we all looked constipated with a shame which refused to pass.

We were children, but we were about to face a very adult— very unconscious— choice.

The shocking violence of the movie essentially told us, "Back in the day, our entire world was centered around the idea that white people were better than black people. And, oh-by-the-way, your ancestors were likely in on it, too..."

And then, seemingly right after, the bell rang and we were all expected to simply go back to our normal lives, our normal social exchanges, and our normal, inane preteen thought patterns.

The movie basically told our integrated class that white people had committed the worst crimes against humanity imaginable against black people... *Now go and play nice.*

And then we, white children, were expected to do *what?*

I remember walking out of the classroom that day glass-eyed.

Am I better than the black kids?

I'd be lying to you if I said it didn't cross my mind.

(More than once.)

After all, our whole *world* had been built around the idea.

Could that many people be wrong?

It, also, felt *good* to believe such a thing, like I'd somehow accomplished something.

Although, I'll admit, it also felt a bit too easy... like a gold medal for a sporting event you cheated at or didn't even bother showing up to at all.

So I kept thinking.

Were my ancestors evil people who believed stupid things? Does that mean I'm stupid and evil since I come from them? And if I'm stupid and evil, wouldn't I be the inferior one?

I knew I wasn't stupid. After all, my teachers called me "gifted."

And I didn't *feel* evil.

The jarring disconnect between my ancestors' alleged beliefs and my own discernable, though increasingly cloudy, conscience raised an even bigger question.

The white child's choice— my choice— essentially boiled down to this: I'm better than *somebody*. Who is it... people who don't look like me or my own family?

I sat, wondering who I should defend: my ancestors or total strangers.

Yet, even though I descended from them, were not my ancestors strangers, too, in the sense that I had never met them?

My mind tossed and turned over itself.

I don't know what the black kids thought about the movie. I never asked them.

I was too busy worrying about my own rank in the system.

The racism in my hometown had a strange past, like it does anywhere, I guess.

Most rural high schools around ours had one— *maybe* two— black kids in the entire school.

Our school had exponentially more black kids than all the other schools around us combined. I have no idea why.

My father was born and raised in that little town. According to him, that's how it had always been.

He told me once how, back when he was in high school, the basketball team was primed for State, but the black players began boycotting and sitting out games.

They were protesting the fact there had never been a black prom queen elected.

As a result, the promising team started losing... not by a few buckets either, but double-digit blowout losses.

Because not a single black player would step foot onto the court, including a few of the team's best starters, the team lost their chance to qualify for playoffs altogether.

And since athletics were the only thing our school was ever any good at, the school administration was flooded with phone calls from town residents when the team lost its playoff opportunity.

'Get the team under control,' seemed to be the general message of most callers.

"The callers were white, right?" I asked my father.

"Oh yeah," he furrowed his brows and nodded confidently.

As he told it, the school administration was under tremendous pressure "from the town" and knew it needed to act, so they simply did away with homecoming and prom courts altogether.

Our school had never had them since.

When my father told me what the administration did, I remember thinking how wild it was that they just *changed the rules* to eliminate the conversation altogether.

That wasn't the last time racial issues had played out through sports in my town.

When I was in school, it was J.J. Jackson, Terrell's older cousin.

He was one of our starting basketball players and one January afternoon, Keith Moore called him a "**that word**" in the hallway during an argument.

Even though I've always hated the term, Keith was, by anyone's definition, "white trash."

I didn't hear the argument.

I don't know who all did.

All I remember is that the whole school was buzzing how J.J. and some of the other black kids were going to beat the ever-living shit out of Keith after school.

I remember hearing whispers how the varsity basketball coach, who was also black, caught wind of it and became involved. Then the gossip just vanished.

And the beating never took place.

Keith walked the halls in the coming days, cocky and ignorant as ever.

The thing is: had J.J. beaten Keith up that day— even *off* school property— he would have received out of school suspension for the longest period of time possible, because that's what every student received who took a swing at another under the school's "zero tolerance for violence" policy.

And J.J. wouldn't have been able to play basketball.

And the whole town knew a D1 college in the next county was looking to recruit J.J., while Keith, on the other hand, had nothing on his horizon.

I never liked Keith much.

During my first month at the high school, I walked into the study hall room as a shy freshman to deliver a note to the monitor from my algebra teacher. I had been wearing pigtails, and from the back of the room, Keith shouted to at least fifty kids: "What do you call a blonde with pigtails? ...HANDLEBARS!"

Most of the male students laughed, as the apathetic study hall monitor plucked the note from my hand with her long red fingernails and lazily told Keith to "keep it down" instead of rightfully giving him detention.

I never felt justice had been served for his degrading remarks.

I, also, never wore pigtails to school again after that.

The black kids and I were *both* disappointed when Keith escaped his beating.

Summer 2003
In honor of Diane Bond
Chicago, IL

I adjusted my long blonde ponytail then turned, as the rest of the varsity volleyball team prepared in front of their respective lockers.

Lifting my right running shoe onto the wooden bench and tightening its strings, I attempted to mentally brace myself for the bleacher runs we would soon endure in the ninety-degree heat.

Ebony Jones was gorgeous and one of our two star players, both of whom happened to be black. She was a senior, six-feet tall, and had D1 colleges all over the country trying to recruit her.

Ebony stood at the locker next to mine, and out of the corner of my curious eye, I stared at her. She must have felt it, because she turned sharply to me.

"Can I help you?" she asked with a playful smirk, continuing to rub the white cream onto her dark skin.

Her wide brown eyes stared down at me with expectation.

"I, um... I just... I just didn't realize that you..."

And I motioned to the bottle of sunscreen in her hand.

I watched her face as it shifted, finally understanding why I was staring at her.

"Do *you* get darker in the sun?" she replied in a patient but matter-of-fact tone which might as well have asked me '*is* there a sun?'

"Ye-yeah..."

"Okay," she chirped simply, turning back to her locker and closing it, "so do I."

Summer 2004
In honor of Frank Jude Jr. and Lovell Harris
Milwaukee, WI

I'll never forget the day I said that word in front of black people.

My volleyball team was on our way to a scrimmage with the neighboring city's team before the season started.

Since it was summer and before the official school year began, by law, our team had to split up and take a few large vans instead of a traditional school bus. Each van was driven by a different coach.

I was in the van with the head coach, as well as Jessie, Sara, Jada, Jazmine, and Aliyah.

The last three names belonged to some of my black teammates. One younger than me, two older.

I was sitting beside Jada, the only star player left now that Ebony had graduated. We were in the van's furthest row back.

In front of me was Jessie, Jazmine, and Aliyah.

In the passenger's seat was Sara.

Our white head coach was still outside, overseeing the loading process of the other vans.

As the radio hummed the most popular rap song at the time, I will never forget what happened next:

39

All of us were staring out our respective windows, watching the rest of our teammates mill about, as a few of us quietly sang along with the rapper...

As soon as the verse escaped my lips, all singing in the van stopped.

My jaw dropped, and my green eyes went so wide, they nearly popped out of my skull.

In unison, Jada, Jazmine, and Aliyah whipped their heads around and stared at me with similar expressions.

The song continued to play quietly in the background, unaware of what just happened.

My teammates' mouths hung open, clearly stunned I had the audacity to sing that lyric.

"I... I'm so... *so* sorry," I stammered, blinking hard.

How could I have done something so stupid?!

I only sang that part when I was alone or with other white people.

It's like I was on autopilot or something.

I had been too busy watching our assistant coach toss the ball bag into her van's trunk.

What an idiot I am!

"I'm really sorry," I repeated to all the expectant brown eyes.

Silence for another moment, and then...

Instantly, the three young black women erupted into laughter.

To this day, I have no idea why.

But I chuckled awkwardly with them, as they each turned around and kept on singing.

I, obviously, did not.

"HER HAIR!"

"Oh my God, look at it!"

"Why is it *like* that?!"

"Trisha, look!"

I turned to see our token black friend with her relaxed hair sticking straight up to the ceiling. Evidently, she had removed her ponytail holder and her hair just... *stayed* like that.

"Oh, wow!" my face crinkled, as I walked over to the sofa where they all were seated.

Becc was half-black and in a moment of candor a few weeks prior, had told me she felt more comfortable with white people than black people because the black kids always told her she was "too white."

She was the kind of black girl you'd hear speak on the telephone and think she was white.

She had, also however, added she often felt "too black" for us.

I conveniently forgot about that conversation and, again, became the living embodiment of it.

"Is it from hairspray?" I asked her, searching for an explanation which made sense to my brain.

Becc laughed, shaking her head, and repeated the new party trick again for her incredulous audience.

I laughed, head cocked to the side and jaw wide, amazed and confused.

For as many black girls as I went to school with, I'd never seen black hair up-close before that day.

> Becc and I would stay in touch after high school. A few years later, she came from her college to visit me at mine donning a gorgeous, natural Afro.

Fall 2005
In memory and honor of the six victims of the
Danziger Bridge Shootings
New Orleans, LA

"This is America," our white teacher fiercely reminded her entirely-white Advanced Placement English class, "What we are seeing on the news of what is happening down in New Orleans is not even *close* to being okay."

We stared up at her in silence.

"This is America, and the federal, state, and local governments have utterly failed entire communities of people, to arguably *murderous* degrees."

We stared up at her in silence.

"This is not okay, and I hope that tonight when you turn on the news and see people standing on their rooftops, or hear stories of people going to the bathroom in the sinks at the Superdome, you realize that these are *people*."

We stared up at her in silence.

"Same as you and me, even though some of us may look differently from one another."

We stared up at her in silence.

"This is America. And this horror is happening in America *right now*."

That night, I watched the news like most of America.

But instead of feeling compassion, empathy, or the rightful outrage which had been assigned to us as homework, I watched, detached as though it were fiction and sickly fascinated by what fresh horror the news cameras would find next.

I rolled my eyes for the twentieth time.

Every black kid, I thought to myself impatiently.

My graduation capped-head shook itself in judgment.

Dozens of black people yelled and rang cowbells in the audience each time a name of one of my black classmates was called.

The crowd's cheering grew tenfold when the black student walked up and accepted their diploma.

It really isn't that big of a deal, I thought to myself, *It's only high school.*

When I was seven, my mother told me I didn't have a choice whether or not I'd attend college. I had to. She told me the only choice I had was *which* school I would attend and even then, she informed me she had the ability to overrule.

I rolled my eyes, as someone in the audience shook a tambourine.

Maybe it's a big deal for them, I thought.

Maybe graduating high school means a lot to them, I thought.

I thought back to my all-white Advanced Placement classes. My all-white-except-Tiya gifted courses.

46

Maybe it's harder for them... or something, I thought.

Fall 2007
In memory of DeAunta Terrel Farrow
West Memphis, AR

Casey was half black and had one of the best smiles I'd ever seen.

That night, he and I were at the same house party and, after a few rounds of beer pong and flirting, I let him walk me home to my sorority house.

We stood on the front steps and drunkenly kissed, then I pulled back and excused myself inside, to go to sleep.

As the large, heavy door to the massive white mansion sealed closed behind me, my high heels stepped carefully over the Persian rug in our ornate foyer.

Just then, my foggy brain pieced together an interesting observation: *I could accuse Casey of raping me, and he would probably go to prison.*

I shook my head, blinking hard, while awkwardly climbing the stairs.

It's a strange feeling to know you could ruin an innocent person's life if you *really* wanted to.

My head shook again.

I obviously didn't want to.

But it had been just the two of us the whole walk home from the party...

A white woman. And a black man.

I could tell the cops anything, I thought to myself, fairly bemused.

He pushed me into the bushes, Officer...

I climbed the final few stairs.

He pinned me down in an alley and forced himself on me...

I fumbled with my keys, with a smirk on my face.

No evidence? Well, I went home and scrubbed my body raw in the shower, of course, Officer...

It would be his word against mine.

I opened my bedroom door and immediately kicked off my heels.

I could ruin that handsome, charming guy's life if I simply wanted to.

I obviously didn't want to.

But, I realized then, my whim would be the only thing preventing it.

As I fell onto my perpetually unmade bed, I drunkenly chuckled to myself.

Can you imagine?

Spring 2008
In memory of Tarika Wilson and in honor of her
then-one year-old son
Lima, OH

I caused black students to walk out of class once.

> I actually didn't put it together that all four
> students coincidentally walked out at the same
> time— right after I spoke— until years later.
> (That's how oblivious I was.)

The class was "Science, Gender, and Race." It was the
third week of class, and we were discussing slavery in
America.

I raised my hand and began with what I thought was
an appropriate question.

The white professor and all thirty students stared in
silence at me. Naturally, I took their collective
reaction as my cue that I was onto something and
generously expanded upon my point for them.

Silence and more staring.

So I spoke more words into the silence and concluded
my thesis by restating a more detailed version of my
original question.

One black student stood up and walked out.

Then another.

Our professor contributed a mere "Umm..."

To which the third, then fourth and final remaining black student stood up and silently walked out.

The professor never did answer my question. She simply moved on with class, leaving my curiosity unsatisfied.

I can't remember if the four black students ever returned to class that day.

After all, I wasn't paying much attention to them.

Later that evening, I was over at my boyfriend Luke's fraternity house.

"You said that *out loud* in a classroom?" he cackled beneath loose brown curls, barely able to keep his blue eyes open.

"Yeah," I shrugged, growing defensive, "It's a science- and race-based class. That's a science- and race-related question!"

He continued laughing.

"It was a question about genetics and eugenics," I protested to him sincerely, "I feel like everything I asked about is probably true."

"It *is* true," he cried out, wiping hysterical tears from his cheeks, "but you don't say it *out loud!*"

I stared at him.

"And you certainly don't say it," he gasped cheerfully, "around *black people!*"

He sniffled, as another joyful tear escaped the corner of his eye.

"What does that mean?" I asked in earnest, "Why can't I ask about it?"

"What did your professor say?" he happily wept.

"Nothing!" I shouted, "She, like, didn't even address it! I'm *still* annoyed by it!"

"Typical," his tone tightened as he shook his head, "P.C. bullshit."

"Why can't I ask a *question*? I wasn't, like, being racist or saying black people are inferior..."

"What did the black kids in the class say?"

"I don't know," I shrugged, "I think one or two of them went to the bathroom or something."

With that, he fell back onto the couch in a fresh batch of giggles.

I stared at him, mystified and mortified.

"What is so funny?"

"I can't wait to tell the guys this story. It's so good, it's almost not real!"

I shrugged again, ready to put the whole thing to bed.

"Whatever."

"I really wish the professor had said something," he shook his head, once more shifting from humor to anger.

"I wish I'd gotten an *answer*."

Fall 2008
In memory of Lawrence Allen
Philadelphia, PA

Barack Obama was elected President.

I voted for him.

I was thrilled by the idea of telling my future
grandchildren how I "courageously" cast my ballot for
the first black President of the United States.

I agreed with his politics and all at the time, but had
he been white, there's no way I would have gone to the
trouble of voting.

I wanted the badge of honor of being part of history. I
wanted to be part of it. I wanted *a* part of it.

And if I'm being *totally* honest: I didn't want to wait
until I had grandkids to receive my pat on the back. I
wanted attention and praise when I posted about it on
social media. I wanted to be viewed as a *good person*.
I wanted to be seen as... *not racist*.

Me, me, me...

I remember the night he was elected.

Luke and I were drinking in his bedroom at the
fraternity house, getting ready to go out.

Luke voted for John McCain. (He *certainly* wasn't
going to vote for Obama.)

54

By then, more states were being called, and then-Senator Obama was clearly on track to win.

We drank more.

At the popular bar down the street, there was a party wherein everyone was supposed to wear the color of who they supported in the election.

I was wearing a bright blue sequin top.

And I was looking forward to going, regardless of the outcome.

I wanted to see which of my friends were wearing blue and which were wearing red. And, equally as much, I wanted out of Luke's filthy little bedroom.

Just then, the news broke that Barack Obama had reached the coveted two-hundred and seventy electoral votes and was, indeed, our next President.

I grinned at the television screen, witnessing history.

In a flurry of silent elation, my cheap beer and I turned to look at Luke.

He was staring down at his phone, texting. And he looked livid.

"Hey," I prompted him with a cheerful tone, "ready to go?"

I couldn't wait to reach the bar.

(...though that was nothing new.)

"I'm not going anywhere," he informed me, still fuming into his phone.

"Who... uh... who are you texting?"

"My brother and my dad," he didn't even look up at me, "You can do what you want. I'm not going."

There was a pause, and then he slid into a cold, mocking tone.

"You guys got what you wanted. You got your history," he shook his head and jutted out his jaw, "This is a fucking nightmare."

I looked at him, devastated that we wouldn't be going out.

I knew I could go alone, but it just didn't feel right when my boyfriend was so upset.

So I stared at him.

He was both seething and sulking.

At once, he picked up the remote control and clicked the channel to ESPN, where the news was but a scrolling footer at the bottom of the screen during an otherwise unrelated sports documentary.

I sighed, slowly coming to the realization that on this historic day, I would spend the evening in this filthy, God-forsaken bedroom instead of down at the bar, celebrating with like-minded friends.

A sudden roar of sirens screamed from outside.

Alarmed, Luke and I jumped off his couch and rushed over to the never-been-cleaned window above his also-never-been-cleaned air conditioning unit.

Peering out into the freshly darkened evening sky, we watched squad car... after squad car... after squad car... after squad car fly down the quiet little street, blaring their sirens and flashing blue and red lights.

I lost count after fourteen police cars.

Our jaws hung open at such an astonishing sight.

"Where... where are they all going?" I turned to Luke, scared.

He looked over at me.

"The black neighborhoods are a few blocks in that direction."

Becc and I bounced out of my sorority house's front door into the windy, snowless afternoon.

The sky was cloudy, and her new hairstyle shone like a black sun against a cold grey sky.

"Nice hair!" I cooed, taking a long look.

She grinned over at me.

"Do you know the *time*... the *energy*... and the *pain* required for a black girl to straighten her hair?"

I looked her way.

"No. Is it a lot?"

She laughed, shaking her head, as her hair— moving as one entity with her head— shook with it.

"You have *no* idea. I met some friends at school, half-black and half-white, and we got to talking."

I nodded, listening.

"I decided to stop messing with my hair and just wear it natural from now on."

I smiled, feeling genuine relief for her.

"Well, it looks beautiful!"

"Umm, slightly on-topic," Becc turned to me with scrunched-together black brows and a wry grin, "Let's talk about how the only black person in your entire sorority is the woman who's your house cook. I almost called her 'Mammy' this morning at breakfast."

I laughed, pulling the zipper on my sweatshirt all the way up.

"I never thought of that. We have a girl who's half-black, though. She's an upperclassman."

"Creeeeeeaaaaaatttcchh!"

The entire chapter room of sorority "sisters" sang out toward the lone black girl in our house (if you don't count our cook).

As usual, I didn't join in.

"Creatch" was her... uh... *loving* nickname.

It was short for "creature."

According to the older girls who had assigned the moniker, it originated one morning when a cluster of them saw Creatch's hair standing on-end after a hard night of partying.

When they told the story to a few of us younger girls, my mind flashed to Becc and I blurted out: "Isn't that kind of messed up to call the only black girl in the house 'creature?'"

The white girls' jaws hung, aghast, and Creatch— who stood beside them as they recounted the tale to us— just laughed. But not a regular laugh.

A laugh with a little something *off* about it. I couldn't put my finger on it.

The white girls were horrified that I'd make such an accusation (especially with Creatch standing *right there*).

"No, it's because of her *hair*," one of the white girls articulated, clearly believing those were two separate things.

Their facial expressions implied that *I* was the racist one.

"Plus, I'm *half*-black," clarified the subject of our conversation.

I recalled the time I first saw Becc pull her relaxed hair out of a ponytail. How it stood straight up. How we gawked and giggled.

Sympathetically, I wagered it was these girls' first time seeing black hair up-close, too.

But I wasn't about to take the time to explain what, admittedly, *very* little I knew about black people and their hair, if the black person in the room wasn't.

I shook the story-of-origin memory loose and watched Creatch stand up with the pledge sheet in her slightly tan hand.

The name "Creature" always struck me as ironic, too, considering she was objectively far prettier than the girls who dubbed her as such. For illustration, she looked like a stunning blend of Rihanna and Christina Milian. She was flat-out *gorgeous*.

"I think she's okay," Creach shrugged nonchalantly about a black girl who came through recruitment that day, "She was cool and everything, but she's a year older than we prefer."

Only about a dozen black girls came through recruitment earlier, out of over five hundred Lindseys and Ashleys.

The recruit's name was Holly, and the three adjectives assigned to her column on the pledge sheet were "nice," "smart," and "alright."

I spoke with her, but wasn't one of the three girls assigned to fill out her form.

After speaking with her for nearly twenty minutes, I concluded she had more charisma than anybody in the entire house, including our President.

Plus, she was whip-smart.

"Okay," our blonde-haired, blue-eyed President confirmed, "Time to vote. Who votes yes?"

Only three of us raised our hands, including my then-roommate.

Holly didn't make it through to the next round.

Neither did Kara, the recruit seven votes prior whose three adjectives included a lowercase "asian."

"Trisha, you ever been with a black guy?" Colin asked me with a taunting grin three weeks later.

"What?" my face turned to horror, as it usually did when Colin spoke to me, "I... what the hell?"

"That's not an answerrr," he chided, in an obnoxious sing-songy tone.

I glanced at Luke. He and I had just walked into the room.

My boyfriend let out a laugh so robust, the skin on the outside of his young eyes crinkled.

"No," he answered for me, "she's not tainted."

"Are you sure she's not tainted? She didn't really answer," Colin looked me square in the eyes, smiling and spinning himself from left to right on the chair he was in.

Behind him was a desk with little white lines of powder on top.

Luke rolled his blue eyes, as Colin grinned at me with his beady little brown ones.

"Tainted?" I sought clarification.

The room of four white guys laughed in unison, and Colin answered for them all.

"It's when a white chick has been with a black dude before."

My eyebrows furrowed above fake eyelashes.

"She's not tainted," my boyfriend repeated, stepping aggressively toward the desk, "And you owe me money."

Colin shrugged carelessly in response, while Luke grabbed the rolled up twenty-dollar bill to reclaim his debt.

"I accept cash and coke."

Later that night, Luke, Colin, another white guy, and I stood in the dingy white stairwell of the fraternity house, sipping mixed drinks in the wee hours of the morning.

Luke was okay, I guess. We'd been dating for over a year by that point.

I was never too wild about him, but the girls in my sorority liked him and thought he was great, so I sort of just trusted group sentiment on the matter.

The four of us held red Solo cups and chatted from varying elevations, while framed composite photos hung on the walls, surrounding us.

Each composite was about four feet high and five feet wide and consisted of a collection of individual photos of the fraternity's members from that year. There were decades' worth of composites in that stairwell.

As my eyes darted around the stained white bricks, I observed matter-of-factly (and aloud): "Everyone in this fraternity has always been white."

The three "brothers" in collared shirts looked at each other and laughed.

True to form, Colin yelled out: "HELL YEAH! NO **THAT WORDS** ALLOWED!"

My eyebrows raised and jaw dropped a bit, while the words echoed from one floor's walls to the next in both directions.

I looked to Luke for a cue. He was looking at Colin, laughing.

I nervously followed his lead.

"Oh," I said surprised, forcing a tight laughter.

"There's an Asian kid in our current pledge class," Luke looked over to me and explained in a tone I couldn't decipher.

"We'll see if he lasts," Colin chimed in, with a cynical grin, "It's Hell Week next week."

Luke shook his head, called Colin "an idiot," and laughed downward toward the floor, glancing at me out of the corner of his bloodshot blue eyes.

I said nothing.

The memory of my wordlessness— even laughter— in the face of that word brings me shame to this day.

I wish that I'd said something, said *anything*.

But again— and this time as an adult— I said nothing.

Between that moment and now, I've learned there aren't enough years in the human life to outrun pivotal moments of our own cowardly silence.

Back then, I didn't understand how long regret could chase a person down for.

Had I known, I'd like to say I would not have stayed so quiet.

But, to be totally honest, even had I known how often this memory would ruin a perfectly good shower or lovely afternoon drive or otherwise decent future moment, I was so beholden to what others thought of me back then, I probably still would have stayed silent... and mortgaged my future for their flimsy approval.

"We cannot accept this hate in our community!" an impassioned Social Work 210 professor declared to a diverse class of twenty-four students.

It was Monday, and over the weekend, somebody had defaced a Martin Luther King Jr. statue in a black neighborhood in town.

They sprayed his hair yellow.

They sprayed blue dots over his eyes.

And they sprayed three swastikas on the base.

It was probably just kids, my inner dialogue repeated dismissively.

I didn't feel particularly inspired to do much about it.

After all, it was probably just a bad joke or something.

But in class, I raised my hand and participated in the planning of "organized action" as though I *did* care and as though I *was* inspired.

If we're going to get right down to it, I took the Social Work class to improve my GPA.

Ever since I had begun partying every night, my grade point average had been in a freefall. I needed all the help I could get.

And I assumed, if I played my cards right, I could score a solid A in *that*.

So I said the right things, in the exact way that made our professor nod approvingly in my direction.

I acted outraged.

I acted appalled.

I acted.

And on the day of the protest in the park which I had helped organize, with the local news station that I had helped book, I wrote an email to my professor, telling her I was too sick to come to class.

And it was true, to some degree.

After all, I was almost terminally ill in a spiritual sense.

But that isn't what I meant.

I didn't even *know* what that meant.

I just knew it was cold outside and that I'd rather sleep off my hangover du jour.

And, if I'm being completely frank, I didn't really care about what happened to the statue in the park.

I cared only about doing what I needed to do to get what I wanted.

Ultimately, I received my A in the course.

Spring 2009
In honor of Ronald Bernard Jones
Dallas, TX

I watched my grandfather cry on his deathbed.

I was home from school and penniless from all my partying, while all my richer friends spent their spring breaks on tropical islands.

The day prior, my mother had asked me if I wanted to go see him, but I was already half-drunk from their liquor cabinet by that point and didn't feel like it.

So— albeit hungover— I went the following day instead, before I started my drinking.

My grandfather was a veteran of the U.S. Air Force during the Korean War, and I had never seen him cry before.

"When I was a child, they burned down my Catholic church," he told me, "the Ku Klux Klan."

I stared into his bloodshot blue eyes.

"I remember the night that it happened like it was yesterday," he solemnly recalled, "We raced to the church, my family. And all we could do was stand there and watch it burn with other members of our congregation and our neighbors. I can still hear the sound of stained-glass windows breaking as the fire tore through the building. I can still feel the heat from the flames burning my young face."

A teardrop fell down his cheek.

And I stared at the devout Catholic man.

"But I thought the KKK only hated black people?"

"No," he looked gravely into my eyes, the round shape of which I inherited, "Just like the Nazis, they hated any minorities, gay people, Jewish people, and Catholics. That's why it's so important to defend each other against hate."

My mind struggled to compute this new information, as well as the realization that *my family* had been targeted and victimized by the Ku Klux Klan.

I looked at him, knowing he always had all the answers.

"So the KKK and the Nazis are, like, *really* similar then?"

"I'm not racist," the clean-shaven white guy boasted at my first party back on campus, "I don't see race."

He belonged to Luke's fraternity, but from a different state, so he was staying at their house that weekend. Any impartial party would have told you he was somehow, almost impressively, ten times more of a douchebag than Colin even.

"You can't say that," I shook my head, preparing to recite what my Social Work 210 professor taught me just last quarter.

Three white guys and two black guys were sitting on the fraternity mansion's front steps. The black guys had wandered up at the tail end of the party, asking for beers.

The white guys, very sheepishly, invited them to share a nightcap with the small group of us who had taken too many amphetamines and were still awake.

So there we were, a motley crew of barely-adults, all of whom should have gone to bed a long time ago.

It was around four in the morning, and my head was dizzy from the cigarette I had just finished.

I didn't typically smoke cigarettes... I only did when I was *absolutely* hammered.

Lately, I'd been smoking a lot.

"You can't say that," I repeated, glancing at the two black guys who were staring at me as I spoke, "Because when you say you 'don't see race' you negate everything that people of color have experienced *because* of their race."

I continued to regurgitate a concept I learned about a mere six weeks prior, occasionally glancing at the black guys.

"You're telling them, 'I don't see what you go through. I don't acknowledge that you've had a harder time because of the color of your skin.'"

My eyes darted over, again.

"It reveals your ignorance because what you're *actually* saying is: I don't see *racism*."

I glanced again at the black guys, who I was delighted to see were nodding.

"Because, let's just be honest, everyone sees race," I sipped my drink in their direction, but stared at the out-of-state white brother, "To say you don't is simply lying."

All the white guys stared at me.

"I'm going inside," the original guy concluded, "I disagree with you completely, because I've never even thought a racist thought, let alone acted in a racist way."

He placed his red Solo cup between his teeth, stood up, and brushed off his khakis.

The other two white guys stood and moved toward the door with him.

The black guys then stood up, and so did I.

"You coming with us or what?" one black guy asked me with an odd tone of expectation.

My eyes widened.

"Trisha," one of the white guys called to me, "you coming?"

"Have a good night," I told the black guys, and my high heels teetered their way inside to pass out on Tanner's futon.

What is it about white people craving approval from black people?

What is it that makes us want so badly for a black person to call us 'cool' or 'different?'

Is it guilt?

Is it some deep desire to rebel against our parents?

I don't know why, and maybe it's different for everybody.

But I do know that your average mainstream white person feels a certain rush of excitement when a black person gives them a stamp of approval... Or, at least, *I did*.

And, like my vote for Barack Obama, I didn't say what I said that night for black people— to sincerely advocate for them and denounce racist tropes— I did it for me.

I did it for how it made me look to the black people who were sitting there.

I did it for the rush of their approval.

I did it to be seen as a "different kind" of white person.

I engaged in performative activism that night for the same reason I silently held the very racism I denounced, as true, in my heart: because both benefited *me*.

It wouldn't be a family holiday unless there were racial slurs. That's just the sad truth of the matter.

I haven't made much direct mention of my father up to now, and that doesn't seem fair.

Once I passed a certain age growing up, I heard just about every slur in existence for other racial and ethnic groups.

Asians, Italians, Hispanics, Jewish people... everybody.

But none more than black people.

Once, when I was twelve, we were out at a restaurant and I unknowingly referred to the spoon in my place-setting right as our black waitress walked up to our table. My father erupted in giggles across from me.

That's how I learned "spoon" was one of them.

This holiday was no different.

Our family gathered around the cleared dinner table and, again, unsuccessfully attempted to reenact a Norman Rockwell painting wherein a white family plays good-hearted card games in a spotless home, sharing in jovial laughter, and creating wholesome memories together.

Instead, per usual, glasses of alcohol littered our table, our home was only spotless because my mother cleaned as a coping mechanism, and my father yelled that word several times throughout the game, each with the enthusiasm and gusto of a comedian delivering the perfect punchline to an eager crowd.

And the same thing that happened every year happened again this particular year: a portion of the table chuckled at his antics (the same half who made their annual "dark meat" jokes to one another while dishing out the turkey) and the other portion of the table groaned and shook their heads, fruitlessly muttering "You can't say that," to my father's deliberately deaf ears.

And all the while, in response, my mother either rolled her eyes exhaustedly or glared scoldingly at him, like she would at a misbehaving child.

I never really liked holidays much.

But like a callus grows on overworked hands, so, too, do calluses grow on overworked souls.

And each time, growing up, my little heart would hear an ugly word spoken about a group of people we didn't know or much associate with, it would harden just a tiny bit more to protect itself from the abrasion.

By this point, I'd long since lost all feeling.

I slurred the obligatory "That's not funny. You can't say that." But, by then, it was more out of pent-up resentment for my father rather than any noble crusade against bigotry.

And so the holiday came and went, like any other.

Except this time, I got *way* too drunk, and when I woke up to go to the bathroom in the wee hours of the night, I tripped and hit just above my right eye on the sharp corner of my childhood dresser.

Hearing the loud crashing noise, my mother rushed into the bedroom and began castigating me while I cupped my hands to contain the mess, stumbling across her white carpeting to the stark all-white bathroom.

There was blood everywhere.

The next morning, it was the only thing noteworthy enough for people to discuss at breakfast.

The first time I said that word outside of a rap song, I was all by myself.

I was living alone in the most depressing, rundown one-bedroom apartment you've ever seen and drinking from the moment I came to each morning until the time I'd pass out each night.

I'd occasionally go to a minimum wage job where I would begrudgingly sober up for a few hours.

One night, I sat on my cheap brown couch in the silence. No TV. No music. No nothing. Just the relentless humming of my refrigerator and thoughts.

I'd never said that word before. *Really* said it.

I'd heard a lot of other people say it, but, I realized then, *I* never had.

I was curious.

What would it feel like in my mouth?

The first time I said it, I whispered.

"That word.**"**

As a rush from the taboo washed down my spine, I said it twice more in a regular tone to the bare white walls, hoping that no one was standing outside my front door who possessed supersonic hearing.

"That word... that word...**"**

I said it three times total.

Then I got off the couch, poured myself another glass of cheap vodka with a splash of cranberry cocktail and made a pizza-flavored Hot Pocket in the microwave.

My father set his wallet down on the desk in the kitchen, then emptied the coins from his pocket and laid them beside it.

Unbeknownst to him, my mother would later swipe all the coins, as she always did.

"I saw the black landscaper today," he announced.

I glanced around the room and saw nobody else.

He must be talking to me.

"Oh yeah? Where?"

"Down by City Hall. I was there getting a form notarized."

I glanced down at the turkey sandwich I had been making.

"Oh."

"He was in the parking lot, hanging some Christmas decorations as I was leaving, and I was chatting with him by his truck like I usually do when I see him."

I nodded at my sandwich, uninterested.

"We're good friends."

My head snapped up.

"You *are?*"

"Oh yeah," my father finally turned and looked back at me, "I joke around with him all the time."

Oh no.

"Today he had a long rope tied to the back of his truck," my pale father chuckled, "I joked he shouldn't get too close to it since he works with branches."

My eyes widened in horror.

"You *can't* say that!"

"Sure I can," my father waved his hand at me dismissively, then picked up a sheet of loose paper off the desk, "We're good friends. He tells me every time I see him that his church prays for me every week."

I stared at him.

"Think of that," he turned back to me, smiling and proud, "I have a whole black church praying for me every week. Isn't that incredible?"

Spring 2011
In honor of the four injured innocent bystanders
of Urban Beach Week
Miami, FL

"is that racist? lol"

I hit send and the text shot off into the ether.

"um, yeah."

Ryan responded immediately and I received a few in succession.

"black ppl drive middle class cars, trisha. they're not all poor single mothers and rich drug dealers. lol"

A pause.

"but you're right. it's weird that a black dude drives a prius hahaha"

I shook my head, smiling with bloated cheeks, then grabbed the thirty-pack of cheap beer off the gas station counter, as my phone continued to audibly ding with Ryan entertaining himself.

"Thank you," I smiled sweetly to the now-familiar Indian girl behind the counter and began walking out.

Once outside in the drizzling rain, I hoisted the giant box of alcohol into the backseat of my car and, once again, examined the massive and mysterious side-swipe damage that appeared on the side of my car last week after I drove home drunk from a local bar.

I never did figure out how it got there.

I slammed the car door shut with relief.

This will be enough to get me to Wednesday morning…

It was Monday evening.

As usual, I wasn't sure what I'd do for alcohol between Wednesday and payday on Friday.

I pondered heading over to the consignment store again, to sell a few more articles of clothes or hand-me-down purses from my sister.

After climbing into the driver's seat, I glanced anxiously to the backseat the way I always did after loading alcohol, like a worried mother, just to make sure it didn't somehow escape or that I had imagined loading it and actually forgotten it.

I thought about how I could possibly afford more alcohol and worse, what alcohol I could actually afford once I found the money.

It had been a couple of months since I'd last drank hard liquor. I sighed.

I'd been doing "so well" on just beer and wine.

I pulled out of the gas station and wondered what the Indian girl thought of me. She saw me come in every couple of days and buy obscenely large quantities of alcohol.

The first time, she playfully asked: "Oh! Are you having a party?"

I answered "yes" out of embarrassment, even though it was all for me.

By this point, she must have thought I was either completely pathetic or the most popular human being alive.

But she smiled kindly at me just the same every time.

"Fuck you," I muttered, alone, to the black girl on my grainy sixteen-inch TV set.

I took a swig of the Nattie Ice in my pink plastic cup. Tomorrow would be payday, and I'd finally be able to afford something other than Nattie Ice.

I listened to Ryan Seacrest give her a quick pep talk and then watched her walk confidently into the audition room.

She sang in octaves I didn't even know existed. She, of course, scored a ticket to Hollywood.

Fuck her, I thought to myself, enviously, as I stared at her giant hair and sparkling purple eye shadow, *she better not fucking win.*

My inner vitriol roiled.

They'll probably make her win because they need a black chick to win or something.

I rolled my eyes hard and started channel surfing.

A familiar sound effect rang out, then music that I knew well...

Intervention.

I used to drink while watching A&E's show "Intervention" so I could tell myself that my drinking "wasn't as bad" as those people's...

By this point, though, it was worse and I'd just turn it on so I wouldn't be drinking alone.

My least favorite part of the show was the end, because I hated either outcome.

I hated hearing they relapsed and either died or are still drinking, because it left me hopeless.

And I hated— somehow even more— hearing they had become sober and were subsequently living an awesome life, because it made me angry and envious.

I had tried quitting every day and in every which way for about a year.

I switched my type of booze.

I tried cold-turkey.

I tried only drinking a six-pack... an exercise which *always* ended in me driving back to the gas station for more.

But I never could quit.

I usually drank alone in my apartment. I'd learned over the years that it was just safer that way.

Later that night, in a blackout, I made a horrible remark to a black woman I'd never met on Facebook.

We had no mutual friends.

I don't even know how I wound up on her page.

But I'll never forget her response: "That's the devil talking. You have to go, in the name of Jesus!"

I couldn't remember anything other than her words the next morning. I didn't even know what I had said. But I know she called me the devil.

And, with how quickly alcoholism had been dissolving any remnant of a soul I might have had left, I knew that next morning: she was right.

But the devil had me in his grips, and he never gives up without one hell of a fight.

Fall 2011
In memory of Kenneth Chamberlain Sr.
White Plains, NY

That morning, I came to, foggier than ever before.

As I pulled on my minimum wage uniform and obligatory black non-skid footwear, I tried to piece together the night prior.

I had gone out, vowing while still sober I would only have *one* beer at a nice bar, go home, and fall asleep.

Two bars later, I drove home in a blackout.

I didn't remember walking to my car in the parking lot.

I didn't remember a single part of my drive home.

I didn't remember climbing the dilapidated stairs of my apartment complex.

And I didn't remember taking my pants off.

As I drove to my job, shaking from dehydration and panic, my mind raced to fill in the blanks.

What happened?

Was I raped?

Did someone follow me up the stairs, push me inside, and have sex with me?

I shook my head repeatedly, hoping against all logic to literally shake loose my dark thoughts, as well as maybe some answers.

Once at my job, I spent all morning dry-heaving over a trashcan in the back.

"You look like you've had better days," one coworker offered, having seen me hungover many times before.

Gary was old, saintly, and, evidently, over twenty years sober himself.

I wiped my mouth with my stained black apron and looked up at him.

"I feel like I was raped last night," I told him in a completely inappropriate moment of candor.

"Well, you were," he responded matter-of-factly.

I stared at him, as my stomach lurched even further.

Does he know what happened to me last night? Was he in the parking lot? Does he know someone who saw me?

"In a way," he began to clarify his point, "you *were* raped, Trisha. You see, once you took that first drink, you were completely out of control of your entire night. Everything that happened after that first drink happened against your will. Every drink that followed was out of your control."

He stared deeply into my bloodshot green eyes.

"Wasn't it?"

I thought back to my aspirations— and downright conviction— for "just one beer."

I thought back to the second beer, then the third and fourth, then, *oh my God,* I suddenly recalled a humiliatingly loud conversation I had with some random divorce lawyer two stools down from me about how I always wished my parents had gotten a divorce...

I thought back to what flickers I could recall during my drive from the first bar to the second. I remembered I had the driver's side window open and accidentally dropped the lucky charm I held while driving.

That would explain why it was missing from the cupholder this morning.

My mind relived arriving at the second bar, ordering hard liquor, and then... *black.*

"That's what happens to alcoholics," his heavy voice cut into my train of thought, "The first drink takes you for a ride you never agreed to go on."

He shook his head with a knowing smile.

"But you just can't resist that first one."

I left work fifteen minutes later— only an hour and a half into my shift— sweating and stunned.

He was right.

I had a problem. A *real* problem.

I went home and laid in bed for the rest of the morning, reflecting on my life's trajectory.

The promise I made to myself in fifth grade, to be a good person without God.

All those gifted classes.

All that praise through school.

Where had my talent and intellect taken me?

To a rundown, filthy apartment I still couldn't afford and working a job that I hated, yet was barely hanging onto by a thread.

> And I'll clarify: there's no shame in doing minimum wage work, but there certainly was no pride in how *I* was performing it, either.

Every day, I showed up hungover and expecting to be fired.

How had I fallen so far?

How had my life resulted in so little?

How had I let hatred and evil grow in my heart *this* much?

God...

My wobbly knees carried the rest of my body to the end of my bed where I sat.

I don't know what You are.

I shook my disheveled, box-dyed blonde ponytail.

I don't even know if You are...

My eyes filled with hot tears and looked up.

But if You are, please help me.

Please.

Please help me.

I can't do this on my own.

And I am willing to have been wrong about You my entire life, if You just please...

"Help me."

Summer 2012
In memory of Rekia Boyd
and in honor of Antonio Cross
Chicago, IL

Nearly one year sober and still trying to find my footing while living in Hoboken, New Jersey, the temp agency promised me this position was a wonderful opportunity for advancement.

It was at a mutual fund and the entire office was glass, overlooking Central Park.

I arrived early, as instructed, and dressed in my best outfit, also as instructed.

The young blonde woman who previously held the receptionist role droned on and on about how hot, but rude, the CEO's son was and how her new boss— who she served as executive assistant to— graciously only made her cry once a week.

She told me if I ever needed to cry, I should go to the ladies' room. At any given point, she said, there's usually one or two women in there doing the same.

As she gave me a tour of the space, I couldn't help but notice a number of inappropriate paintings of nude women on the walls of the mixed-sex professional space.

When I asked the young woman about them, she explained how the CEO loved art and they're originals from an Italian painter whom he adored. She kept walking— and talking— quickly.

I watched her slender frame slow as we returned to the front desk where I would spend the next three weeks of my life.

"And the CEO is gonna love you," she blurted out, "He likes blondes at the front desk."

My head cocked itself, confused.

"We had a Hispanic girl come last month for this position and he hated it. Then they sent a black girl for, like, four days," the fellow blonde's eyes grew wide and she shook her head to me ominously, "He didn't talk about anything else the whole time she was here. He says it works best when there's a blonde as the first impression for the office."

She smiled and nodded reassuringly to me since, frankly, we looked like funhouse mirror versions of each other. (I, obviously, being the chubbier of the two...)

My eyebrows scrunched a bit, and for the next few days, I considered if that exchange, plus a handful of wildly sexist moments I experienced at the behemoth mutual fund, was somehow worthy of going to the press... or something.

I never did, and I never considered it even noteworthy enough to share with my parents back home.

I simply continued working there for the few weeks I needed income and then refused the full-time job they offered to me after.

My parents were incredulous, accusing me of insanity because I could have made more money than I'd ever seen.

But everyone who worked there was so miserable.

Millionaire investment bankers screaming at lunch delivery guys over forgotten guacamole...

Powerful female executives cutting down *any* woman their junior...

The married VP who was very obviously cheating on his wife/mother of his kids with another young blonde assistant...

And the CEO's son, who constantly looked hungover and barely spoke two words to anyone...

Who knew people with more money than God could be so unhappy?

I didn't, but I learned it there.

"I've got a hell of a story for you," my father announced to me as I picked over a plate of Christmas leftovers in the adjoining kitchen of my childhood home.

Anytime he was overly convivial, I tensed up, never really knowing what to expect.

"My friend Dan, the banker, was in my office last week, and he and I get along great. We golf together every week in the summer," the local real estate developer fragmentedly explained to me, "and so I'm there, and I'm telling him about this new family— this *black* family— who wants to move into the neighborhood..."

Oh God, here we go.

"And Dan points to the map of the empty lots on the wall and asks where they'd move," he paused for suspense, "And I laugh and shout 'NO COONS ALLOWED! YOU KNOW THAT!'"

I sighed, utterly exhausted.

"But then we walk out of my office and into the waiting room, and there was a *black guy* standing there!"

My fork fell from my hand into last night's mashed potatoes, as I pictured the scene.

"And there was no way he didn't hear it," my father further clarified, "My door was wide open."

I blinked hard.

"What did you *do*?"

"He wasn't there to see me," my father shrugged, "I just walked past him, with Dan, and walked out."

Summer 2014
In honor of Jannie Ligons
Oklahoma City, OK

I realized I was racist on a Tuesday.

It was a pretty normal day aside from that.

Nearly three years sober, I woke up in my cluttered studio apartment in Bayonne, New Jersey, a little later than I should have if I had wanted to arrive to work on time. As usual.

I threw on some clothes I don't remember, but certainly only half-matched as I'd been gaining weight at a pace steadier than paycheck increases to afford new outfits.

I grabbed my makeup bag from the medicine cabinet, the keys off the small white table I'd salvaged from a former Hoboken neighbor's trash and my phone.

I rushed out of the apartment, heavy metal door sealing shut behind me.

I checked the lock. Then again. And again.

That door was part of the reason I felt okay moving to Bayonne. It was heavy like a bank vault door, with double deadbolts.

My parents had never been invited to see and *would* never see my apartment there.

People like me didn't live in Bayonne. Or, at least, so I had been told repeatedly by literally everyone who ever learned I lived there.

I had recently insisted my parents stop helping with my rent so, at age twenty-six, I could fully support myself and feel more freedom as an adult.

A friend of mine had suggested that my parents might feel less entitled to critique my life decisions if I were no longer on their payroll, so to speak.

With that, I downsized from a spacious park-facing one bedroom apartment in the insanely expensive city of Hoboken to the place I would spend perhaps the most formative year of my life. This place.

I didn't realize it then, as I raced past several blocks of graffitied and caged storefronts to the Light Rail Train, but it was Tuesday.

That Tuesday.

PART II: LEARNING LOVE

"No one is born hating another person because of the color of his skin... People must learn hate. And if they can learn hate, they can be taught to love, for love comes more naturally to the human heart than its opposite."
Nelson Mandela

The New York City subway floor feels sticky, as usual, beneath my $30 black booties, while the metal cars lurch and clatter between stops.

My body sways from side to side with the movement of the train and other commuters.

I never hold any poles to balance myself while commuting, due to the often-crippling OCD that I developed toward the tail end of my drinking.

As a result of it, I check the lock at least three or four times whenever leaving my apartment. And germs? Forget about it. I'm a lunatic in that arena.

"I CAN'T BREATHE," my wandering green eyes read.

They are big, bold, capital letters on the front page of a newspaper the white man standing beside me is reading.

My eyes move, and I look out the large dark window above the seated heads in front of me as grimy cement subway walls race by, peppered with occasional graffiti or piping.

That's the newest story about a black man who was killed by police, I remind myself.

It happened a day or two ago, and a video of the whole thing recently surfaced.

Since then, the city has been even more tense than usual.

The train jerks noisily to a stop, and I almost lose my balance.

"Shit," I mutter, quickly twisting my cheap, treadless boots with momentum's sway, desperately trying to avoid the inevitable.

But my hand instinctively reaches up... and grabs the metal pole above me.

Aghast, a loud sigh escapes my chapped lips.

I feel the cold, greasy pole beneath my skin and panic over which diseases will now surely come my way.

Licking my lips then pursing them quickly, my angry eyes dart illogically around the messy and crowded car, searching for somebody to blame for the city's overpopulated public transportation, as well as the newfound contamination of my right hand.

I watch a red-haired man clear his throat as he sits in front of the "I CAN'T BREATHE" newspaper man.

I glance down at my chunky plastic heels.

Then back at him, sitting.

I'm wearing heels and am a woman, I think to myself with hostility, *he should let me sit.*

My face scrunches in disgust as my eyes notice other men sitting, as well.

My mascaraed lashes squint at them.

Then my repulsion turns to the middle-aged black woman seated directly in front of me.

I stare down at her.

And I feel the anger in my chest grow.

This lady...

I can feel a heat rise in my face.

THIS lady.

My eyes roll.

And my teeth grit.

And then suddenly...

It is as though my six months of frustrated attempts at meditation have led me here.

To this revelatory moment.

I *see* my thought, as though undergoing an out-of-body sensation with my mind rather than body:

I feel angry with her.

Entitled to the seat she is sitting in...

the same way I felt about the seat of the red-haired man.

Except...

Why?

I look at her.

Her black hair is short, frizzy, and coarse.

Her eyes are exhausted, as though they've seen too much for several lifetimes.

I gaze down at her shoes and recognize them as the black, minimum wage, non-skid footwear I knew so well from the days I worked— usually sweating and nauseous— on my feet with Gary.

Why was my immediate reaction to be angry with *her*, of all people, for sitting?

No.

My stomach doesn't just drop; it plunges.

Is it...

No...

No, that's not it.

I have forgotten about the deadly germs on my right hand.

Instead, my mind wars with itself.

It's not...

Is it...?

It can't be.

Is it that she's sitting...

and I'm standing...

and... I'm...

...white?

My green eyes dart up, frantically searching for a way to escape the looming realization.

There's a purple ad for a local community college above the old woman's kinky hair and the subway car's filthy window. Scribbled across it, in thick black marker and graffiti font, are the three words now echoing off every taxicab and street sign in the city: "I CAN'T BREATHE."

In this moment, neither can I.

Oh my God.

I stare hard at the words.

I'm racist.

The jarring discovery continues to haunt me at random moments throughout the rest of my day.

...in the office bathroom, while washing my hands.

...standing at the coffee machine, waiting for the pot to finish brewing.

...in between cold calls, when my mind would wander.

At 5:05 that evening, I dejectedly walk out of our building, into the hot city summer air, my mind still reeling:

What did it all mean?

Do I have those thoughts often?

Am I simply unconscious to them?

Could I be that unaware?

Warring thoughts race through my mind the entire commute home from Manhattan to Bayonne.

As my now excruciatingly cheap boots speedwalk themselves in the final stretch between the Bayonne Light Rail station and my waiting studio apartment, I decide to reach out to Stacey for advice on the matter.

I've always hated the name Stacey. My mother always hated the name Stacey.

When I was younger, my mother would turn to me any time we heard the name.

"I hate that name," she would whisper, reminding me, "It's so tacky and trashy."

I suppose I inherited the hate from her.

Yet here I am, seeking wisdom and counsel from a red-haired Italian woman named Stacey.

I guess I should back up to how I met her.

Summer 2013
In memory of Jonathan Ferrell
Charlotte, NC

Mental health had never been a strong suit of mine.

And when Oliver dumped me, I couldn't even pretend to stay sane anymore.

I pleaded to him that I would do anything, change anything, *be* anything if he stayed.

I believed he was my soulmate... even though I never really liked him that much.

After he escaped my park-facing Hoboken apartment for the last time, I laid there crying on its immaculately cleaned hardwood floor, waiting for him to come back and help me up.

After over an hour, it finally dawned on me: he wasn't coming back.

So I climbed to a seated position and began to plan out the suicide that had, frankly, always felt somehow inevitable for me.

Overdose seemed risky since Candice had tried that approach three times in high school and woke up after all three.

Slitting my wrists was an option, too, I supposed.

But she had, also, tried that once. In the middle of art class, actually. And she survived.

I didn't have a gun, so that option was clearly out.

I could drink myself to death, or intentionally overdose on drugs... Go out in a blaze of glory, I figured.

But I didn't know where to score drugs. Not since college, anyway.

And to drink myself to death seemed a gamble considering there had been too many occasions to count where I had technically drank enough to die, yet through some merciless hand of fate had woken up the next morning.

No... I needed a sure thing.

Suddenly a foreign thought crowded out all others in my mind:

Go for a walk.

Clear your head.

Then decide.

Sniffling, I pulled myself to stand, changed out of my work clothes, then laced up my rarely-used sneakers.

I started crying as soon as my feet hit the sidewalk outside my building. It was quite a display for the old man who had the unfortunate timing of walking past me.

But I did what the thought told me to do, and I pressed on.

Ten minutes later, I found myself at the uptown pier, staring at the brilliantly lit and ever-iconic New York City skyline.

The sky continued to darken.

I cried myself all the way into nightfall, I realized, almost impressed by my capacity for self-pity.

As I sat on a bench with warm tears dripping down my face, I hoped with everything in me none of his friends would walk past. Or worse, *him.*

My breath exhaled time and time again, as I watched the city lights grow brighter against the increasingly black sky, above the glistening-yet-filthy Hudson River.

And, finally, as the few stars appeared that could with such light pollution, I felt the urge to say a prayer into the vast night sky.

God, here I am again.

Desperate...

And hopeless... again.

I shook my head, as humiliated tears fell from flushed cheeks to the concrete beside my shoes.

I don't know what You want for me.

I thought You wanted him for me. I thought he was Your plan for me.

I'm out of ideas and out of direction... again.

Please.

Help me.

Show me what You want me to do.

I have nothing left.

I stared down at the ground, wondering how it would feel to exist without him.

I never possessed much patience, so naturally I expected an immediate booming voice, meteor shower, or some other instantaneous supernatural sign from above.

Alas, no such thing happened.

And as I stood up and began to walk back to my lonely apartment, I felt angry with God.

Here, I had put myself out there... really laid myself bare at His/Her/Whatever feet...

And *nothing*.

I kept walking, bitterly entitled steps pounding harder and harder against the dark sidewalk.

As my self-pitying tears became hot, resentful ones, I turned an unfamiliar corner and realized... I was lost.

In a town of only one square mile, in which I had lived for almost two years, I was lost.

Now, in *every* sense of the word.

I never learned how to navigate Hoboken. I just followed him around, it dawned on me.

Furious at God all over again for allowing my humiliation to mount, I roamed around quiet, confused uptown blocks until...

Until I heard laughter.

Group laughter.

As I approached the nearest street corner, I looked to my left and saw an eclectic mix of people standing outside a demure building, socializing. Somebody was locking the weathered brown door.

What...

A few of their members glanced over at me and smiled, as I tried to nonchalantly wipe tears from my face.

In the strange night air, I felt drawn to them.

Compelled to walk over... despite the fact I knew nobody, looked like shit, and had absolutely nothing to say.

My suicide-decision sneakers mysteriously walked themselves up to three women who were chatting.

"What is this group?" my voice broke.

The Italian woman with wild red hair smiled into my bloodshot eyes.

"I'm Stacey," she placed a hand on her chest and then introduced me to the two women beside her.

Back to Summer 2014
Still in memory of Eric Garner
New York City, NY

"Oh, hey," I greet Stacey, as the lock unclicks to my apartment.

"How's it going?" her calming voice coos back at me.

Awkwardly, I position the phone between my cheek and shoulder, simultaneously shuffling through the door, jumbling with my keys, and re-locking both locks behind me.

Once secure inside, I drop my too-heavy work bag and, of course, remove my boots.

I glance back to make sure I re-locked the door. Of course I did.

I hated Christianity before I met Stacey that day.

Allegedly Gandhi had once said: "I like your Christ, but I do not like your Christians. Your Christians are so unlike your Christ." That epitomized how I felt growing up, only I didn't like what little I knew about Christ either.

The Christians I met that night— a year and a lot of desperation ago— were very different Christians than the stereotype I held in my mind.

First of all, not all of them *were* Christians. In the group of about fifteen people, there was one Buddhist, and two were agnostic. One was formerly Jewish, but now identified as Christian.

113

But it was a Christian group. They spoke about Jesus, God, and the Bible.

And they welcomed non-Christians to sit in and join, though they never pressured the non-Christians to change.

That's what I liked most about them in the beginning. They weren't trying to sell me anything.

Blame it on the day job, but I hate being *sold* anything.

I always figured if I've been eating shitty, microwave pizza my whole life, then stumbled upon the greatest pizzeria in the world, no one would need to sell me their pizza.

I'd smell the perfectly browned, melted cheese.

I'd see the vibrant, tangy red sauce peeking through.

I'd hear the crunch of people devouring the crust and mentally compare it to the flaccid, rubbery microwave crust I was used to.

I'd sit in that pizza shop for all of five seconds before rushing home to grab my wallet.

So far as I was concerned, if what Christians have is truly better than anything else, I should see it plain as day, not have to be *sold* on it.

In that group, I saw it plain as day.

And over the course of the last year as a member, I've seen changed lives, restored relationships, happy and loving people.

I've heard miracle stories on a regular basis.

"It's okay," I respond while preheating my oven, then turning to open the freezer.

"Just okay?" she prods.

I pull out the box of French bread pepperoni pizzas.

"Umm... I think I may be racist."

I blurt the words out to her, laying the box on the countertop and turning to make the very short walk to the bathroom.

This is my nightly ritual, sans tonight's admission of bigotry of course.

"Oh," Stacey reacts, so surprised she somewhat laughs, "and what prompted this realization?"

I breathe in heavily, remembering.

"I was on the subway today and realized I felt hostility toward a woman, and I'm not sure, but I think it was because she was black and was sitting down, while I had to stand."

A quiet on the other end. And then...

"What about other instances in your life?"

I think about how, when I used to have a car, I'd lock my car doors when a black man would walk by. Or at least always double-check. (After all, my doors are always locked.)

Reminded, I lean out of the small, tiled bathroom just long enough to re-confirm that my front door is still locked. It is. Then I lean back into the bathroom.

I think about how loud black women bother me just a *little* bit more than loud white women.

I think about how I felt in high school, when I heard several of my black classmates received athletic scholarships, and how I assumed many of them wouldn't have been accepted to those colleges on academics alone, despite knowing nothing about their grades.

I think about how I've never dated a black guy, fearing other white people's opinions of me if I did.

"Uh, yeah," I realize, slowly turning the bathtub knob to start the water.

My hand lowers to feel the rush of water beginning to warm, and I stand up more slowly than usual.

"Yeah, I am," the confidence in my tone feels foreign, but finally honest.

The oven's preheat timer beeps a few feet and a flimsy wall away in the kitchen, but I don't move.

I watch the clear water pour out of the spotless metal faucet.

"Okay," Stacey begins cautiously, but compassionately, "well the good news is, you're not the first person to ever deal with the demon of racism."

She laughs lightly, and I kind of do, too, because this whole scenario feels very surreal.

I've just told someone I've only known a year that I'm racist.

That's like some shit you only tell a therapist... if anybody... *ever... at all.*

"The solution is simple," she declares, snapping me out of my water-induced trance.

I shake my head lightly, and a few tired blonde wisps fall out of the bun I had worn to work today.

My panty-hosed feet begin walking across the tile floor, back to the oven, continuing my nightly routine.

"You need to pray for them," Stacey instructs.

"What?" my feet stop.

"Any person, or especially group, you hate or feel negatively toward, you need to pray for them."

"I thought we just prayed for our enemies," I inquire, genuinely puzzled.

"And people we have hatred towards and to whom we've caused harm," Stacey adds, as I can hear her opening what sounds to be a bag of chips in the background.

"Okay," I absorb the news slowly, "but, like, *how?*"

The background noise on her end stops, and I begin to smell the cheese from my previous frozen pizza burning off the charred black bottom of my oven where it had dripped.

There is silence for a moment.

"God, I have sinned. I have hated my brothers and sisters because of narratives passed down from the enemy. I reject those hateful narratives today, and I lift up each of Your children in this group who have ever been persecuted or discriminated against, and oppressed due to the color of their skin. I am so sorry. Please lead me past this hatred and into Your everlasting love for all of Your children, especially my black brothers and sisters."

"Did," my voice starts then stops, "...did you read that somewhere? Can you send that to me?"

"Honey, I just said it," Stacey answers in her no-nonsense tone, "If you truly want this hatefulness and darkness to leave your heart, a scripted prayer won't help you as much as an earnest cry for help. God will meet you at your level of readiness. Reading someone else's words can work for a time, but you're past that stage, Trisha. You need a faith all your own now."

I slowly step toward the kitchen.

"And I just... *pray for them?*"

"Pray for them, that they have all the things you want in your life, like love, financial prosperity, good relationships, safety... then pray for forgiveness for yourself, and finally, ask God for His help."

I nod as though she can see me.

I don't have any of those things in my life, but I certainly do want them.

"When we can't, He can," she reminds me, "and He will, if we let Him."

I walk over and unwrap the pizza from its loud clear wrapper, then open the oven door and drop the frozen pizza directly on the wire rack.

"Okay."

As I shut the door and stand upright, Stacey adds: "You do it every day."

"Every *day?*" my eyebrows raise high, as my fingers instinctively unzip the back of my black pencil skirt and drop it to the floor.

"You probably feel racism every day at some point— whether you know it or not— so yes, every day. Plus," she adds, while I peel off my black pantyhose, "racism is a big one, with a lot of group and historical momentum behind it. It needs all the spiritual warfare we have."

"Shit," I hiss, as my fingernail snags the thigh.

"I know," Stacey laments, even though I was swearing about my pantyhose.

I sigh.

"Alright."

"Alright," she confirms, "anything else?"

"Well, I definitely swear too much, I think," I answer honestly, but impatient to hop in the shower and begin relaxing.

She laughs for real this time.

"Easy does it. Let's focus on one thing at a time. That first one will be plenty big to take up all your focus for awhile."

My mind turns to the French bread pizza and inevitable reruns of The Office I'm going to watch.

"Alright."

That night, like every night, I kneel down beside my mattress on the floor to meditate for five minutes and say my final prayer.

Only tonight, I awkwardly piece together a 'please-God-make-me-less-racist' prayer.

It isn't nearly as eloquent as Stacey's.

Late Winter 2014
In memory of Tamir Rice
Cleveland, OH

"Grand Jury Won't Indict NYPD Officer in Eric Garner Chokehold Death"

I should be making cold calls, but instead my eyes scan the headline on my work computer.

Not knowing much about the Eric Garner incident, I click into the article.

I haven't watched the video.

To be honest, I just... it hasn't felt right.

A man died.

How do I *watch* that?

But this headline today has mysteriously stirred something in me.

The city is now boiling over with rage and dissent at every turn.

And all I know, really, are three things:
1. A black man died at the hands of a police officer.
2. This black man was both a father and a criminal, although I had no idea his crime(s).
3. A small voice inside me defends the police officer every time I hear or see the phrase "I CAN'T BREATHE," even though I have no idea what actually happened.

Suddenly, I decide to watch the video.

What if it scars me to watch? I briefly wonder.

A friend of mine once told how he watched a video of a beheading on YouTube one day while bored at work, and it messed him up mentally for years.

Shrugging yet determined, I pull out my headphones and pull up YouTube on my phone.

I'm bored at work. There's nothing better to do.

And, frankly— I strangely realize— if I'm going to take sides with the police officer on such a hot-button issue, I should at least watch the damn video to know for sure.

I quickly glance around and see that, as usual, no one is paying any attention to me.

I click Play.

And I watch.

I watch one police officer escalate a situation needlessly by wrapping his arm around Eric Garner's neck.

I watch other police officers pile on, supporting their colleague's efforts.

I watch Eric Garner being taken down by a mob of small, aggressive police officers like a strange re-enactment of that one scene from Gulliver's Travels.

Only this time, the giant man was black, face-down, and slowly suffocating to death.

I watch, although my vision blurs from the unexpected tears which pool in my eyes.

And when it's over, I sit.

Stunned.

The small voice inside me which, moments ago, was defending the police officer was... *wrong*.

I'm not saying every police officer in the whole country is wrong. But *this one* is.

This was wrong.

And *this*... is not okay.

An unfamiliar breed of anger surges beneath my pale skin.

And suddenly, I'm reminded of the lyrics from a praise song that I listened to on my commute this morning...

It spoke about the things that break God's heart, and then asked the listener whether or not their heart breaks for those things, too.

My heart is broken. And I'm filled with anger. But what can I do?

Quickly, I blink away the tears, remembering I'm at work.

And then, an idea.

Google.

I lean forward at my work computer: "eric garner protest nyc"

"Bingo," I whisper as the list pulls up results from local news stations.

After clicking into a few different sources, I notice the trend.

People wishing to participate will meet at Union Square Park at 6pm. Tonight.

Tonight?!

But my mind doesn't have a fighting chance against the righteous anger in my heart.

I have to.

I don't have a choice.

And I can't explain it.

I'm a classic millennial, who is always looking for excuses to bail on anything that isn't on the internet.

But *this*... feels different.

This energy isn't mine.

And so, I stand up and walk downstairs to the Duane Reade store beneath our office.

I'm going to need some granola bars to make it from now until tonight, and, thankfully, Friday was payday.

Four hours later, my nervous boot bounces itself against the stained maroon carpet of our office.

I've never done anything like this before and feel the way I did before big track meets in high school. Excited, but also ready to throw up.

I reflect on the email sent to my Social Work professor the morning of the protest back in college. I told her I had gotten food poisoning.

Shaking my head but unable to shake the shame, I realize while I can't go back and relive that moment, I can move forward from here.

So I light up my phone again to check the time. 5:24pm.

I could probably leave now.

My eyes glance down at the box of unopened blueberry granola bars shoved into my fake leather bag. And then I close them to pray.

God, please give me the strength and courage to act tonight, to do what is right, and not bail like I always do...

And before my mind can talk me out of it, my fingers grab the tangled cord of headphones off my desk and my cheap bag off the floor, and I walk briskly out of

125

the office, toward the subway which will take me
down to Union Square Park.

I crumple the empty blue metallic wrapper, still
chewing, and stuff it into the now-opened box jutting
out from my tote bag, as my other hand grips tighter
to my cell phone.

I see a group of loosely gathered people.

I would guess there are about forty of them, but I was
always terrible at those "guess how many jellybeans
are in the jar" exercises, so I really have no idea.

It's 5:55.

As I near the group of racially diverse people, I
certainly don't look the part like the others.

For one thing, I'm not wearing a canvas backpack of
any sort.

For another, I am not donning a sweatshirt with any
of the following emblazoned on it: the black power fist
symbol, tie-dye, a marijuana leaf, *any* band name, or
the anarchy symbol.

I am wearing tweed slacks beneath my black coat.

*God, please help me not to judge these people, and
help me to do Your will.*

A metallic, echoing voice rings out over the casual
crowd: "We will wait here until 6:20pm exactly, and
then we will begin our march uptown."

My chunky-heeled boots turn toward the sound of leadership and see a black man holding a megaphone. He is wearing a red, green and yellow tie-dyed shirt with black writing I can't make out under a black unzipped zip-up. And he has dreadlocks down to his waist.

My eyes scan the slowly growing crowd and I feel enormously out of place, as my knuckles grow even whiter against my cell phone.

In a strange way, though, I also feel energized and inspired.

I'm finally doing something for a cause I believe in.

I blink hard, not even recognizing myself, and wonder for the tenth time if the other people in the group assume I am lost.

A heavily-necklaced white man to my right begins playing bongo drums which hang from a cord around his neck.

Of course he's playing the bongos, my eyes roll loudly.

Judge not, the angel on my opposite shoulder quietly reminds me.

The crowd is about three-quarters young people, and probably over eighty-percent people of color.

At this moment, I feel more awkward than I ever have in my life.

All those times I stayed uncomfortably silent in the face of racial slurs do not compare to the ironic discomfort I feel standing here, finally showing up to do the right thing.

So I pretend to scroll through my phone, like any good millennial in uncomfortable situations.

This lasts about five minutes, while small clusters of people continue joining the group.

Again, I'm no expert at counting jellybeans, but I'd guess there are now around sixty-five people gathered.

Nearly everyone who has joined is black, I notice, sprinkled with only a few white people, a very disproportionate amount of whom have their version of dreadlocks.

As I look around, most all of the white people here resemble cast-offs from a community college job fair. The few that don't look like stereotypical stoners are around the age of seventy and have faces so wrinkled, it's clear they've been angry for awhile.

"We're going to leave in ten minutes!" the dreadlocked-man with the megaphone shouts to the crowd's cheers.

I clap with one hand against the other, still holding my safety blanket.

"We will march up Broadway..."

I tune the rest out, and tune into the side conversations going on around me.

"The video was repulsive. That cop deserves life..."

"I just don't understand how many more times this needs to happen before..."

"There won't be any justice here. There never is."
    "Then we'll march 'til there is!"
        "What if marching isn't what's going to work?"
            "It *has* to.... It *has to*. People *have to* listen eventually."

I look at the two people having that particular conversation.

Two young black women, one with glasses, both with braids. Both around my age.

I wonder if, in some strange twist of fate, either of them were among the students who walked out of my college class that day.

I lick my lips, anxiously, then begin reading everyone's signs.

I don't have a sign.

Nor do I have any materials to make one.

I glance around and see several people holding onto various newspapers with headlines from today's news, of which I, also, do not have.

Among the homemade cardboard signs are slogans that read as new to the American lexicon:

"I CAN'T BREATHE"

"BLACK LIVES MATTER"

Then there are tried and true slogans which have seemingly been around forever, such as:

"NO JUSTICE. NO PEACE."

As well as the clever riff:

"KNOW JUSTICE. KNOW PEACE."

I see several red sweatshirts walk up with the same logo on it and, beneath it, some sort of "Workers' Party" phrase denoting communism.

I sigh with raised eyebrows.

If I haven't been placed on a government watchlist up to now, I guess today's the day.

"Alright, everyone," the man with the megaphone tries fruitlessly to wrangle all the jellybeans.

There are about ninety(ish) of us now.

Everyone's chatter seems to grow louder, despite his call for attention.

I just stand here and watch.

A few people are chuckling, some hugging, a few shaking their heads— clearly pissed off— and one black girl is crying...

It's an interesting thing to bring together people who all feel the same way about a cause, but don't all feel the same way in a given moment.

"We are going to begin!" he announces, and hearty cheers erupt as my heart skips a beat.

This is it.

I'm actually doing this.

My sweaty fingers clutch harder to the cell phone in my hand.

"WHAT DO WE WANT?" he shouts into the metallic megaphone.

> "JUSTICE!" everyone around me calls out, as we begin moving.

Oh God. We're moving.

"AND WHEN DO WE WANT IT?"

> "NOW!"

"What's going on?" I ask the light-skinned black guy beside me. He looks at least five years younger than me and has the tiniest ringlet curls I've ever seen in an enviably voluminous shoulder-length haircut.

"The cops are blocking us," the sleeve of his puffy coat points up at the now-dark sky, "They've got their choppers on us, too, and are trying to flank us so we can't make it to the Rockefeller tree lighting."

I glance up and see blinking lights hovering, stationary against the dark sky.

It's an ominous sight, knowing they're looking down on an "us" I'm now a part of.

I nod to him with conviction and move my eyes to the row of riot-geared police behind the metal crowd control barricades, thirty feet of protesters in front of the two of us.

By now, there are hundreds, maybe even over a thousand people marching with the group.

I stopped trying to count after the first hour or so of marching.

Scanning the crowd, I see a diverse collection of New Yorkers and, in my case, New Jerseyans. Still, though, mostly black and varying shades of brown faces.

I shuffle through the crowd, naively, up to the police officers.

I stare at one of them sweetly, thinking my old tricks will work under this new dynamic I've placed myself in.

"Hi sir," I smile, batting my eyelashes at him a bit, "Why won't you guys let us go down this road?"

The white officer keeps his strong, gloved grip on the silver crowd control barrier and stares above me.

"Excuse me," I attempt again, in my whitest, most feminine tone, "Why can't we go down this way?"

He looks down at me with tired eyes, as though staring right through me.

"You're not going down that way," he sternly informs me in a tone which, frankly, startles me.

My brows furrow. *This is new.*

"But why? We're not doing anything wrong," I point out in a way which few in the crowd can.

An order calls out behind him, and the entire row of police officers suddenly begin marching forward, pushing our bodies backward with the metal barriers.

"What the?!" I shuffle and shout, trying not to fall, "You can't do that! We didn't even touch you!"

My white voice drowns in a sea of shouts from both sides.

Evidently they can... because they <u>are</u>.

The officer I spoke with pushed his barricade into me with no more aggression than anyone else, but it feels personal, as though he is trying to tell me: "Honey, that sweet, pretty white girl act won't work here today."

It doesn't feel *mean,* per se. But it does feel... *intentional.*

The hard, metal fencing continues to force my feet backward, awkwardly, as the officer continues to stare out above me.

I sink back into the protection of the crowd and notice the light-skinned black guy again.

I wave at him, concerned about what I just went through and, also, grateful to see a familiar face.

"How'd it go?" he asks eagerly.

"Well they're pushing us back now with the barricades," I shrug with a sarcastic and nervous laugh, "so I wouldn't say I contributed much."

He extends a smile, as well as a few pieces of paper, to me.

"You want a sign? We have some extras," his brown eyes glance over to a heavier-set brunette white girl with braided pigtails behind him.

She turns and smiles at me.

"You come here from work?" the girl asks through horn-rimmed glasses and a septum piercing.

I nod, half-smiling.

"Good for you!" they both grin.

The guy extends four sheets of papers to me. I see one sheet that says "No Justice, No Peace," as well as three with large letters "I CAN'T BREATHE!"

I grab one of the latter, not wanting to be rude and take the last one of anything.

"Thanks," I smile.

"Are you here alone?" he asks me.

"Uh, yeah," I look around, feeling like a very uncool kid at school, then lie, "I may have a friend around here somewhere, but I haven't seen him yet."

"Well, come walk with us!" he offers, ringlets bouncing enthusiastically.

He and the brunette girl link arms, and he extends his other to me.

I glance down at his puffy-sleeved arm and link up, smiling, feeling as though I might belong here for the first time in the two hours I've been walking.

I hold up the small sign with my unlinked arm, as the three of us march onward together, like a strange Wizard of Oz trio.

There's Braided Dorothy with the septum piercing.

Me as the Timid Lion, trying to find courage in all of this.

And the light-skinned black guy who, frankly, feels like The Good Witch at this point with his unprompted kindness and how safe I feel now that I've made a few "friends."

As we walk down the street together, there is little time for small talk as we recite the words "I CAN'T BREATHE" over and over and over again.

My mind flashes with memories of the video I'd watched hours earlier.

Then suddenly, a strange, familiar feeling descends on me.

Inside me wells with a very unholy pride at the fact that *I*, a white person, have joined arms with *him*, a black guy.

With my nose rising higher in the air and swelling grandiosity, I imagine myself righteously sitting at segregated soda counters with black people "back in the day," and I begin to think about how cool I must look in this particular moment... before my gag reflex can stop me.

I cast my eyes down at the passing pavement, immediately ashamed.

And let out a tired sigh.

God, please forgive me.

Let me remember this is not all about me. In fact, it's not <u>at all</u> about me.

Help me forget about me right now.

Rid me of the obsessive thoughts about what I look like to others... And bless this guy and his friend who have been so kind to me.

My prayer screeches to a halt as a cluster of photographers clamor toward us from the sidewalk, jumping out in front of our merry trio, snapping photos of us.

My eyes dart over toward my two compatriots.

Their eyes are fixed ahead, determined.

My panicked eyes shift and stare into the lenses, as mixed emotions surge within me.

Hope and pride quickly give way to fear, concern, and near-paranoia.

What if they are photographers from large national papers and my family back home sees me?

What if they are local papers and my boss sees me?

What if the guy I've been talking to recently sees me and doesn't want to date me anymore?

My eyes widen as the bright flashes erupt in our faces.

But despite my thoughts swirling with worry, my feet keep on walking.

"HANDS UP!"

    "DON'T SHOOT!"

"HANDS UP!"

"DON'T SHOOT!"

Somewhere about five blocks ago, the three of us parted ways.

Hipster Dorothy had to duck into a diner to use the restroom. I kept marching so I could finish sooner and begin my long commute home.

Normally my commute home from my midtown office is almost two hours, one-way. But tonight— as we head further and further uptown— who knows?

Maybe I'll just get an Uber from the Hoboken train station back home to Bayonne tonight...

After all, Friday was payday.

As I ponder the impulsive spending I've done in the last couple of days, everyone begins laying down on the street.

"What the hell?" I actually spoke out loud.

"It's a die-in!" a faceless man with a rather feminine voice shouts from behind me, "Right in front of Fox News!"

I gaze up in the direction we are all facing as more and more people lower themselves to the ground.

Sure enough, on the second and third floors, there are signs for Fox News. I can see the large cameras inside and everything.

As I look around, I notice I'm the only person still standing in a quarter-block radius (if you don't count all the cops and their horses).

I slowly lower myself to the filthy New York City street and lay down, succumbing to peer pressure and trying not to imagine what I am laying in.

I'm going to have to burn this coat when I get home.

For the what-feels-like eternity that we lay there, I try to talk my OCD down off the ledge: *Thisismoreimportantthangerms.Thisismoreimporta ntthangerms.Thisismoreimportantthangerms.Thisis moreimportantthangerms.Thisismoreimportantthan germs.Thisismoreimportantthangerms.Thisismorei mportantthangerms.Thisismoreimportantthangerms .Thisismoreimportantthangerms.Thisismoreimporta ntthangerms.THISISMOREIMPORTANTTHANGER MS.*

From the pavement, my tense eyes watch slender silhouettes in the floor-to-ceiling windows of Fox News raise their phones and snap photos of us.

They are, literally, looking down at us, and suddenly I feel cartoonish, embarrassed, and like a... *loser* or something.

I watch from the hard black asphalt as three or four bodies around me rise, and I pop up off the disgusting street like a piece of toast out of the toaster.

Everyone else slowly begins to stand up, too.

Last one down, one of the first ones up, my guilt nags me.

And how the hell am I going to afford a new coat?

"We're going all the way up to Columbus *Circle?*" my voice breaks.

Adrenaline began seeping out of me around the time of the die-in and now my cheaply booted feet ache, as my right shoulder throbs from my tote bag that is, as always, too heavy.

No one answers me. I moreso pleaded it to the night sky rather than inquire to any one specific person, anyway.

But, yes, we are going all the way to Columbus Circle.

I sigh and continue the trudge.

Specks of light, cool rain begin peppering my forehead, as though God, Himself, is trying to revive the dwindling group back to life.

I slowly gaze around the crowd. There are still hundreds of people marching— most with signs— but it's a calm group now.

I haven't seen Hipster Dorothy and the light-skinned Good Witch since they parted with the group over an hour ago. I suppose it was unrealistic of me to even expect that I might.

Eyes scanning the weary crowd in the now-damp, brisk night air, all I see are signs filled with phrases that, a year ago, would have meant nothing to me.

HANDS UP. DON'T SHOOT.

I CAN'T BREATHE.

BLACK LIVES MATTER.

They mean something to me now.

Forty-five minutes later, I climb down the filthy staircase to the concrete subway platform, groaning with each excruciating step.

$30 boots are not made to walk the length of Manhattan. *Now we know.*

Yet, despite the searing pain, I feel... happy.

I feel lighter, despite the fact my bag and body have only grown heavier.

I feel proud of myself and all the other peaceful protesters I saw tonight.

I glance at my phone. It's 10:07pm.

And as I stand waiting for the train, I think of the angry ones.

On one occasion, a half-filled water bottle was thrown from the back of the crowd up toward the line of police.

And occasionally, I heard angry shouting at the police.

There weren't many who acted on their anger. Only a few. Certainly not enough to sully my remembrance of the event on the whole.

The rickety subway pulls up, squealing to a halt.

I briefly wonder if the police will typecast all the protesters tonight due to the angry and unruly ones in the same way some protesters seemed to have typecast all police by the actions of their untrustworthy and abusive colleagues.

The chime tolls and the flimsy metal doors slide open. I climb on-board the nearly empty car, mercifully lowering my body onto a plastic seat.

Thank You for opening my eyes on a lot of things today, God. Thank You for giving me positive action to take. Help me to take more positive action, and even more impactful action going forward.

My eyelids blink heavily, and I light up my phone to, again, check the time.

10:14pm.

My foggy mind does some quick math and at this rate, I'll be walking home from the Light Rail around 12:45am.

The last time I walked home late, it was only 10:30pm and a woman across the street threatened the man walking twenty yards in front of me with a gun because he had been yelling out to her.

I'm definitely taking an Uber home from Hoboken.

Fall 2015
In memory of Brenden Glenn
Venice, CA

I barely make it inside before the Light Rail doors seal shut.

I can already tell the red coat I'm wearing isn't warm enough for today's weather, but I've gained too much weight to fit into my other jacket.

Damn.

I shake my ponytailed head and catch a glimpse of a miraculously empty seat near the back of the train.

Shuffling my way past bookbags belonging to nurses whose scrubs I can see beneath their enviably puffy winter jackets, I whisper the obligatory "excuse me" every few feet despite the fact nearly everyone is wearing headphones.

Hardly anybody on my commute is white.

I plop myself down in the empty seat, next to a black man in his forties or fifties who is wearing a nice suit underneath his black wool coat.

Still breathing heavily from running up to the train, I sit still for a moment, trying not to be a total spaz next to this professional man who's clearly on his way to somewhere important.

He continues staring serenely out the window, not even glancing over at me.

After about forty-five seconds of trying my best to pretend I'm not a frenzied, perpetually late, disorganized mess of a human being, I slowly bend down and reach into my fake leather work bag to pull out the daily devotional Stacey gave me at the start of the year.

I pull out the white and purple softcover book, as I do every morning.

I glance around and see nobody looking at me, despite how it feels.

The gentleman beside me is still gazing out the window.

My fingers turn the thick beige pages to today's date and I begin to read the entry for November 14th.

I read how our thoughts and beliefs are like the ingredients one would use to bake. If you add cinnamon into the batter, it will appear in the finished product. If you don't add cinnamon, it will not.

Our thoughts and beliefs have the same effect in our lives, I read.

Then the Bible verse: "...those who plow iniquity and sow trouble reap the same." (Job 4:8)

I look up, pinching my thin lips together as I often do while in thought.

My thoughts and beliefs... "plow iniquity"... "sow trouble"...

Without moving my head, my eyes roll to the right, toward the black man beside me.
I think about racism.

That's certainly got to qualify for "plowing iniquity."

After a moment of hesitation, I begrudgingly admit to myself that to hold those beliefs is sowing trouble, as well.

My head drops a bit and hangs, as I look down into the messy contents of my open work bag.

Wallet.

Bottle of water.

Empty granola bar wrapper.

Then my eyes find what they're looking for: a pen.

Stacey had suggested I write down the year and issue I'm struggling with in the devotional so that when I go back to use it, year after year, I can see all the growth God's brought into my life.

I bend at the waist as the doors open, letting in a blustery autumn wind and seven more commuters.

I grab the exposed pen cap amid the mess in my bag.

Being that this is my first year working through the devotional, there are only the notes I've taken since January.

I place the pen to my mouth, gripping the cap between my teeth, and firmly yank on it.

With the cap still between my teeth, I quickly glance over to confirm my black seatmate is still looking out the window.

He is.

I half-close the book so no other commuters can see the shame-filled word I am about to write.

"2015: racism"

Then I quickly close the book and stuff it deep into the bottom of my bag.

My green eyes finally catch his enormous brown ones across the room.

Brown hair, dark beard, a slight tan, torn jeans, and cool Ray Bans hooked onto his signature black t-shirt's collar.

His name is Brad.

And from the moment I noticed him sitting in the back row at Bible Group, I'd been convinced God created him just for me.

He's everything I've ever wanted.

He even works high up at Google.

And he's a Christian.

He stares at me, and the left corner of his mouth turns up slightly.

Every cell in my body electrifies.

I smile back, not hearing a word of what the chatty woman is saying to me.

The young woman standing in front of me whom I am ignoring is new to the Group, and tonight is only her second time attending.

I know in my heart I should be paying attention to her instead, but... *damn, is he handsome.*

"So tell me about this guy," Stacey prods playfully through the phone the next night.

"His name is Brad," I don't hesitate, as I speed-walk home, "He's in the Group. Brown hair, brown eyes, with a full beard."

I groan as if I'm a thirteen-year-old girl swooning over a popstar.

"He's *perfect!*"

"Brad," she responds with pause, "Hmm."

I wait for her to continue. When she doesn't, my heart skips a beat.

I immediately try to pry a positive reaction out of her.

"You know him? Isn't he so great?"

Stacey says nothing for a moment.

"Um," she finally begins, obviously measuring her words, "I've heard him share in Group several times. I'm, um... I'm not sure if the two of you are on the same path."

Insecurity sweeps over me.

"You don't think I'm a good enough Christian for him?" I half-plead into the phone.

"That's not at all what I said."

She falls silent.

I am silent.

We're silent.

"I, uh... How do I put this to you?"

I am still silent.

"I heard him share last week when you weren't there and, um, it led me to believe that while he *says* he's a Christian..." her tone rises considerably on the word 'says,' and she continues, "Mmm... He's not really pursuing the Christian path of making one's heart ever-nearer to Jesus."

My eyebrows scrunch together, trying to compute her words, then they loosen.

I'm too Christian... *for him?*

My eyes widen.

Well, this is a first.

"I don't mean to sound as though I'm judging," Stacey clarifies, "That isn't our place. I just, I'm looking out for you. And I've just heard some things he's shared that aren't, well... on the spiritual beam, so to speak."

My eyes blink hard in the cold, dark air.

Why do I always forget gloves?

My mother would kill me if she knew I forgot gloves.

"Hmm," I pause, trying to defend him, "but he's been in the Group for so long? Like *way* before me."

"And I've seen him date many young women in it, Trisha," Stacey seems to finish my sentence, as jealousy and comparison swell within me.

She continues.

"He usually only comes to the mixed-gendered meetings when he's looking for a new girl, which is likely why you've been seeing him lately."

My heart simultaneously skips with excitement and drops from disappointment.

"But look, you're on your path," she offers the line I hear from her often, "I don't know God's Plan for you. Maybe this is part of it. I just don't, personally, see the two of you aligning from a spiritual perspective with all the good work I see you trying to do."

My shoulders slump as the wind in my sails grows still.

"Hmm," I consider her words, "Well I have a date with him this weekend."

"Okay," she chirps in a falsely encouraging high pitch, "Well, pray on it! God will lead you to who you're supposed to be with."

I know Stacey is encouraging me not to pursue him.

I know she has her reasons.

And deep down— if I'm honest with myself— I know she's probably right.

But... *damn, is he handsome.*

Late Fall 2015
In memory of Natasha McKenna
Fairfax County, VA

A month later, I receive a voicemail from Stacey. In it, she recounts how she was in morning prayer and felt the Lord lead her to encourage me in my career.

She knows I hate my job.

"Maybe focus your energy now on finding a fulfilling career," she imparts.

"I know you've been struggling with jealousy a lot with Brad, and I just feel like once you discover what God wants you to do for work, a lot of your insecurities will fall away and you may be in a better position to date with clearer direction."

I feel judged. Rejected. And bossed around.

I love Stacey. I do. But sometimes she's just so annoying.

As always, however, I listen.

Not because I'm one of those blind follower Christians who idolizes a person... but because the advice she has given me up to now has been sound and *has* led me closer to God.

What <u>do</u> I want to do for a career?

It's a question that's plagued me for years.

"Oh," Stacey concludes in her message, "and if you're not feeling a strong direction toward one career or another, maybe pray and ask God what He would have you be."

It's 9pm and my tennis shoes pound hard against the treadmill.

Les Brown's confident black voice echoes in my headphones, as I gaze out over the fluorescent-lit gym.

He tells me that, for a long time, he wasn't sure what the purpose of his life was.

I raise the speed on the treadmill by 0.1 mph, feeling my overweight breathing begin to labor.

He tells me that he had no idea what his life's work was supposed to be.

I stare down at the red numbers, knowing that story well, and then raise it another 0.2, up to 6.3 mph.

He tells me that he wasn't sure about anything.

I think about how much I hate my job in insurance as I burp up some of the weird acai berry-flavored pre-workout drink I chugged before walking across the street from my apartment.

No one is destined to work in insurance. I know few things in this life for sure, but that is certainly one of them.

I hate my job.

I hate every day in it.

The motivational video continues as I watch people of varying races mill about the weight machines and front desk area.

He tells me that I need to make a conscious effort to find out what I'm supposed to do.

I push the up arrow until the red numbers read 6.7 mph.

He tells me that finding *that thing* will literally save my life.

Then he repeats that it will literally save my life.

I raise the number to 7 mph.

He tells me that 85% of Americans hate their jobs.

I look down at my racing feet, knowing I'm among them.

He tells me that when people go to jobs they hate, it destroys their self-respect and throws them into a state of inner turmoil.

I stare down at the speeding tread while he speaks— it would seem— directly to me.

He tells me that my life is worth finding.

I blink hard and push the button up to 7.1 mph.

He asks me: "What is it that you're supposed to do?"

"how was your run?" his text reads.

I smile, staring at my phone like an idiot while walking across the street.

"good... hard. what are you up to?" I type back.

I finally look up, climbing the steps to my four-story apartment building's front entrance.

"watching the news. pretty exciting lol. what do you want to do this weekend?"

I lift my key fob and hear the intense metal lock unlatch, slipping into the building away from the cold night air.

I enter the white stairwell, as lately I've been trying to take the stairs rather than the elevator.

"I don't care! just hanging with you is so much fun!" I add a smiley face emoji, as I take the stairs two at a time to cool-down.

I can't believe I'm dating Brad.

THE Brad.

I smile, pushing the heavy metal door to my floor open and turning down the hall toward my studio apartment.

My phone lights up and I look down to read: "you like me so much, lol"

I smirk.

"guilty lol" I respond, shamelessly.

I don't see why Stacey warned me about him.

I certainly haven't seen any red flags.

I climb down onto my prayer carpet, as Enya sings in the background.

I sigh as heavily as I feel, gazing into the glowing flames of the flickering votive candles lined up on top of my metal radiator.

Dear God, I know we're working on a lot.

I'm sorry I felt racist toward those two young black men on the train home this evening. Help me to see rightly. Help me to see my brothers and sisters as just that: brothers and sisters.

Help me. Help me to be more like You. More like Jesus.

God, You know that Stacey told me to focus on what I should be doing with the time You've given me here.

Warm tears fill my eyes at the thought of all the time I've wasted up to now, as one lone tear drops to my cheek.

I know that time is a gift, but I don't know what You want me to do with mine.

I don't know why I'm here, which, I guess makes sense since I didn't bring myself here. You know the dreams I have... the talents I possess... after all, they're Yours. From You.

I shake my head with pinched eyes, as a second tear escapes my eye.

I just... I don't know where to go with any of it. You know I float from job to job and never feel satisfied. Bouncing from crappy career to crappy career, never truly using the gifts You've given me.

Please show me why I'm here. Even if I don't want to see it. Tell me my purpose.

With still-closed eyes, I let out a sigh, digging deep for more strength to pray honestly.

And once that's established, God, please clear away everyone and everything that is not in service to that call, in service to You and the work You have laid out for me.

Finally opening my eyes, I stare out the large window into the black Bayonne sky, sparsely peppered with glimmering white stars.

And God...

I pause heavily.

You know I have a habit of muddying the waters and making things overly complicated. Please make this so simple, even I can't screw it up.

Thank You. I love You. Amen.

The wirey fibers on the aged maroon and beige rug burn their way into my knees, and I manage to slowly climb up off my prayer rug, wiping a few tears from my ripe, pink cheeks.

My phone buzzes almost immediately, bringing me back to reality.

"you up and want to talk?" he asks.

"I guess" I send back with a flirtatious wink emoji.

A half hour phone call later, I kneel down for my five minute meditation and final prayer, still gripping my phone— and lifeline to him— smiling.

Every morning when I wake up, I move directly from bed to my knees on the floor.

Otherwise I'll forget.

I don't even walk the ten yards to my prayer rug.

Most mornings the cold beige tile that lines my entire, small apartment sears too deeply into my volleyball-damaged knees, so I simply spin around and sit, leaning my back against the mattress on the floor.

This morning is no different.

Dear God...

I don't know why I always begin my prayers as though I'm writing a letter. It's just what I do.

Good morning. Thank You for this day, I begin out of habit.

Suddenly, the air is sucked from my lungs as I am struck with a truth that a deep part of me knew since late last night in my sleep, after saying that prayer about finding my career:

I am supposed to be a pastor.

What?

I stare down at the floor for a moment and see how the statement feels when compared against my soul.

"I am supposed to be a... pastor," I whisper so low, even I can barely hear.

But the statement feels confident... certain... and... *right.*

This is it!

I can't explain the sensation inside me.

It just *is.*

I am supposed to be a pastor, but didn't know it until... today? Last night?

Always... somewhere... deep down?

I don't know, but I know now what I am called to be.

"Is this for real?" I say out loud to God, astonished.

My mind races.

And then the doubts flood in.

I swear a lot...

and slack off at work...

and am racist...

and I binge eat...

and usually all four in a given day!

I'm not the right pick to be a pastor, I realize, *I'm in no position to be telling people what to do.*

So I pray again.

God, I, uh...

I don't even know verses from the Bible like other Christians do!

And I don't raise my hands during worship like everybody else.

And, I didn't go to school for this... I'm not in the church I was raised in... I don't post about You on social media like others do... I'm a, uh, I'm a woman.

I pause.

I mean, not like You didn't know that, I stammer to Him in my head.

Or any of that, I realize, *I just...*

My face feels like it does when somebody asks me to do complicated math off the top of my head. Scrunched, confused, and struggling.

"This can't be right, is it?" I whisper, shaking my messy bunned head.

I look at my open closet across the room and think solely of the statement "I am supposed to be a pastor."

And then, a shift: "I *am* a pastor."

My mind is telling me a million reasons why this calling is wrong.

But in the silence of my heart, staring at those thick wooden closet doors, it just feels *right*. It feels true in my soul.

It feels the way I feel when I think about any other fact.

Confident.

Unwavering.

Right.

The sky is blue.

Birds fly.

And I... have just been called to become a pastor.

I blink hard on the Light Rail home from church.

I forgot my headphones and have spent nearly every moment since leaving my apartment this morning thinking about what "becoming a pastor" would mean, what it would look like, what topics my sermons would be on...

I, obviously, mentioned nothing about it at church.

My thoughts are suddenly derailed by the opening of the train's doors.

With a blustering gust of wind, in rush a group of four black boys, about thirteen or fourteen years old, all laughing.

One boy is wearing a black winter hat and my aching ears envy it.

The four boys make their way up the stairs to my right and sit down three rows behind me.

As the train doors close, I stare out my window at the season's first whispery flakes of snow. The wind blows them against the glass, causing them to melt on contact mere inches from my nose.

Suddenly, the boys behind me erupt into loud laughter and one of them lets out a small shout.

The laughing continues as my gaze hardens, now staring through the beautiful snow, angered by the disruption.

I glance around the sparsely populated train car, as their rowdy laughter continues.

My eyes are drawn to the black travelers.

Will <u>nobody</u> say something to them, to keep it down?

My eyes dart, looking for somebody to hold these troublemakers accountable for disturbing the rest of us.

And then I see her.

A black woman, about forty. She's wearing scrubs under a long puffy blue coat and looks tired, as if on her way home from a shift.

Her large, round eyes are warm, though. And they seem to be smiling up at the boys.

They're children, the thought slips into my mind.

I turn backward briefly and see one of the boys showing his phone screen to the other three as they all laugh together, happily oblivious to me.

I stare at their round cheeks and the braces one of them wears on his teeth.

They're children.

And if they were white children, it dawns on me, *I would see them as such.*

I envision a group of theoretical white children laughing, how young and innocent their energetic faces would look as they savor these precious few years before adulthood wounds them, if their childhoods haven't already.

My body turns me back around, and my neck bends my head downward, toward the floor.

Not out of shame, although maybe it should have been.

More out of amazement at how my initial reaction toward these boys and their presence was authoritative, if not even tyrannical.

The realization is humbling. Its gravity, sobering.

I close my eyes and listen to the boys' laughter.

"That's crazy," I hear one tell another.

I never thought I was part of the problem.

I've never attended a klan meeting. I've never committed a hate crime.

I've never called anyone that word. And I don't follow black people around in stores, accusing them of theft or anything else crazy.

I don't belong to any shadowy Internet forums that propagate ideas of racial superiority.

I've never even called a black person "articulate," because I know it's a loaded word.

I thank my black baristas.

I wave at my black doormen.

I smile at black strangers and hold doors open for them.

Just then, a certain Bible verse springs to my mind: "Catch us the foxes, the little foxes that spoil the vines…"

I don't know where in the Bible it says that, but I remember a recent sermon I listened to which referenced it.

It's saying the little sins, the little aggressions, the little thoughts of iniquity ruin our ability to rest in the loving presence of God.

And who knows? Maybe these thoughts aren't "little" sins at all.

They feel little, by comparison to what they *could* be.

But does that line of thinking really hold water? Theoretically, one murder is small if you compare it to Hitler.

And it's been a tough thing to realize I am racist. I don't want sympathy necessarily, but I just want you (whoever you are) to know— it's a really tough pill to swallow.

It's humbling at best to acknowledge one's own ignorance and stupidity, downright crushing at worst.

No one reasonable wants to be racist... that horrible, one-toothed stereotype of some poor, white guy in the swamps of the Deep South who bangs his sister and can't piece together a coherent sentence.

No one wants to belong to that category. Like I said, at least no one reasonable.

And I'm reasonable. Reasonable *enough*, at least I guess.

But as I listen to the children's laughter on the train, children's laughter that I, mere moments ago, wanted to abolish, condemn, and punish, I can't help but realize the propensity in me to view black children as adults, to hold them to stricter standards of behavior than I would otherwise, and even *look for* opportunities to rule over them, in a position I somehow assume I have.

But where did I receive this right to lord over anybody?

...I didn't.

Perhaps I am part of the problem by pushing the label "racist" toward that nearly fictional example of a klan member living in a one-room shack.

Perhaps, as a white person, that's been convenient for me.

It's been forgiving to me.

It's been comfortable for me.

I stare down.

Dear God, forgive me for seeing any of Your children as anything other than that. Please soften my gaze, soften my heart, soften my thoughts and attitudes toward children of color. Please help them, as they grow in a world that has people wanting to punish their laughter.

My eyes focus on an empty water bottle rolling around the floor.

Help soften me, Lord, so as not ever to be one of those people again. Help me to see all Your children— no matter their age— as Yours. From Your creation and made in Your image.

I close my eyes, praying to the melody of their laughter.

Protect these young boys, today and always, for their whole lives.

My mind turns toward all the stories in the news lately of black boys and men being shot and killed by police officers.

Protect them God. Please.

"Amen," I whisper, opening my eyes.

The train pulls to a stop.

I watch the black nurse with the round eyes stand slowly, and smile with her mouth this time at the young men behind me, then exit the train.

I imagine her older, knowing smile trying to tell them: "There's a lot in this world working against your happiness. I'm proud of you for being happy anyway."

When I arrive home, I will tell Stacey about my experience on the train as I make myself a late lunch. And she will tell me that she's proud of me, but that there's still work to be done.

She will tell me that prayer is where we *start,* but not where we end.

She will tell me that I can donate to causes which promote children of color and take tangible action to bolster my efforts in prayer.

I will look at my bank account that night and see twenty-seven dollars standing between me and payday, which is five days away. I will calculate my most basic food and transportation needs. Then I will visit the Black Girls Code website and donate all I can.

The next afternoon at work, I google how to become a pastor.

A few blogs pull up, which seem to be written exclusively by men, and I settle on the wikiHow page as my roadmap.

Along with reading the instructions, I notice all of the illustrations are of men. Not a single woman.

My lips purse.

That's a conversation for another day, I suppose.

I quickly locate where I am on the to-do list.

"Earn a degree in theology or attend seminary school."

I sigh.

When I dropped out of college, my parents freaked out, as I was the first and only person in my entire family to not earn a college degree. To quell my mother's panic, I promised her one day I'd go back and finish my degree. That never happened, as it often doesn't.

As such, I hastily type "do I need a college degree to attend seminary school" into the taskbar and hit enter.

As I click through link after link, most websites say I will need an undergraduate degree. However, occasionally I stumble across the hopeful phrase "but not in all cases."

I look up and notice that it's 5:02.

Closing my laptop and standing up to put my coat on, I resolve to research seminary schools in my area tomorrow.

Later that night, Brad calls me to iron out our date for tomorrow evening.

He'll pick me up at my apartment at six, and then we'll drive over to the show.

"Oh," I perk up, wanting to share with him my good news, "I figured out what I want to do for a career!"

"Oh yeah?" he muses, "What's that?"

"So I prayed on it the other night, and it came to me that I should become a pastor!"

He is silent.

"And I mean, it makes sense," I continue, pacing excitedly in my small apartment, "I love public speaking and what a great use for my talents, sharing the Word of God!"

He is still quiet.

I finally prod him: "What do you think?"

"That's kind of weird for a woman," he confesses, "I don't know. That's weird."

My eyes fall to the floor and my feet stop walking.

For a moment, I forget to even breathe.

"Yeah," he decides, laughing, "I'm not really sure how I feel about that."

"Well," I respond optimistically, "it's new, and who knows, maybe it will change? Maybe I heard Him wrong?"

I laugh lightly, despite feeling utterly crushed.

And that's the last time becoming a pastor would cross my mind for the next thirty hours.

Tomorrow at work would come and go, and I wouldn't google a single seminary school.

I would, however, stare anxiously at my cell phone all day, waiting for the next text from Brad.

I lean toward the driver's side to kiss him goodnight.

"Oh," he coughed, waving his hand to shoo me away, "I don't want to get you sick."

"Okay," I nod eagerly, "Drive home safely! Thanks again for tonight!"

As I bounce out of his Ford Escape, I turn to look at him before closing the door.

He gives me a look I can't decipher, alongside a bare half smile.

He recently shaved his beard, which I'm hoping he changes his mind on. To be frank: I don't find him nearly as attractive without it. The rest of his face is not *at all* as handsome as I once thought.

Nevertheless, I grin one last time at him and turn on my high heels to walk inside.

As I try to walk as attractively as possible— in case he's watching— my mind begins spinning as it always does when I leave him.

Future plans, past conversations, everything...

Like an Olympic judge, I reflect back to score my own performance that evening.

Did I come off as cool? Was I overly eager?

It's so much pressure to date who you're meant to be with.

I tap the elevator button in my apartment lobby with my knuckle to avoid contamination.

When is he going to ask me to be his girlfriend?

We've been dating for a month and a half.

Why won't he ask me to be exclusive with him?

You'd think with how serious we are, he'd want it to be official.

As the elevator doors open to the lobby, I pluck my phone from my bag to re-read our previous text messages on the ride up.

My eyes scan the messages, unblinking.

Guys are so funny, I shake my head incredulously, looking at his one-line responses contrasted with my texted paragraphs, *They're so brief in their texts!*

The doors open. And I walk to my bank vault door, eyes still glued to the screen.

As I let myself in, my thumb scrolls all the way up to the very beginning of our text thread.

I had asked for his number after one of our Group meetings. Technically, I texted him because he was the outgoing refreshment volunteer, and I had volunteered for the following month (as an excuse to talk to him more).

That was a little over two months ago. At a certain point, I got tired of waiting for him and finally asked if he wanted to "grab coffee in a non-platonic way."

He agreed.

As I unfasten my painfully high heels and start preparing for a shower, my head continues spinning.

I look at our text thread once more and decide to text him "Thanks again for a great night!" with a smiley face.

I smile, thinking he may enjoy pulling up to his apartment and seeing an appreciative text.

An hour passes with no response from Brad, despite the fact his drive home is only fifteen minutes and I've been picking up my phone every fifteen seconds to check-in.

I pause The Office re-run I'm watching, lift myself off my pale green loveseat and adjust my favorite maroon sweatpants on the walk to the freezer.

173

Pulling out a pint of Ben & Jerry's Cherry Garcia, I slide the silverware drawer out and grab a small spoon. I've learned that I don't blow through the pint as fast if I use a smaller spoon. But, make no mistake, I still finish it in one sitting. It's simply a matter of how *long* it takes.

On my walk back to the loveseat, I am overcome with the desire to call him. To find answers. *Am I his girlfriend? Am I not? If not, <u>why</u> not?*

I can't explain where this sudden surge of confidence emanated from, but here it is and as impulsively as I make many of my decisions, I pick up the phone and call him.

I'm done suffering, I decide.

I'm done fidgeting.

I'm done wondering.

I'm done staring in anticipation at a notification-less phone.

"Hey," Brad answers after the third ring. He sounds as surprised as I am by my bold phone call.

"Hey," I respond quickly.

"Uhh, what's up?"

"Are we going to be exclusive soon or not?" I stare at Steve Carell's frozen face on my television screen and decide to fill the silence with more, "Because we've been dating for over a month and you haven't made any mention of us being exclusive."

There's more silence, so I decide to be blunt.

"It's time to fish or cut bait."

The month of agony and frustration surrounding this boy not doing what I want and what I think he should be doing has reached a boiling point. I have no idea what makes tonight the night, but it's time to tip me over and pour me out...

"Umm, wow," he responds, characteristically without commitment to one side or another.

"I mean, do you see this going any further?" I press him.

"Umm, honestly, I wanted to tell you tonight, but I chickened out, so I was going to tell you next time I saw you in-person."

I listen, as he finally says it.

"I don't think this is working out."

My heart drops, as a simultaneous wave of rage overcomes me. We see each other once a week, maybe twice.

He was going to wait a whole week— respond half-heartedly or not at all to my texts for a whole week— and meanwhile I'd be the sucker with a gun's laser on my forehead the whole time?

Blinking twice hard, I stare at Steve Carell, wondering what I should do.

After a few silent seconds, I inhale sharply then sigh, praying silently for grace and the right words in this moment.

We were going to get married.

We were going to be the picture perfect couple of the Group.

We were...

"Thank you for telling me," my words interrupt my train of thought, "and thank you for the opportunity to get to know you better."

He says nothing.

"I really enjoyed it and learned a lot from our time together."

He is silent.

This time, so am I.

"Wow, um," he starts, "I thought you'd be more sad."

My eyebrows scrunch.

"I really thought you were going to cry," he confesses.

My brain reminds me of all the times he flexed his biceps to a giggling schoolgirl version of myself, and I shake my head, angrily trying to loosen the utterly cringe-worthy memories.

He must think he's really something.

How could I have thought he was really something?

I think of Stacey and her words about him.

Glaring now at Steve Carell, who is certainly at no fault, I snap out of my thoughts quickly enough to salvage the last scraps of dignity I try to convince myself I have left.

He thought I'd fall to pieces. Well, maybe I will... but not for him to see.

"Nope," I chirp eagerly, laughing lightly, "Again, thank you for the opportunity to get to know you better, Brad."

I smile and I know he can hear it when I say: "Good luck with everything, sincerely."

He stammers and fumbles over his words, clearly taken aback.

"Have a great rest of your weekend," I articulate cheerfully. And then I hang up on him.

Setting my phone down and staring at it, I can feel the hot tears start to pool.

Breathing in, I again stand up and walk over to my familiar prayer rug to kneel down.

Years ago, I'd heard Oprah recall how Dr. Maya Angelou once advised her to say "thank You" up to God in very difficult moments.

To hear her retell the advice, you don't need to feel like saying "thank You." You don't even need to know what, exactly, you're saying "thank You" for. Just say "thank You," knowing that, even in this, God has your best interests at heart and is leading you there.

Disappointed tears now stream down my face, as I start to whisper, "Thank You. Thank You. Thank You."

Looking up out the window in front of me as I often do in prayer, I can see a few stars in the dark sky.

"I don't know why this is happening, but thank You."

I stand up and walk back over to where I set my phone.

It's black now.

I open it and text my friend from Group, Jill.

She doesn't know Brad. She only attends the women's meetings, which is where I know her from.

"Hey, can you talk?"

"Of course," she responds immediately.

And I hit the button to dial her.

"Oh honey, I'm sorry," Jill coos at my tale.

I can feel empathy oozing from her voice, as I click the button to place her on speakerphone, lifting my spoon to begin eating.

"I mean," she begins again, "I don't know him, but I do know that if it's not him, God will bring you someone better."

I nod as countless tears stream down my hot, red face.

"Ugh," I groan with a mouthful of Cherry Garcia, "I wanted *him,* though."

"I know," she commiserates, "I'm so sorry."

I wipe my cheeks.

"I'm just so disappointed."

"I know," the sweet brunette agrees, "Trust me, I know that love stories don't always go how we thought they would."

She is, of course, referring to the fact that she is engaged to Brock, a guy who used to be in our Group before he moved for work, and lately she's been sharing that she doesn't feel called to marry him anymore.

I sigh, slowly releasing my own self-pity.

"How's everything with you and Brock going?"

"Ugh," she coughs, laughing a bit, "I don't know. I brought up my fears and reservations to him the other day on Skype."

179

"How'd that go?"

"Oh man, *so* badly!"

She laughs, and I decide it's okay to join in a bit, to empathize.

"He was so confused, like, he didn't see it coming at *all*."

I nod. *How can you?*

"He told me the next morning that he's going to move back. And we're going to try to live together for a little bit to see if this can be saved."

I nod.

"That's a good idea," I advise, "I mean, then you'll kind of know what marriage is like."

"Right, I just..." she trails off.

I listen to her silently search for the right words.

"I already know where it's going, you know? Like, I already know where this ends... I just feel too guilty to end it right now. It's the worst."

I nod.

Maybe she's right...

Maybe all the love stories before your husband are supposed to be terrible. Because, if they weren't, how would you know when it's finally right?

"I'll say some prayers for you guys, for sure," I promise.

"And back at you, girl! You'll make it through this, but I'm so sorry you have to go through it!"

"Thanks. You too, obviously."

She laughs and we say goodnight.

I think about her comforting tone and, after sobbing so heavily, I actually feel a bit better.

I pop another bite of ice cream in my mouth and then examine the creamy, empty spoon.

I glance up at Steve Carell's frozen face and then pinch my eyes closed again.

"Thank You. Thank You. Thank You..."

Monday morning, I google seminary schools.

While browsing page one of the results, one link in particular is jumping out at me.

New York Theological Seminary.

The name of it sounds good, and there is something pulling me to click it. However, I dutifully click through the page results in order.

In website after website, I see groups of white men who are, evidently, trying to become pastors, too. They're laughing in semi-circles with Bibles on their laps. I see young men diligently taking notes in class. Some of the pastors-to-be, I notice, are *very* attractive and it dawns on me: there are no girls-only seminary schools. At least not anywhere near me.

As such, I would likely be the only woman in my class.

My heart sinks as my mouse scrolls.

I couldn't do that. I'd basically just be auditioning the whole time to become a pastor's wife.

I know how I am around men. I know it needs to change. And I know I'm not strong enough to remain authentic in a room of men, especially if I find even one moderately attractive.

What is it about men that makes me lose myself?

I've been obsessed with boys since I was in nursery school where I spent all my days staring at Andrew White. I even once confessed my love to him when we were supposed to have been napping. He didn't return the sentiment.

I visualize myself in a class with these well-coiffed young white men and can't imagine that would do anything but hurt my situation and make me lose focus.

I click back to the search results, utterly dejected.

The New York Theological Seminary school's link sings out to me two hyperlinks down from where I currently am.

I decide to skip the next two entries and follow my gut. I click it.

Immediately I see three black women in a video still-frame on the homepage. I turn off the volume, glance around my office, then click into Full Screen mode and click Play.

The scene opens to an old black man talking to the screen and cuts to the scene of those three black women laughing, then back to the old black man who now is standing beside an even older black woman.

I feel a rush of excitement I can't quite put my finger on.

As I click out of the partially-played video and click into "Course Offerings," my manager Sandra walks up to my desk. I quickly minimize the screen and look up at her, caught.

Sandra has bright blonde hair and always wears her signature black eyeliner. She is only about four feet, eleven inches tall, but has enough charisma to fill Madison Square Garden. I don't know how charming people do it, all I know is that I try to emulate her social skills at every opportunity.

She smiles warmly, having not seen my screen, but understanding as both a mother and a boss that I was certainly just caught slacking.

"Hi Trisha," she greets me in her thick Brooklyn accent.

"Hi," I smile, nervously.

"I just wanted to see how that giant deal you're working on is going. I know you were the only agent to establish any traction on that Tier 1 list of leads."

I lick my lips and glance at my cup of pens and highlighters before looking back to her.

"It's going well, actually. The manager has invited the controller into our next call, so that's definitely a good sign..."

I trail off, looking again at my collection of pens.

Probably only half of those still have ink.

"Do you think it would be beneficial to bring me in on that call? It won't affect your commission at all, and if I can help in any way, I'd be happy to."

I look up at her still-smiling face.

She continues, "Whatever you're comfortable with. I just know you've been an agent for a little under a year and it would be our company's biggest deal of the entire year... but if you feel it makes more sense for you to continue solo, we support and trust your judgment totally."

I smile up at her.

"Thank you so much for the offer," I mirror the response I've seen her give to people, "That sounds really valuable. Can I think about it and let you know by lunch?"

Her smile grows.

"Take til the end of the day, sweetheart. How's everything else going?"

I don't know why, but she always asks me that. Maybe she knows I live in a crappy neighborhood. Maybe she knows about my OCD. Maybe she knows I'm a recovering alcoholic.

"It's good," I nod a bit too eagerly, "That guy I was seeing ended things with me this weekend, but..."

I trail off again.

"Ohh," she coos like she would if I were her own daughter, "I'm sorry, sweetie. You know what, from what you told me about him, I didn't like him for you anyway."

She waves her hand.

"You deserve better."

I smile, reminded of Stacey.

"You know," I remark, raising my need-to-be-plucked eyebrows, "you're not the first person to tell me that."

"Well, there ya go!" she brightens, "Okay, sweetie. You let me know by end-of-day. I'm happy to block out time on my calendar. What day is the call again?"

"Thursday afternoon at three."

"Okay, you let me know."

As she walks away, I bow my head.

You can't really tell your manager you need to 'pray on' a thing before you decide, unless you want to be labeled the office nut, which let's be honest, I may already reign as if anyone counts how many times I Purell my hands in a day.

I swallow hard, then begin: *God, You know what's best here. You can see all things. Please help me to see if Sandra should be in on this next call on Thursday.*

As I raise my eyes and look up, I see Ernest staring at me.

Ernest is the Hispanic guy who sits beside me. Despite having more experience in sales than me, he's worked here for about half the time.

"You okay?" his round face asks from behind his tiny glasses.

I smile, feeling caught in my deskside prayer.

"Yeah," I chuckle, "just hoping they show up to the call this Thursday."

He smiles.

"I'm impressed you were able to gain so much traction," he tells me, "I haven't gotten anywhere on that Tier 1 list. I'm proud of you, kid!"

My lips tighten into a forced smile, feeling resentful toward him. He's only a few years older than me, and he definitely doesn't need to sound so surprised.

"Thanks," my tone is artificially bright.

Then I promptly turn my chair toward the drawers in my cubicle, opening one and pretending to search for anything other than this conversation inside.

Later that night, I conclude my usual five excruciating minutes of meditation in front of my mattress.

I don't care what Stacey says, I swear it's making me crazier.

My eyes open and I try, strenuously, to adjust my legs in their present kneeling position.

As a former volleyball player, my knees aren't exactly aging like fine wine... more like an opened, half-drunk bottle of beer.

The entire five minutes of "meditation" were spent thinking about Brad.

I sigh.

I'm *deeply* flawed.

I'm chronically late. I judge people. I'm racist. I think *way* too much about men and, also, too often of myself. I binge eat. I have credit card debt. And I'm a terrible employee.

Not exactly Reverend King over here...

My eyes roll impatiently at myself as I turn and face the mattress, preparing for my last prayer of the night.

And yet, somehow— despite all the flaws— I don't think I heard God wrong.

I do believe God called me to be a pastor.

But *why?*

Suddenly a cold wave of electricity shoots through my body, and my vision tightens on my pillow, like an eagle catching a glimpse of its prey.

Brad ending things with me was an answer to my very plea for guidance.

My mind races.

I asked God that night to tell me what I should be and then asked Him to clear away everything... and every*one*... that wasn't going to support me in His calling.

Then God took away Brad.

I shake my head incredulously, suddenly remembering Brad's discouraging words when I told him of my pastoral ambitions, and how I had laid down all my seminarial goals when I didn't receive his approval.

How could I not see this before?

I was willing to abandon THE. CALL. OF. GOD. based on this one man's flimsy rejection of the idea.

So God cleared him away.

Answering my prayer.

And yet, it dawns on me, God is keeping all these flaws in me... at least, for now.

As I sit on the cold tile, leaning against my mattress, I recall what Alex, a member of the Group, said in our last meeting: the most arrogant thing I can do is ask God "why?" and believe that He somehow owes me an answer.

Why He called me a pastor...

Why He took away Brad, but left me all these sins...

God...

I begin.

I don't need to know why. I <u>don't</u> know any of the why's. But I trust You. And I thank You, for doing for me what I didn't have the strength to do myself.

For clearing Brad away.

Bless him.

Open his mind about women in church leadership.

I don't know why You left all these sins in me. But I don't need to.

I trust You. And I trust that You will clear them away, like You did with Brad, in Your perfect time.

I climb into bed, roll over to one side, and begin involuntarily fantasizing about Brad trying to win me back.

Like I said... *deeply* flawed.

I wore my winter coat today, thank God.

This one was a gift from Oliver.

You remember Oliver... he dumped me and that was the night I met Stacey.

It's a long, heavy black coat, much nicer than I could have ever afforded myself.

My fingers play with the holes in the pocket linings of the now years-old coat. It has lost its softness, as well as a button or two, but it still does the job of keeping me warm.

As I stand on the subway platform awaiting the first of three forms of mass transit I'll take home to my dark, but warm, studio apartment, I shiver with each late fall breeze that still somehow fights its way underground.

A sigh escapes my mouth, as I wait with a small group of shivering strangers.

I hope there's a seat for me.

I stare down at my $20 black, fake suede boots. They're flat and don't have any arch support, but if I pair them with the right socks, they stay cozy through the day.

Heading home is always exhausting, but also exciting because once I'm there, I'm *there*.

I can relax.

I can breathe.

The subway train slows as it approaches the platform, and I watch a rat scurry under the third rail and presumably back to a warmer home of its own.

Sucking in one last cold breath, we all start moving toward the slowly-lurching piece of screeching steel. The doors ping and open, allowing the small pool of cold commuters to gush inside like blood-letting from the wound of a city too cold and not yet ready for winter.

I watch as people of every color find seats of their own, including me.

And as I stare at people in that certain way that only non-New Yorkers do, a small group of four people enter the opposite end of the train car at the last moment before its doors seal shut.

Four people.

Two young black men.

One young half black, half Hispanic man.

And one slightly-less-young white woman who appears dressed in a way so as to keep her gender a secret from everyone.

All four are carrying the same black, white and yellow colored pamphlets.

"Cops are killing young black men in our streets," announces the white woman sharply.

I watch the three men behind her approach young men who look like they do and hand them pamphlets upon which my straining eyes vaguely make out the words: "You Have Rights."

"Stop and Frisk disproportionately targets men of color in this city," she continues to proclaim, handing pamphlets to both interested and ambivalent people of color nearer to me.

They continue their slow walk down the train car.

I notice several buttons on the woman's denim jacket and wager she must be cold, as it's clearly not heavy enough for the frigid fall air.

One is a black fist on a red background.

One says "NAACP."

And another is that well-known picture of Che Guevara.

I watch her short brown hair and glasses walk toward my long blonde hair and contact lenses.

"Um," I speak lightly, causing two or three sitting commuter heads between us to turn, "Can I have one?"

I feel my voice ask the question as my body feels the train slowing at a stop.

The young white friend of Che Guevara turns to me with venom behind the lenses of her glasses.

"NO, WHITE PEOPLE," she hurls at me and evidently every other white person on board, "YOU CAN'T GET EVERYTHING YOU WANT ALL THE TIME!"

I feel the entire car's eyes on the two of us as the train stops and the doors ping, then open.

I furrow my brow, confused and publicly embarrassed, as she races out of the car with all of her remaining pamphlets in tow.

"Come on," she barks from the platform to the three men of color still on board.

All three of them move to exit the car, the third man— one of the two black men— glances down at me with confusion and sympathy in his eyes.

Then they walk out, as a handful of new commuters enter.

The doors ping again, then close, and I can still feel eyes on me as my brain tries to process what has just happened.

As my face contorts into a sarcastic facial expression for the crowd, my ego casually remarks "She knew she was white, right?"

Two or three people who saw the exchange chuckle, but most do what New Yorkers do best during public spectacles, of which I just became a part: they pretend it didn't happen and go back to minding their own business.

I watch the group of four through the window walk onto the subway train across the platform, no doubt to continue their doubtlessly worthy campaign.

But what my sarcastic defense mechanism will never tell the crowd it sought to defend itself to is that I prayed for them this morning.

I prayed for those subjected to racism big and small, individual and systemic.

I prayed to God to help me overcome the racism in me.

I prayed that we all learn to love each other as brothers and sisters of the same Loving Father.

And when I asked for that pamphlet, I *meant* it. I want to learn.

But I suppose I can't always get what I want... or at least, so I've been told.

As I stand by the printer, I pick up each sheet of paper before the machine even sets it down.

I can't afford for anyone to see what I'm printing. For a few reasons, honestly.

The leaves of paper are warm in my left hand as my right one patrols, snatching them up.

The booklet I'm printing is seventeen pages.

It's the coming semester's course offering list at the New York Theological Seminary.

After this, I'm going to print the admissions process booklet.

It's 12:15 in the afternoon now, and most people are either out eating lunch, at their desks eating lunch, or at their desks daydreaming about their lunch.

I decided now would be a good time to print personal things from my work computer. No, I didn't ask anyone to use the printer for personal use. I figured that wouldn't be prudent considering what I'm printing entails a career change.

Do I feel guilty about it? Of course I do.

It's like stealing, in a way.

(Okay... it *is* stealing, stickler.)

I guess what I'm trying to tell you is: I'm a Christian, not a saint.

I don't even really know if God would think I'm a very good person.

I'm racist, remember? And I, evidently, steal sheets of printer paper and their ink from my employer.

I sigh, holding these classes in my hands, feeling both excited and like a fraud.

But this is the first thing I've felt excitement about in a long time. (The classes, not the illegal copies. Those, I still feel guilty about.)

I don't even feel this excited over guys. That excitement is too clouded by relentless anxiety and crippling self-doubt.

But these...

I glance down.

"Women in the Bible" I read, and my heart skips a beat in elation.

I haven't told Stacey about this career path yet. I guess a part of me is scared she'll tell me I'm not ready or I'm not Christian enough or something.

And honestly, I wouldn't dispute either of those points.

I'm *not* ready, and I *definitely* don't feel "Christian enough."

I still tense up when I say the words "in Jesus' name." A relic of my former atheism, I suppose...

I used to brace myself every time someone would bring up Jesus.

Nowadays, when I talk about Him, a deep part of me still winces.

I know it's something I need to release, especially if I'm going to become a pastor, but...

The printer suddenly beeps aggressively.

Oh no.

I look down, jolted out of my thoughts.

"Out of Paper!" the tiny green screen blinks.

It beeps angrily at me again, and I almost shush the inanimate object to be quiet.

Frantic, my eyes race around the area to see if I can find any paper to shove in the tray to get it moving again.

Carol pops up over her cubicle.

"Oh, I'll come help," she promises, walking toward me.

My left palm begins to sweat on the contraband.

"I, uh..."

"Is it just out of paper?" she asks over thin wire-framed glasses, beneath blunt blonde bangs.

I nod, not even speaking at this point.

"No problem," she waves her forty-something year-old hand and bends over to the tan, metal drawers at our right.

She opens one to reveal a seemingly endless supply of thick white computer paper.

Ripping the red plastic covering off of one stack, she expeditiously loads it in the printer's drawer and slams it shut.

"Thank you," I barely smile.

"You're lucky I like you," she grins, beginning to walk back to her desk, "I just poured my Diet Coke and didn't even take a sip yet."

She winks at me, and the printer gears up to start printing again.

I glance down at how many pages I have left to go. Eight left to collect.

I look around nervously, praying nothing so dramatic happens again.

That evening, I push my cart through the aisles of the grocery store down the street. I usually go during the day, but this weekend was too cold and I had enough food in my fridge to afford procrastination.

When your shelves are empty, it's not too cold to go to the grocery store.

When you can eek out a few more days of pantry meals, you can afford to roll the dice.

Could I have checked the weather and planned ahead? Sure. But checking the weather seems like something only Type A people do, the kind of people who are never late to work and never run out of paper in the printer.

Plus, it was the first of the month on Friday, and the store is always a zoo around the first of the month. It's filled with ten times the normal amount of people and countless families shouting to one another, pushing three carts each. It took me two or three months of living in this neighborhood to piece together that the first of the month is when government assistance gets doled out.

Today was payday for me, so I won't have to charge it onto my habitually maxed out credit card.

While I push my half-full cart up to the register, I see an obscure granola bar brand that I used to buy back when my parents contributed to my rent each month. They're four dollars a bar, but so delicious.

I stare at the open boxes for a long moment and then bend forward, grabbing only two bars.

I can't afford to splurge much more than that at this point, but eating one of these would be a nice pick-me-up at work this week.

I grab one cherry flavor and one cashew butter.

Then I look at my cart and, for the millionth time, mentally estimate what my total will be.

I always overdo it at the grocery store.

A young black woman stands in front of me, loading her groceries onto the small rubber conveyor belt.

She's not dark-skinned. Fairly light. And with very short, natural hair that resembles a smaller scale version of the Afro I saw years ago on Becc.

I watch her place organic almond milk and large cage-free humanely-raised brown eggs onto the belt, followed by non-GMO organic chicken and some of that super healthy cereal that's eight dollars a box and a quarter of the size of a normal box of cereal.

I stare at her groceries and remember longingly the days when I could afford such luxuries.

I look down at my cart.

$1.99 per pound store brand ground chicken (all dark meat) that I would turn into chicken burgers to last me the rest of the week.

Large and evidently caged-and-tortured white eggs that are $2.99 a dozen.

A half gallon of whole milk that I will add an occasional shot of water to, in order to stretch it further.

A cylindrical container of generic brand instant oats to make my own breakfast oatmeal pouches that I take into work and pour hot water and the office coffee cream over.

Staring self-consciously at the rest of my groceries, I hold my chin up high, knowing that I'm trying.

"$110.72," the cashier tells the young woman, who looks to be about my age.

My eyes catch the $4-a-pop granola bars amidst my otherwise humble groceries, and I feel a sudden pang of guilt.

Those are so indulgent and I don't really get much bang for my buck since they're only snacks.

I should buy those when I get a raise or close that large deal I've been working on or... *WHAT... THE... HELL?!*

I see the young woman hand over a debit card with the acronym "SNAP" emblazoned across it.

My eyes immediately narrow.

WHAT.

THE.

HELL?!?

IS THIS A JOKE?

I feel fire well up inside me.

This chick is on food stamps and is eating exponentially better than me, as I commute over three hours every day to a shit job that I *hate*.

Here I am pinching pennies and paying taxes so that... *this lady can eat like a freaking king?!*

She smiles politely at the cashier as the worker types in some magic code behind the register.

The cashier hands her back her colorful card and helps the young black woman fill both of her reusable grocery bags.

With a warm energy, the Afro-haired woman leaves. And I'm left, floored.

I'm working a full-time job and, evidently, I'm poorer than someone on food stamps.

There's no way I could afford her groceries!

As the cashier begins ringing up my items, a resentment builds in me that I have never felt before.

A rage, even.

This is a broken system, and I'm not on the receiving end.

As the cashier begins placing my items in plastic bags for me, I think about how my redistributed wages just paid for that woman's groceries when I can barely even afford to pay for my own.

I cast a sigh so heavy, the woman behind the register looks up at me.

I give her the socially obligatory half-smile.

"Sorry, rough day," I explain to her quickly.

I know what Stacey would say...

That I should mind my own business.

That I should stop comparing, stop envying.

That I should be grateful to be in a position of giving rather than receiving.

Would I prefer to be receiving government assistance than paying my own way?

I stare down at my generic brand peanut butter and think about the young black woman's organic almond butter.

Would I prefer she buy junk food and booze with the money she receives?

"67.17," the cashier tells me.

I slide my debit card through the machine, grasping for perspective, but still unable to see anything other than red.

That night I fill out everything in the seminary school's application packet, except for the essay.

Instead of writing the essay, I turn on more reruns of "The Office" and reward myself with a French Bread Pizza and another whole pint of Cherry Garcia.

Briefly wondering if I could afford cable, as this is my second time re-watching The Office and there's nothing left on Netflix which interests me, I quickly conclude that I cannot.

Intermittently through the episode, I recall the question which must be the basis of my admittance essay: Why would you like to attend seminary school, and what led you to make this decision?

The essay must be between one to two pages.

Filling pages with writing has always been a fairly easy task for me. In my early twenties, I quickly went through a phase of blogging, as most white women that age in that time did.

I light-heartedly imagine writing down: "I would like to become a pastor, and God."

And turning it in. *That's it. That's my essay.*

I chuckle to myself as I fish out a chocolate chunk from the cardboard pint.

And I go back to watching Steve Carrell...

The next day finds me on a frosty Light Rail coming home from work.

I spent the entire day scrolling Instagram at my desk and doing what amounted to only about an hour of real, actual work.

As I sit, pondering the reality that I am *actually* going to apply to a predominantly— pretty much *exclusively*— black seminary school, my mind recalls the young Afroed woman from last evening, who had a SNAP card and organic, fair-trade groceries.

I look out a suddenly snow-flurried window, silently wondering what racism really *is*.

I know slavery is racism.

I know segregated lunch counters are racism.

But in the quiet of my heart, I sit— surrounded by strangers of color— and wonder if that young black woman would be able to work so little, as I did today, and still retain my title and salary?

I wonder...

I wonder if she showed up to the interview instead of me and handed her resume over, same as I did, would the white woman and white man who interviewed me have given her the job? The *same* job? The *same* salary? The same near-immediate opportunity for advancement?

Would I have this job if I weren't white?

I'd like to think it's an outdated question to ask, but is it?

My mind flashes to that old temp job at the mutual fund, where the chatty receptionist informed me of the CEO's mandatory "white" and "blonde" credentials for front desk hire.

As the train doors open, allowing freezing air and another group of non-white people in, I shudder.

(To clarify, I shudder at the cold, not the people. I'm not a *total* monster.)

I stare out at the fresh all-white snow, yet untainted by car exhaust fumes.

It's so hard to stay white without getting stained.

I glance down at my coat and outfit, all black, for the same reason.

Would I be this far into that large deal of mine if I weren't white?

Everyone else involved in the deal is, also, white.

If I weren't white, I imagine, it would feel as though there is an extra hurdle, no matter how kind everyone else is or how subtle.

I'm not sitting here saying all white people's successes are because of their skin tone. Not at all.

But I'm a recovering alcoholic, with a terrible job history, and no degree.

I just can't help but wonder how much of *my own* successes are.

I was unqualified for the job I currently hold. The interviewers told me they wanted to "take a chance" on me, because they "had a good feeling" about me.

I don't even have good feelings about me.

And now that I'm in the role, I'm not particularly driven at what I do.

I show up late. I do the bare minimum.

And yet, they give me a paycheck every fifteen days in a sum too large for me to qualify for the government assistance which, apparently, can afford almond milk.

I stare out the window.

I think back to my father "joking" about not allowing a black family into our neighborhood.

I think about the black man in the waiting room of his office, right outside his door.

I think about all the laws in place which seek to prevent housing discrimination.

I think back to the mutual fund CEO and how he allegedly spoke of nothing else for those few days the temp agency sent him a black girl for a receptionist.

I think about that black girl who was not hired, no matter how pleasant and qualified she might have been.

I think about all the laws in place which seek to prevent employment discrimination.

I think about how impossible it is to legislate a person's heart and secret motives, but how necessary it is to do *something* about this.

I think about how many people of color would kill to have a job like mine and how much I take it for granted.

God, please help me to be a better worker.

Help me to earn the money I'm given and to include You in each one of my work days.

Help me to help people through my job. Help reduce my pride and let me see my own shortcomings and where I can come up higher.

Help me to behave honestly at work and to see things honestly in my life.

And please be with that black receptionist, that black man in the waiting room, and that Afro-haired woman in the grocery store. Bless them, and promote them. And help us all to know You ever more closely. Amen.

As we pull up to my stop, I do what I always do: stand and check the place I had been seated for anything I may have dropped as many times as I can before the doors close.

I'm sure I look insane.

It's the OCD.

I know I need to work on it, but Stacey was right, working on my racism has proved to be a task weighty enough.

The doors shut and my body finds itself on the platform, surrounded by gentle snow flurries, even though my eyes are still back inside seeing if I dropped anything.

It's all exhausting.

I adjust my scratchy black scarf so that it goes all the way up to my chin and begin walking with my too-heavy tote bag.

I have roughly seven blocks through not-great neighborhoods to go before I reach "home."

As the bells ding and the train pulls away swiftly, the two dozen or so other people and I make our way across the platform toward the concrete staircase down to the street.

A group of young, preteen black and white boys laugh and jostle each other in front of me as we pass the well-worn yellow ticket machines near the top of the staircase.

"That's what I'm talkin' about, my **that word**," I hear one small male voice call out.

The group continues laughing and moving as a unit.

An old black man appears seemingly out of nowhere, staring down at the kids over his round silver glasses. He appears to be in his fifties or sixties.

"YOU, YOUNG MAN," he points firmly to the brunette white boy who was, evidently, the source of the comment.

The whole group slows to a nervous stop as commuters continue brushing past them toward the staircase which carries everyone down to their respective walks home.

The old man points his finger in the young man's face.

"YOU DON'T EVER SAY THAT WORD."

I slow down like a true non-New Yorker in order to see how this whole thing plays out.

"NEVER!"

The group of youngsters stare silently at the angry grey-haired man.

"SOMEONE SHOULD HAVE RAISED YOU BETTER, BUT YOU DON'T EVER SAY THAT WORD. YOU UNDERSTAND ME?"

The white boy looks up at him with somehow the most confused expression I imagine his face can create. It's clear he's baffled by why this old man is yelling at him.

The old black man turns his attention to the young black boy the white kid was, evidently, speaking to and continues yelling as I walk directly past the group, trying not to make any eye contact but, also, still wanting a voyeur's look.

"AND *YOU*," he points into the black boy's face mere feet from mine, "YOU NEVER LET ANYONE CALL YOU THAT. SOMEONE SHOULD HAVE TAUGHT YOU YOUR HISTORY."

I blink hard, stomach dropping vicariously, as though he were yelling at me.

"YOU DON'T EVER LET SOME WHITE BOY CALL YOU THAT."

My eyes try their hardest to resist widening. (They fail.)

As I move past them all, some of the boys on the outer edges of the group begin walking nervously toward the stairs.

Slowly the group trickles apart into smaller ones. They're all silent.

I glance backwards and see the two main boys slowly following the rest of the group, now making their way down the stairs like me.

They remind me of a classroom which has just been scolded by their teacher. How quickly their collective tone went from jovial to horrifyingly awkward.

The white and black boys each stare at the hard cement steps they're walking down, as I turn back around.

I'm sure they can feel people staring at them. And, by people, I mean me.

My cheap boots hit the sidewalk and two of the young boys behind me start talking about basketball practice next week, clearly trying to infuse some normalcy back into the group's social dynamic.

Reaching into my bag, I pull out my headphones for the remainder of my walk home.

For as equal as young people may believe they are nowadays, I can almost guarantee those two young men have never felt more disparate than in the exchange I just witnessed.

The old man's words ring in my mind as Sanctus Real sings in my ears.

In both scoldings, he essentially blamed the people who raised each of the boys.

And I have so many questions...

Now home and well-bathed for the night, my unpainted nail scrolls my phone, reviewing the latest Facebook updates.

Seeing a status posted by a black former classmate of mine, I set my phone down and look around the room I live in.

I think about the two boys from earlier this evening.

And I think about the whole group of boys.

Then I think about the old man.

I wonder what they're each thinking right now, at this very moment.

I wonder if the two boys will tell their parents.

I wonder if they both *have* two parents.

I wonder if that last thought would even cross my mind, had both kids been white.

And I know that last answer is "no."

Do they even understand what happened earlier this evening?

For that matter... *do I?*

I think about the old man's words: "WHO RAISED YOU" and "SOMEBODY SHOULD HAVE TAUGHT YOU," clearly implying family on each.

I think of my Grandma GiGi.

And my father.

And myself.

A child's ignorance is their parents' fault, I realize, *But an adult's ignorance is their own.*

At a certain point, we all must take responsibility for our beliefs. And, if we don't like what we've been given, it's up to us to change it before we pass the poison on.

Moments later, I climb down to my knees on my prayer rug, before binging on Netflix.

God, I don't know what you want me to think and what you don't.

I've been trying to meditate, because I know that's good.

But just... take my mind. The whole thing. And all the thoughts in it. Please.

Take it and replace all of my thoughts with Yours. Show me what You want for me.

Do You want me to pursue NYTS? Show me. I'm tired, and I need Your help.

Well, my mind corrects itself, *I <u>always</u> need Your help.*

Just please help me.

Please. And God, please be with those kids I saw today and the old black man. Be with all of them. And help us all learn how to be better brothers and sisters to one another.

Help us to love one another the way You love each one of us. Amen.

Sandra, my director, hangs up the phone.

"Well I think that went great," she beams over her desk at me.

I concur, nodding.

"I'm excited to meet them in-person next week. After all these phone calls, it will be nice to put faces to the names!" I chuckle, and then Sandra adopts a more serious expression.

"I think now would be an appropriate time to connect with them on LinkedIn, if you haven't already."

I nod, taking down the note on my pad.

"After that," she informs me, "I'll connect with them tomorrow or the next day through LinkedIn."

I look up.

"That way they'll know who to expect when we come into their offices," she instructs, "Plus, it will help them to know we're professionals, who look professional."

I nod, and after a moment or two more of debriefing and discussing next steps, I return to my desk where I won't work on anything for the rest of my day except my admissions essay.

It closed.

The deal closed.

The huge, bigger-than-any-other-deal-in-the-company actually *closed*.

I stare at the signed six-figure contract.

Twelve percent commission.

Twelve percent.

I stare at the signature of Ted, the client's CFO.

After all the prayers and all the hurdles, it actually closed.

I think about what twelve percent commission will be.

Sandra already warned me about the ungodly tax that New York State puts on commission income.

"Basically cut your commission in half," she cautioned me.

And while that makes me angry, it's still more money than I've ever seen.

It's enough to afford the application fee to NYTS and, in the off-chance I'm accepted without a college degree, it would be enough to pay cash for my first class.

I blink hard.

And it *happened*.

It actually *happened*.

Chad, my coworker and boss' son, saunters up to my desk with his over-gelled black hair.

"You buying us all lunch now?" he laughs.

I laugh, hoping he's not serious considering how many potential uses I have for the money.

"But seriously," he slows, "Congrats. I'm jealous as hell."

I smile, and blink.

"I just can't believe it," my ponytailed head shakes.

My chipped maroon-painted index fingernail hits the send button.

I shouldn't be sending personal emails from my work email. I know that.

But something about the momentum here feels *different*.

I just sent an email to the seminary's Director of Vocational Discernment.

In it, I had asked for clarity regarding the school's stance on my lack of an undergraduate degree.

Not five minutes pass and her response appears in my inbox.

The fear of rejection towards my newfound dream looms large over my spirit.

I stare at the email, then glance around the office. As always, no one is paying attention to me.

My finger can't help but click into the letter, and my eyes race over its words.

They'd be happy to explore alternatives. They do make exceptions if the candidate has appropriate life experience. She wants to meet with me in-person, next week.

A giant grin crawls itself across my lips.

How is this all coming together?

How is this actually working?

I stand up and, with shoulders back for the first time in a very long time, I float over to our mustard-yellow employee kitchen.

It's small, but at least I'm alone in it.

My smile somehow grows even wider and, from within another mismatching outfit, I do a happy spin— just once— in the dingy kitchenette.

Looking up at the inexplicably stained ceiling tiles, I simply mouth the words: "Thank You."

I'm on the phone with my mother that night in my apartment.

"So I have some pretty big news," I lead her, excitedly.

"Oh God, you're not pregnant, are you?"

"What?" I pull back sharply, "No!"

She sighs in relief.

"Why would that be your first thought?"

She stammers.

"I... I just wanted to make sure..."

"Whatever," I shake my head and roll my eyes, "I decided to go back to school!"

There's a pause.

"Oh," she responds with genuine surprise, "Um, the same major? Which school?"

"Seminary school!"

"Oh," her tone drops in obvious disappointment, and my heart and stomach follow suit.

She sighs again.

"What, uh, what brought *this* about?"

"I want to become a pastor!" I exclaim to only more skepticism.

"A pastor now? So you closed down your mobile app, and now you don't want to become a fitness instructor anymore, is that right? Now it's a *pastor?*"

Her tone says what little her words hold back.

Now it's my turn to sigh.

"I'm really excited about it," I try, as my body lowers itself onto my pale green sofa, "There's a school here in New York where they make exceptions for people who don't have bachelor's degrees."

Dead air.

"I could leapfrog my bachelor's and jump right into getting my Master's!"

She exhales loudly.

"Is this school even reputable?"

"I mean," I hesitate, "I think so... It's a real school, if that's what you're asking."

"What's the name of it?" she demands.

"New York Theological Seminary," I tell her in what will very soon prove to be a costly error on my part.

I hear typing.

"Are you at your computer?"

"Yes, I was just checking my emails when you called," her voice trails off, "Hmm…"

I lean forward, trying to hear what she's thinking.

"What is it?" I ask with sincerity.

"Looks very, um, *diverse*," her tone jumps three octaves at the last word.

"Yeah," I grin naively, "I don't know. That's just where I feel God's leading me."

"Hmm," and another pause, "Well I'm going to share this with your father and see what he thinks."

"Well…"

"Are you saving money to pay for this school? Because I don't think we can…"

"No," I cut her off proudly, "I *have* the money. I just closed that huge deal at work!"

"And you're putting that money toward *this?*"

My eyes move to the floor, the same way they once did when she told me I couldn't have the black babydoll.

"Well, I…"

A disappointed sigh.

"You still owe your father that money he loaned you last year."

This time I sigh.

"I know. I can pay him in part."

"And the rest of the money is going toward this?" she chirps harshly.

A pause.

"Yes," I answer in a whispered tone.

"I just don't think you're going to be happy at a place with all that diversity."

I nod, heartbroken.

How did I possibly think she'd be as excited about this as I was?

Why do I bother to tell her good news?

"I'm gonna pay him back," I promise.

"Well, it seems like you now have the opportunity to and you're choosing not to."

Her words hit me hard.

"I'm going to talk to your father," she informs me again, "Was this the good news? This... *school?*"

I exhale like a deflated party balloon.

"Yes."

"Okay, I'm going to get back to clearing my inbox. We'll talk tomorrow night with your father."

"Well, this isn't really, like, a group decision," I try to assert.

"We'll talk tomorrow, Trisha."

And she hangs up.

And I sit there.

And the shattered, all too familiar, tears begin crying.

"WHY DO I GO TO HER WITH GOOD NEWS?!" I shout into the phone, as my feet walk themselves back to my bed, where I just was.

Stacey exhales and laughs a little.

"Because you love going to the hardware store for oranges, Trisha."

I stop my angered pacing.

"What?" my face scrunches in confusion, still seething.

"You're going to the hardware store asking for oranges," she explains to me, "and they tell you they don't have any. And then you go back the next day and ask for oranges again."

I listen, perplexed.

"And they tell you 'no' again. And you just keep going back to the hardware store asking for oranges."

I am silent, wondering if I've lost my mind or she, hers.

She correctly senses I need a literal, rather than metaphorical, message.

"You keep going to a place to get something you've never been able to find there."

My eyebrows loosen a little.

"You keep going to your mom," she continues, "to get approval and reassurance about your choices, even though you never get it from her."

My mouth opens and my face smoothes out.

"I... never thought of it that way."

"When has she *ever* given you an excited reaction to a big, unique idea or, no pun intended, *unorthodox* career path you've wanted to try out?"

My feet start walking slowly in a circle around my maroon prayer rug, as I stare down at it.

I try to remember.

"I, uh... I don't ever remember a time."

"Okay," Stacey resolves steadily, "so why are you blaming her for not giving you something you've never gotten from her, instead of blaming yourself for going to the hardware store asking for oranges again? You've never gotten that form of support from her before. Why on *earth* would you think she would start tonight, with this idea?"

"I just hoped... I mean, shouldn't..."

She cuts me off.

"If you live that way, you're going to be disappointed a lot," and then she adopts a slightly softer tone, "Your mother is loving you the best she can. She thinks she's keeping you safe by doing what she's doing."

Tears well up in my eyes.

"I just wish..."

And she cuts me off again.

"Your wishes are breaking your heart, Trisha. You'd be a lot happier if you just accept that this is who she is."

I am quiet as I stare downward, examining the white spots within my prayer rug's ornate pattern.

Stacey speaks into the silence.

"There are people you can go to with your big and exciting ideas who will be excited for you and be positive, and then there's your mom. And, again, honestly, she's probably not doing this to be cruel or unkind. And how tragic for her that worrying is the best way she knows how to love you. You should feel compassion for her. She's clearly hurting. She clearly has her own trauma which needs healing. Worrying and looking at potential risks is how she cares for you and loves you and tries to protect you."

There is quiet.

"But is 'diversity' a risk?" I ask, sincerely.

"Some people think it is," her voice calmly explains, a mother, herself, to a toddler, "Many people are afraid of the unknown. You're not one of those people, but you have to understand that your lack of fear when taking big, bold steps into the unknown can scare others. I don't think your mom's a bad person. I think she's far away from her child and genuinely believes that an unfamiliar situation is one to be scared of. Being scared for you is the best she knows how to love you right now."

I sniffle.

"I just wanted her to be excited."

"You just wanted to go to the hardware store and buy oranges."

"Your father and I have been speaking," my mother begins on a phone call where the two of them are on speakerphone against me.

Her tone is not even pretending to conceal their disapproval.

I stare down at the familiar beige tile of my studio apartment floor which has been growing colder and colder with each passing number on the calendar.

"We just don't think you're going to be happy at that school you told us about. We don't think that's a good fit for you."

The familiar sinking feeling returns to my chest, pooling in my lungs as tears pool in my eyes.

My father remains a silent, but menacing, presence on the call.

"We just think this money from your sale would be better spent somewhere else," she pauses, "like maybe paying your father back."

I blink hard.

"I already paid the application fee and have an interview set-up with Admissions this week."

A very familiar heavy sigh from my mother and quiet muttering on the end inform me that I certainly should not have done either of those things.

"You'll still need to pay him that money back," she clarifies.

I stare down, knowing that, just two days ago, I had written down a projected budget for my new money. I had wistfully placed one month's rent into my savings account, and looked forward to utilizing that feature on my online banking account for the first time.

"I mean, I can pay him fourteen hundred," I offer it up.

"Is that all you have left from your big sale?" her tone is now incredulous.

After doing the math using a very aggressive tax rate, per Sandra's warning, I had set aside the anticipated amount for my first class already and the extra month's rent in my savings account used the remaining balance.

I feel ashamed and begin hoping the taxes won't be as high as my coworkers warn... which I already know, in New York, is fruitless.

"Yes."

"You can mail a check to your father," she instructs me bluntly, "It's a start."

"Okay."

We say our goodbyes and hang up.

My mind races with the thought that, soon, after I mail my father the check and pay for my first class— if I'm accepted— I'll be right back to where I started financially. Living paycheck to paycheck, struggling just to break even.

Something's different, though.

I'm not back to anywhere I've ever been spiritually. This is new ground.

And, as I set my phone down on the counter, I recall my mentor's words: "Don't go to the hardware store for oranges."

I briefly wonder if I should stop talking to them altogether, but then I ask myself what Jesus would do.

I stare down and, although shattered (again), I am undeterred.

Their disapproval isn't moving me.

And I feel an energy surge within me that I've never felt before.

I don't know why God is leading me to this school, but since He is, it dawns on me: I don't need a permission slip from anyone else.

This time, I'm buying my own babydoll.

I am the only white person in the waiting room.

I glance around nervously, remembering what few times I've ever been the *only* white person in a space.

That one time I accidentally took the wrong Light Rail down to the Martin Luther King Drive station in Jersey City.

Sometimes on my commute for brief periods between stops.

I think that's it.

Whenever it's happened, I'm always viscerally aware of the fact. Maybe it's something primal.

I don't know why, but it feels somehow unsafe to be the only one who looks the way you do.

I look around.

Two black men, both older than me and one wearing glasses, are seated across from me and respectively reviewing paperwork.

The one with glasses looks up at me. I give him a polite half-smile and he nods, without smiling, and looks back down.

I pick at the snag in the hem of my black sweater I noticed earlier today at work. This is going to cost me at least twenty dollars to replace, and I'm not happy about it.

Maybe I should learn how to sew.

I look over at the black woman to my right who looks only a year or two older than me.

Her hair is natural and styled up, like a mohawk.

She wears round clear glasses that, I deduce from the lenses, are real and not simply fashionable, like many people my age wear nowadays.

Her entire outfit is magenta. I try not to stare.

Looking down, I glance at my phone to see if my mother texted back. She wants to speak with me again tonight, with my father.

No text.

While immediately relieved, I still feel the undercurrent of dread, at what the future text will say.

I glance up at the clock. 6:12pm.

My appointment had been for 6:00pm.

I won't be able to answer my parents' call unless I'm home in my apartment, especially considering the content of our to-be conversation and the general demographics on any given leg of my commute home.

I sigh, and the non-glasses wearing black man glances up at me.

I keep my eyes down.

I don't want to stare at anybody.

All four of us hold paperwork. Mine is the admissions form. It's almost completely finished now, due to my time spent in this waiting room. There isn't much else to do.

I'm not sure what everyone else's paperwork is.

"Trisha," I hear a welcoming voice call.

I look up to see a black woman with braids, draped in purple, yellow, and black African attire smiling at me.

I smile back.

"Hi, yes," I nod, while gathering my things to stand, "That's me."

"I'm Ayanla Brown, the Director of Vocational Discernment," a warm smile creeps across her bare lips again. She wears no makeup, but has on very ornate white earrings. I would place her at around forty years old.

"I so enjoyed reading your email," she tells me as we both walk toward her office, "I had such a good feeling as I read it."

I smile back at her, following her into the well-lit but small white room with bookshelves lining every wall.

God, please give me the right words and help this to go according to Your Will.

"Have a seat," she motions at two forest green fabric armchairs with a small table in between, on which stands a tiny green pot and sprig of fresh bamboo.

"It's so nice to meet you in-person," I tell her as she finds her way around the somewhat cluttered desk into her chair, "I appreciated your quick response to my email and willingness to meet with me today."

"Well," she begins with a smile, "anytime a potential student is looking to attend NYTS, it's my job to help assure they land at the place God wants them to land,

232

even if it's not here. Although," she outstretches her hand for effect, "like I said, I have a good feeling about you from your email."

"I don't have enough money to cover a whole semester," I confess outright.

She nods and tells me they have some great financial aid programs.

"I think I want to do one class for now and then build from there," I pause slightly with my stream of thought, "If I stick to one class, I can pay cash for it, too, which would be helpful because my credit is terrible and I don't think anywhere would loan me money anyway."

Two months ago, my boss above Sandra— Chad's dad— pulled me into a conference room with a piece of mail he'd received. It was one of my late medical bills. Evidently after several unsuccessful collections attempts, collection companies can go to small claims court and begin garnishing wages. He told me he'd received a copy of the letter which said a medical provider was taking me to small claims court to do just that.

The humiliation of that moment stuck to me like napalm.

Not to mention I am still paying off a bank loan from my old mobile app. (And I, obviously, still owe my father.)

"Okay," Ms. Brown shrugs, still smiling, "what made you reach out and pursue NYTS, might I ask?"

She stares at me quizzically, as I glance around the room at her stuffed bookshelves.

I notice title after title of books relating to African American culture, racism, sexism and, of course, Christianity.

"I just felt *drawn,*" I tell her as my eyes settle on one title in particular, "I felt the call to become a pastor, so, honestly, I googled seminary schools."

My eyes are glued to the one book.

"And I just felt drawn to NYTS's listing," I conclude, finally looking back at her.

I smile, as if on cue.

She smiles and looks down at her desk.

I glance back to the title.

"Now in your email you had stated you don't hold a bachelor's degree..."

She leaves it open-ended, and I turn back to her.

"Sorry," I shake my head, "this one title is really jumping out at me on your bookshelf."

She looks over at that wall of books.

"Just the one?" her eyebrows briefly scrunch above a bemused smile, "which one?"

"That one," I point, "Tyranny of Kindness."

Her head cocks and she grins.

"Why does that one jump out at you?"

I can't break eye contact with the title on the bind.

"It's just such a provocative title, to position kindness as tyranny or vice versa."

I purse my lips and furrow my brow at it.

"Take it," she tells me.

My head jerks over at her.

"What?" I almost laugh, "Oh, I couldn't do that!"

What an absurd idea. I come into somebody's office and stare at something, then they just *give* it to me?

I could never...

"Of course!" she waves her hand at me, laughing, "I've already read it, and it clearly is drawing your attention for a reason."

"Seriously?" I lean forward to her, floored.

"Of course!" she waves both her hands at me this time.

I stand and slowly walk over to it.

"I don't know what it is about this book," I tell her as I slowly remove it from the bookcase.

"I hope you enjoy it!"

I sit down, as my eyes and fingers examine the book.

"So," she begins again, "you don't have your bachelor's degree."

I look up at her.

"No."

"May I ask why?"

I lick my lips and look down at my new book.

"I attended college for a couple years," I begin, glancing up at her eager brown eyes, "Um, I love school. I've *always* loved school. But I'd been an atheist for awhile at that point."

I shake my head, in awe of my disjointed response.

Why didn't I prepare better for this meeting?

God, please give me the words.

"I was young," I admit, looking around the room at nothing in particular, "and impressionable, and *very* ego-driven."

The Director places both elbows on her desk and props her head in her hands, continuing to listen intently.

I clear my throat to continue.

"I fell in with the wrong crowd and a fast lifestyle, and sacrificed an amazing schooling opportunity for things that were so shallow," my head shakes, remembering the parties, money, and power I had tried so hard to surround myself with.

"In that crowd, I met others prioritizing the same things I was... which were all the wrong things."

Ms. Brown begins to nod silently, watching me.

"And then one day, I wanted to stop. To give up the partying lifestyle. But it wouldn't let me."

I cross my hands on top the book, recounting addiction's tyranny into the kindness of her eyes.

"It took a long time and a lot of humbling experiences to get to the point of having an open mind regarding the idea of God. And once I asked for His help, the cravings didn't go away at first, but I was somehow able to resist them."

My mind flashes to a past version of myself, struggling to pace the carpeted floors of my depressing one bedroom apartment in those early days, counting the minutes until 1AM, when my usual gas station closed.

Then, sweating and praying, I'd count my way to 2AM, when all the bars had to close.

At 2:01AM, I'd finally exhale.

"But, with God, I know now all things are possible and I'm better now than I've ever been. I share about those experiences and how God has delivered me from them in the Christian Bible Group I belong to, where I get to learn more about Him every week."

Ms. Brown nods.

"That's a powerful testimony," she tells me, "and it sounds like in many ways, you *did* continue your education after school, just not in the traditional sense of the word."

She smiles, and I smile back, sighing with relief.

"I never thought of it that way."

Her smile grows.

"I think you'd make an excellent addition to our school, no matter how many course hours you choose to take," she nods and gathers some papers into her hands, straightening them out.

My fingers fidget with my new book.

"Me too."

I fold the note back up and shove it into my pocket.

Wiping the tears away, I glance around the expansive military cemetery.

There's nobody here but me.

Well...

And all the people whose names surround me.

I stare at my grandfather's name, reflecting on all the time I missed out with him due to my addiction.

I came here today, in order to redress it all.

Just me and him and God.

I think back to my freshman year of college, when I vowed to be his pen pal. I wrote him a note or two, but then partying took its priority.

I think back to the letter he wrote me expressing excitement over Barack Obama and Hillary Clinton being front-runners in the Democratic Primaries.

"To witness this moment of history is so thrilling and exciting! Such a long time coming!" the old white man had written me.

I think back to all the conversations he and I had, before my drinking took hold.

I stare at the letters on his tombstone which denote his military service.

I wonder what might have been had I talked to him more as I grew older.

Would I be so deep in this problem of racism if I had?

My anxious fingers pull out the wrinkled note again, staring at its edges.

"Grandpa," I whisper once more, beginning to weep with regret and praying for release, "I hope that you were able to hear me somehow."

I suck in air, looking at the modest note my heart pored over, wondering what he would think of my life now and the decisions I've been making.

About the fact I'm still single.

About the fact I'm dead broke.

About the fact I'm considering attending seminary school.

"Please let me know you heard me."

I breathe in, looking up at the pink and orange glowing sky, and begin walking slowly back to my car.

Once inside, I sigh once more, pleading to God to *please, please let him have heard me.*

I turn the key and hear the first few notes of an impossible song.

Gasping, the lyrics echo off every inch of me...

It's the OneRepublic song.

Preacher.

I have been flooded with memories these last few days.

Memories of interactions I've had with black people or things I've seen or thought.

There's no way I've grown enough to be applying to NYTS, but yet, here I am, still with this insatiable urge in the core of my soul.

I stare at the attachments on the email one last time, counting them to confirm I've attached everything they need.

I glance over the short text of the email.

Staring at the Admissions email address in the "To" field, I move the mouse up.

I exhale deeply and shut my eyes, thanking God for leading me this far and asking Him to continue guiding me from here.

And I hit "Send."

I sit in the back since I arrived late.

I haven't been going to Group as often lately.

The weather's been cold and, frankly, I've just been tired and lazy.

I listen to a fairly tall brunette man with weathered white skin share in the church basement, surrounded by a double semi-circle of filled chairs. He is wearing a long-sleeved white cotton shirt and jeans. I stare at two faded tattoos on his neck, one cursive word I can't distinguish and the other, a shield-shaped emblem with a hint of red ink to it.

"Back in the day, I used to look at women purely for sex," he confesses to the Group. He's a good-looking older guy, maybe in his late forties or early fifties.

"Only when I found you guys and found Jesus and found men who taught me better did I even know that how I was thinking was wrong. I was sexist to the core."

I think of my own racism, then stare down at my shoes.

I had stepped in a puddle getting off the bus here, so my left tennis shoe is wet and looks darker purple than the right.

"I used to see women as what I had been told they were, by society or by other shallow men, or as some fleshly purpose I thought they could serve to me or what I thought I was owed."

He continues in his candor behind a cracked wooden podium donning more chips than paint.

"As the years went on, my resentment toward the whole mass of women grew. Not surprisingly, not many women wanted to be around me back then. I feel like they could just tell what my soul looked like, how ugly it was toward them."

I watch him fidget with his hands at the podium and watch one of his feet tap nervously.

"The few women who let me be around them hated themselves even more than I did. I fell down a dark, despairing hole of pornography and was badly addicted to it for many years."

He looks up from his fidgeting fingers at us.

"I didn't know there was a better way until I met you guys," he professes.

I notice a few men's heads nodding around the room.

"I found this place, and it was like my whole life opened up, and I learned that much of what I'd been raised to believe about other people, women, and myself were mostly lies... Everyone is a child of God. *Everyone.*"

His words hit me hard and I stare at him, beginning to nod now myself.

"I am special to God, but no more special than anyone else."

More heads nod around the room.

"I am made in God's image, but no more than anyone else."

He exhales hard.

"And I am no more entitled to God's goodness and the innate dignity that comes with it than anyone else. *Everyone* deserves to be treated with dignity."

I look down again and close my eyes softly.

God, I know you brought me here tonight for a reason. Please help me to have fresh ears and an open mind to new ideas and ways of being in Your world.

"I learned here that women are daughters of God and deserve more than today's popular concept of tolerance. Tolerance is such a cheap word. I tolerate a hot day, but I still can't stand it."

The speaker's tone quickens.

"I tolerate a line at the DMV, because I have to. I tolerate traffic and resist the urge toward road rage because it's a crime. I tolerate things I don't like all the time. And there's two parts to that," he tells us.

"One, I tolerate *things*. People are not things. A person is not an undesirable set of circumstances which I am exposed to and need to endure. Each one of you has been brought here to this earth by our Almighty God for a divine purpose, and I'm going to have arrogance to just *tolerate* you? Jesus didn't call us to *tolerate* one another."

Almost everybody in the room is nodding along, and a few people have their arms silently raised in worship.

"He called us to love one another. I tolerate what I don't like. I can't tolerate someone I love, because I love them. I can't mistreat or look down on or judge someone I love, because I love them."

I can feel my own face grow hot.

Yes God, You brought me here tonight for a reason.

"I can't feel superior to my wife of seven years, who I met in this room," he motions to his right, "Wendy, you're my queen. I couldn't look down on her if I tried."

A collective smile sweeps over the room.

"Most of the time I'm actually trying to get on her level," he laughs and the room follows his lead, "but I'm faithful to her today. She comes before anyone else today and I will defend her honor and worth with everything in me today. I learned how to be an honorable man from this Group, in this room, and in our breakout sessions."

I look around and silently wonder what everyone else here is struggling with that's causing them to nod along.

"I learned how it's not just enough to pray for others."

My eyes dart up. And he continues.

"We have to perform the action of loving them and supporting them, the way Jesus teaches us to. Love them enough to correct their course, gently, like men in these rooms did to me. Love them enough to give them grace when we don't feel they deserve it, like the men in this room did for me. Love them enough to prioritize God's direction to us— to love one another— over my own petty ego telling me I'm somehow above or superior or *owed something*."

He sighs and the room is more quiet than I've ever heard it.

"You guys taught me how to love myself and others through God's eyes. You guys taught me about God's unending grace and power to heal and redeem. You guys taught me not by telling me, but by *showing* me that love."

I see nodding heads around the room and hear one older white woman whisper the word "yes."

"You guys called me at night, when you knew I'd be struggling, and you asked me how I'm doing and actually listened. You guys instructed me which stories in the Bible to read that would change my views on women and show me how valuable they are in God's eyes. And Trevor, Joe," he turns toward two older men seated near his wife, "you guys were there last night when Wendy and I received word that our adoption fell through."

I look to his wife, Wendy, who is probably in her late forties.

She begins crying.

"And you guys reminded me," the speaker's own deep voice breaks, "that while weeping may endure for a night, joy *will* come in the morning. And our child is still out there... waiting for us to find them."

With one finger, he wipes away a tear.

"You guys taught me how to cry. Heck, if Jesus is man enough to cry great tears of blood, there's no pride to be had in my holding back," he quips to smiles and tears around the room.

"Thank you," he concludes, "for showing me what life is truly all about."

He bows his head and then moves slowly to his seat as applause erupts. I watch his wife reach over and rub his forearm as he sits down in the only empty metal folding chair in the room.

He glances at her with a modest smile.

It takes a lot of courage to stand in front of a room of people and confess your sins.

It takes even more courage to first admit them to yourself.

"God," I begin in a whisper on my knees later that night, "I don't know why You haven't taken this racism from my heart yet, but I know You will.

I know You will for me, because You've helped so many others.

I know You will, because You've helped me so many times.

I know You will, because for Your children to love one another as You do is Your greatest wish.

Please let me know what I need to do, what I can do to help this process.

I'm going to keep knocking, until this door is opened. *Amen.*"

"I mean, Sasha, what would you do?"

"If I were *racist?*"

I nod as though the fellow young white woman from Group can see me through the phone.

"I gotta be honest, Trisha. I don't think you *are.*"

I listen.

"I think a lot of this stuff is super normal, like locking the doors and having some of these other thoughts," she pauses, "It's *normal.* It's not racist."

I look out my apartment window at the dark night sky.

I don't think she understands.

But I relent.

"Okay," not pressing her on the matter.

"How do I become less racist?" I quietly ask Kylie the next night on the phone.

Sasha is the closest thing to a friend that I have in Group; Kylie is second.

"I don't think you seem that bad," my almost-friend sounds almost-reassuring on the matter.

I blink hard, silently.

"Like, I don't know what it's like to be racist," she pauses, "but I definitely think it's worse than what you're describing."

I stare straight ahead at Mindy Kaling's frozen face on my screen.

"Like it's just *thoughts,* Trisha," she suddenly sounds impatient on the other line, "I really think you're making too much of this and overthinking."

I politely thank her— although I'm not sure what for— and tell her goodbye.

I stare at Mindy's dark black hair, now plagued with frustration, as well as a silent, gnawing desire to accept the ruling of Judge Kylie and let myself off the hook.

Before actions are actions, they're thoughts, though...

My mind debates itself.

So maybe I'm not racist in <u>actions</u>, but the premeditation for racist actions is there if the thoughts still are.

There is no shortage of other issues I need to work on— binge eating, seeking validation from men, becoming a better employee, paying off all my debt— but I feel obligated to embody Christ's love in the world.

And I can't recall anywhere in the Bible where Jesus told someone to "Go, and be 'good enough.'"

He told people repeatedly, "Go, and sin no more."

And suddenly my mind recalls a warning from Jesus regarding adultery.

He said: "If a man even looks at a woman with lust, he has committed adultery with her in his heart."

So if I look at a black man with fear, what does that mean I commit in *mine?*

I am sitting on a stained floral chair in a bustling hallway.

When will they call me? I wonder for the umpteenth time.

It's been forty-five minutes since the time I was supposed to meet with the President of the school.

Anecdotally, I haven't seen a white person walk by yet and have silently marveled at *at least* half a dozen women's hair as I sit here.

No one has even looked my way, let alone called my name.

I'm not even sure I'm sitting in the right place to wait.

I want to ask someone, but everyone is bustling about so busily. I don't want to interrupt, especially not to be seen as some arrogant, bossy white lady.

My foot continues to bounce nervously, as I carefully reach into my bag and pull out a compact, to check my makeup again.

I dressed up for this, as I should.

After all, the President will be making the final decision whether I am advanced enough in my knowledge of doctrine (I definitely am not) or devout enough in my heart (still TBD) to be accepted into a Master's program without the otherwise requisite bachelor's degree.

I glance around the sterile white corridor and milling contrasting bodies, all operating atop too-dark navy carpet.

"Trisha?" a male voice calls out from one of the rooms almost right across from me.

I guess I'm in the right spot.

"Yes," I sit up perfectly straight as a reflex, looking in that direction and seeing a small, white-haired Caucasian man.

"Thank you for your patience. I'm ready to see you now."

I gather my fake leather tote off the floor. It contains a printed-out copy of my application, entrance essay, apartment keys, wallet, compact, and perhaps, somewhere, a stray crushed granola bar.

Walking across the wide hallway toward the man, I give a nervous smile and glance at the bronze name plate on the door.

Dr. Alfred Nelson, President of New York Theological Seminary.

An email pops up from Dr. Nelson two days later.

I glance around my office to see— surprise!— no one even remembers I'm here.

My mouse clicks into it.

I see the NYTS letterhead graphic at the top and below, the following words:

"Dear Trisha,"

My eyes blink hard.

"We are pleased to inform you of your acceptance..."

My mouth breaks into a shocked and involuntary grin.

My eyes gloss over the rest of the form.

A representative from the Registrar's office will be in touch with me shortly to begin scheduling me into classes.

Little do they know, I've already memorized the class offerings for the upcoming semester and won't need any assistance.

I can't explain what I'm feeling as I look down at my phone.

Five-figures in a bank account that typically reads single digits.

I blink hard, stunned.

I'll have to mail the check to my father for fourteen hundred dollars tonight.

I swallow hard, trying to force the dread back down, and simply try to enjoy this surreal moment before I say goodbye to all of it.

After the giant company's CFO signed the final contract with us (and back in the privacy of her own office), Sandra asked me how I actually managed to pull off such an astonishing sale.

I knew she was serious.

I don't have the experience, social skills, or talent to pull off such a feat, and I'd be the first to admit it. She's, clearly, the second.

But I smiled at her, and responded honestly: "Prayer, Sandra. Just a lot of prayer."

As I look down at the money that's evidently mine now, I know it's anything but.

I realize it's no coincidence that God is opening these doors for me: granting me admission into NYTS without a degree *and* giving me the money to pay for it.

I know it's God who gave me this money.

And I know it's the devil who took so much for taxes.

After my parents cashed their check, I still have enough money left to pay for one class in cash.

Frankly, with NYTS being uptown around the Columbia campus, it's all I could commit to time-wise, as well.

After doing the math, I will leave the office at 5:30 each Tuesday and Thursday evenings and won't return home to Bayonne until at least 10:30 those same nights.

That means two days a week, I will leave my studio apartment at 7:30am and return back home to it at 10:30pm.

I don't need to take out loans and run myself ragged each night of the week to pursue this vision, I realized this morning in prayer.

Slow and steady wins the race, right?

I glance over my purple letterheaded course selection form, hit Control+S, and then attach it to my email.

Double-checking to make sure the email address is correct, I sigh in relief.

It was hard to decide, but I did it. I chose just one class.

The one that jumped out at me most.

The one I felt God drawing me to.

The one I was most excited about.

"The Art of Biblical Storytelling"

I say a silent prayer, asking for God's blessing in this venture and click "Send."

That's it.

Tomorrow I'll likely receive the email confirming my enrollment.

Now the only left to do: is start.

I hate myself.

I really do most of the time.

And the other times, I'm just distracting myself with something else, like my phone.

But if I'm really honest: I hate who I am and who I've been.

A passionless career, a crappy apartment, no car, no man, no money... When I look in the mirror, I see only what needs fixing and nothing I've aspired to be.

I see nothing to be proud of, short of sobriety, and, even that, I take for granted.

Sometimes people pretend like the moment they get "saved," everything except bliss disappears.

And while I haven't been Christian for long, I know that's not my story.

I once heard an old lady in Group say: "If you walk twenty years into the forest, sometimes it takes you twenty years to get out."

I know God can do it quicker. And I really hope He does.

Because I thought I'd be something great as a little kid.

I never dreamt of myself as a menial insurance salesperson. No child does. (At least not one who wasn't already suicidally depressed.)

I never imagined myself twenty pounds overweight. Yet here I am.

And most of all: I never grew up wanting to be racist.

In fact, every time I witnessed racism as a kid, my soul recoiled in horror.

I'm reminded of a young man in Group last week who shared that he had an abusive alcoholic father he swore he'd never grow up to be like and, yet, he confessed, he knows he drinks too much now, himself.

I never wanted to be racist.

And I never wanted to be overweight.

I never wanted to sell insurance.

Or be broke.

Or stay single.

Or live in a crappy, "dangerous" neighborhood.

I never even wanted to be a Christian.

You know how motivational speakers always talk about how to "get what you want" out of life? I could sell out arenas giving speeches on the opposite.

Because I'm racist.

I'm overweight.

I sell insurance.

I'm dirt poor.

There isn't a prospect for love anywhere *near* my horizon.

I live in one room.

And I'm a Christian.

But the funny thing about that last one… is that it starts a countdown on all the rest.

When I gave my life to God, I gave Him *everything*.

And although I don't know much about the Bible, I *do* know it says: This has not come to stay. It has "come to *pass*."

So I lace up my old suicide-decision sneakers, pull out my phone and find a sermon by Bishop T.D. Jakes on YouTube. Then I pop in my headphones and walk downstairs, across the street to the gym.

And when I arrive back home in about an hour and a half, I will make myself a frozen banana and peanut butter smoothie, to substitute my previous routine of eating an entire pint of ice cream each night.

I came to God as the wreckage of who I became without Him.

And although He could fix me in an instant if He wanted to, He and I both know: I would learn nothing from that.

Late Winter 2015
In memory of Freddie Gray
Baltimore, MD

I'm on my way to the Women's Prison on Rikers
Island.

(No, I haven't been arrested.)

Three other women from Group and I came out here
to carry the Christian message to any woman in this
place who has ears to hear it.

And even though Carey, the young woman who
organizes this monthly outing for our Group, has been
here countless times and was certain that, a week ago,
we all submitted our information perfectly to clear
through security, we nonetheless, sat there in the
front office for over an hour waiting.

Thank God— no pun intended— for the vending
machines. I purchased a packet of blueberry Pop-
Tarts and browsed my phone until its battery dropped
below thirty percent.

Now I stare out the foggy bus window, at the
darkening sky, and fidget in my no-doubt-filthy seat.

Good thing I packed extra Purell.

No one on the shuttle bus speaks as the black prison
guard drives the four of us across the massive
concrete "campus" of different prisons.

There's one other woman on the bus. She must just be
visiting someone here.

I think I heard the one guard mention to her that the women's prison is the farthest away from the main office or something.

I sigh and tap the heavy soles of my black, gold and white DC sneakers on the floorboard of the bus and watch a plane pass through the frozen winter sky.

No one can hear my nervous foot tapping because of the vigorous diesel engine gurgling us along.

It feels as though we've been driving for miles.

I swear the sky has grown darker since this ride began.

"This is it," the driver declares and based off his flatline tone, it feels as though he is merely explaining "this is it" with a period at the end, rather than introducing us to the place with an exclamation point.

I look out the massive, exhaust-painted windshield at the ominous concrete building.

This is it.

I've never been locked up, although I've certainly done more than enough to qualify.

I was once rightly pulled over for a DUI. When I refused to take the field sobriety tests and told the officer I would need to call my (fictitious) lawyer, he simply let me go.

A year ago, I anxiously went with Carey and a few other women to a local jail to share the message, but that was only jail.

This is *prison.*

This is the real deal.

My mind races with stereotypical images of orange jumpsuits and shackles until I am interrupted by Carey.

"Okay," she announces, standing, "Those grey lockers outside the entryway are for visitors. You *literally* have to lock up everything except what you're wearing and your ID."

The brunette stares at us with earnest brown eyes.

"You have to leave your coats, too," she remembers, continuing, "Then we'll head inside where you'll present your ID one last time. The guards here will need it to match the list the front office guards sent over."

Her explanation is seamless, which makes sense considering I asked her yesterday how many of these trips she had arranged over the last year as Head of Correctional Institution Outreach.

Over forty, she said, with over two dozen of those trips being here at Rikers.

She told me the inmates know her by name and likewise.

My heavy sneakers plod down one bus step, then the other and finally, onto the concrete.

Another plane soars across the sky overhead.

I counted at least eight others on our never-ending bus trip over here.

I stare up at its blinking lights set beside a couple of bold stars contrasted against the steel blue sky.

"Is this by an airport or something?" I ask naively.

The native New Yorker in the group, Gina, laughs and points.

"That's literally LaGuardia right there."

My eyes widen.

"So they see airplanes taking off and landing all day here?"

She laughs again, removing her heavy coat and purse, cramming them into the small one-foot by one-foot metal locker.

"Yeah."

I stare up at yet another new plane rising toward the clouds with its taunting blinking lights.

"Well, that's ironic."

Gina and Carey continue to stare at me, as I stuff my belongings into my locker.

"Oh shit," I mutter, remembering I have to take out my ID.

Rolling my eyes, I dig around and find my wallet to extract my ID.

I look up and still see them looking at me.

"...because people are flying all over the world," I gesture upward to conclude my thought, "and then everyone's pretty much in cages on this side of the water, unable to go *anywhere*."

Carey looks at me, half-smiling.

"I wouldn't lead off with that inside."

I smirk.

Noted.

I jam my wallet back inside the small locker and push it hard to shut it with my bulky hole-pocketed black coat stuffed inside.

The woman we rode with is already well inside by this point and the rest of us gather our bearings before moving toward the double metal doors.

There's Carey, who recently shared at the women's meeting, revealing her father is white and her mother is half-Hispanic and half-white.

Gina, who is 100% Italian.

Loreen, who has hot pink hair and brown eyes.

And me, who looks like a chubby, asymmetrical Barbie. Like a Barbie that was accidentally left out in the sun and melted a little... plus sixteen extra pounds.

Suddenly I realize that, with the way this day has gone so far, I will not have time to workout tonight.

The corners of my mouth droop.

I've been making such good progress...

"Okay," Carey announces to her group of Rikers rookies with a grin, snapping me out of my thoughts, "You guys ready? These women are amazing. So sweet and so eager to hear what we have to share with them."

I smile a forced, anxious smile back at her as I recall those cringeworthy moments in junior high where I changed my vernacular based on how the cool kids spoke.

Dear God, please help me to stay authentic in this experience.

Help me to bring Your message here, one of hope and faith and light.

Help me to be who you made me to be and not some phony version of a person I think other people want me to be. Amen.

Pink-haired Loreen pushes hard on one of the doors and enters.

As I follow her and the other young women in, I see a second set of doors beyond two female guards to our left behind bulletproof glass.

"IDs, please," the brunette guard with the no-nonsense bun commands.

We all lay our respective IDs loudly down in the hole on the metal counter, the only place not shielded by the one-inch glass.

She looks at all of them individually, then hands all four to her uniformed black colleague who makes photocopies of each before handing them to the bunned first guard who slides them back to Carey through the metal hole. Carey redistributes them to their rightful owners.

I wonder why they make copies...

Do they keep a file? Do they keep a record on us?

BUZZZZZZ!

A loud metallic buzz makes it clear they are unlocking the next set of doors into the building.

The four of us move as a unit through to the next set of security.

This time, it's five guards of varying genders, with two metal detectors.

My eyes widen.

This is elaborate.

How do people even sneak in contraband for prisoners here?

Contraband is a big problem on the show "Lockup" that I sometimes watch.

I almost ask the question out loud, but as my mouth opens to, it dawns on me that perhaps asking such a question in front of armed guards may not be the best idea unless I'm in the mood to be strip-searched.

And while it's been *awhile* since any hands have been on me other than my own, I decide to keep my mouth shut.

After we each walk through the metal detector without issue, we are escorted by a black male guard down a long, painted white cinderblock hallway and up to a heavy metal-barred drop point.

The familiar, jarring *BUZZZZZZ!*

The heavy metal bars slowly slide open in a sound I'd only ever heard on TV or the movies.

They didn't have this kind of security at the jail.

A uniformed black woman waits on the other side to escort us on the next leg of our journey.

We slowly step on the other side of the bars and I suddenly jolt, as I hear them riveting on their tracks, closing behind us.

That's it.

We're caged in now. Just like the inmates. Just like the murderers.

I know that Jesus preached the gospel to all people, including murderers, I think as the black woman leads our group around a large corner and through more painted white cinderblocks, *but I, also, know that I'm not Jesus.*

I glance around nervously as we approach another door made of metal bars.

The next set of dilapidated metal bars begins to creak open, and we make our way through.

I see a giant plexiglass booth at the end of this hallway, as the echo of closing metal bars repeats itself on seemingly every brick in this place.

There are four guards inside— two women, two men— and we are moving toward it.

"You guys will wait inside here until the inmates file into the cafeteria from their dorm," the guard tells us in a no-nonsense manner.

The guard approaches what appears to be the prison guard command center, drawing an ID out from a zip-cord on her hip and placing it up to the glass.

A muscular blonde woman buzzes us in.

"These are your speakers tonight," our stoic tour guide informs the guards inside, before leaving us.

We walk in. One of the new guards shuts the door and double-deadbolts it behind us.

Oh my God.

I watch a white man, a black man, a black woman, and the muscular blonde woman bustle about in this "office" which is only half the size of a subway car.

They're trapped in here for their whole shift?!

"How long until we go in?" I whisper to Carey.

"Usually not too long," she points and my eyes draw upward with her pale finger, "Look, the first women are already trickling in."

I watch as two black women and one white woman laugh far off to the open space to our right. There are about ten tables which resemble the round lunch tables we had in my hometown's high school cafeteria.

One black woman has much darker skin and longer hair than the other, and it's pretty apparent that the white woman had dyed her otherwise black hair fire engine red before her stay began here. From the length of her roots, she's been in here for awhile.

I watch the three of them chuckle and jostle one another, and the paler black inmate sits first.

Then, three white women walk in together.

I can tell all the way from here that two of them have skin resembling meth addicts.

I intently watch as more and more women pile into the open cafeteria.

A few Hispanic women, many more black women, and a few more white women, including one with grey hair who looks like a cozy grandmother.

They are all wearing loose but starchy grey t-shirts and matching grey pants.

On their feet are either grey plastic slide sandals or a mundane variation of white sneaker.

Some are wearing their hair up in messy buns. Some in braids. Some down and loose.

I watch the group of women like I'm at a zoo.

Then my eye catches her.

An older black woman, maybe in her fifties.

She looks skinny and scattered.

My eyes lock in on her, and I begin to build a shamelessly stereotyped story about her in my mind.

Crack addict.

Former prostitute.

Maybe she got picked up by an undercover cop posing as a John...

I glance around the group and briefly estimate how many might have been sex workers.

But my eyes keep going back to the old black woman.

She probably grew up fatherless.

Maybe she was addicted to male approval as a result, and an older boyfriend first convinced her to try crack.

Maybe she got picked up for possession.

Or maybe she was in a drug-fueled craze and attacked a police officer, biting them...

"They're ready for you," the white male guard announces to Carey.

She looks mean.

I'll bet she's the meanest woman here.

The other members of my group begin moving toward the plexiglass door on the other side of the half-subway car office.

I come to from my made-up story and follow suit.

As we walk from the guard's office to the round table at the front of the cafeteria, one inmate compliments my shoes.

I turn to see the paler black girl of the original trio.

"Thank you," I smile weakly, continuing to walk.

We arrive at the front table and take seats.

270

There are about forty women of varying ages, sizes, and shades staring back at us.

"Big crowd tonight," muses Carey with a warm smile, "For those of you who are new or are just joining us for the first time, welcome! My name is Carey. We are here from a Christian Group out of Hoboken, New Jersey and we are here to, hopefully, share some hope and light with you tonight."

I glance out a small, barred window to our left and see yet another airplane departing, jeering at us all with its blinking lights.

I look back at the blank-faced group, my eyes scanning the women an- *shit!*

It's the black woman I was staring at earlier.

Her black eyes are glaring directly at me.

I look away, to Carey at my left, and then casually back.

Shit!

She is still staring at me.

Oh my God.

I glance up at the guard booth. None of them are looking this way.

I look at the prisoners. None of them are shackled or even cuffed.

What if she's about to shank me or something?

What if she fashioned a shiv earlier and now wants to kill me because I'm a little white girl coming in to... what? Save her?

Oh my God, my mind races, *why did I come here?*

I'm going to die tonight.

And why did I wear these shoes? What if that girl mugs me and robs me of my shoes before I leave?

"Here to start us off," Carey's faded voice re-enters my consciousness, "is Trisha! She's going to share with you guys her story of finding God, or..."

She chuckles.

"...rather how God found her."

I stare at Carey, blinking.

She grins back at me encouragingly.

She didn't tell me I was going first.

I glance over at the old black lady.

Shit! She's still giving me the evil eye.

I look away and feel the air leave my chest.

"Hi," I swallow hard and greet the room, "Can everyone in the back hear me?"

One young black woman in the back smiles and gives me the thumbs up. The rest just stare at me as though they already hate me.

Why did I come here?

I look to the light-skinned black girl who complimented my shoes who has a friendly-by-comparison expression on her face.

She will be my anchor in the crowd.

God, please give me the right words tonight...

"I used to drink alcohol every day," I hear my voice begin, "I grew up in a so-so house."

I glance anxiously around the room, reminded of the homes the popular girls in my junior high came from.

"We had enough money and everything," I stumble to clarify, always uncomfortable about that topic, "I just... nothing was super healthy. And I'm not talking food. I'm talking everything else."

I see two brown heads nod in what is now blurred vision.

"We went to church," my head shakes, quietly remembering Isabelle, the attractive reader my father always gushed about, "and we *looked* the part, but we'd barely be out of the parking lot before the arguing and dysfunction would start up again. So I didn't really want much to do with God."

I feel eyes on me, as I glance to the guards' bullet-proof glass encasement.

"I felt like a prisoner in that house."

I shake my head, coming to, realizing what I just said is hugely offensive.

"I mean... I'm sorry..."

I stammer.

"I just... As a kid, I couldn't leave no matter how much I wanted to."

I notice a few sets of eyes soften, as though they know all too well what I mean.

"And I *definitely* wanted to leave. So when I found alcohol in junior high, that was it. That was the release I'd been searching for."

A few more nods.

"And that addiction took me to the gates of Hell," I breathe heavily, "I dated people I didn't love, hung out with people I didn't like, and looked in the mirror at a person I couldn't stand."

Almost everybody's nodding now, as I finally look toward the old black woman.

Her dark eyes are no longer shooting daggers at me, but she's not nodding either.

I briefly wonder if she is fantasizing about killing me.

We are in a prison, after all.

I suck in the institutionalized air.

"I didn't want to stop until I did. But, that's the thing... by the time I *did* want to stop, I couldn't."

A chorus of knowing hums ring through the fluorescent-lit cafeteria.

I begin to cough.

Shit.

Several coughs... I can't stop.

One black woman in the back walks out of the room, obviously bored and uninterested.

"And I..." *Cough.*

"Sorry."

Cough.

"I don't know what's..."

Cough. Cough.

Cough.

A thick, clear plastic cup of water appears in front of my right hand.

I look up.

It's the black woman who left the room, bored.

Humbled and still coughing into my palm, I try to thank her, as my mind does some quick OCD math of the general demographic who have drank out of this very cup before me.

I watch the room watching me cough and, against my mind's better judgment, slowly lift the cup to my parched mouth.

I take a sip.

Pause.

Then another.

"Thank you," I properly thank the black woman who has since returned to her seat in the back.

"Sorry," I direct toward the room again, "Where was I?"

"You couldn't stop drinking," a black girl one table away offers.

I smile, glancing at the cup of water again, wishing I could bring myself to drink more.

"Thanks."

My green eyes blink hard.

"I was a slave to the substances, a slave to my ego, and a slave to what people thought about me," I pause and then relent, "I still can be a slave to those last two."

"I used to do everything with a buzz. Go to work, drive in the car, see anybody... I even started drinking before I would work out!"

A few women chuckle.

"Not that I worked out much," I shrug, recalling the temporary habit's onset after I met Oliver.

"I tried everything before I tried God, but once I tried God, I was able to stop trying so hard in the first place. That first day I prayed, something broke inside me. A stronghold, a curse, an addiction, whatever you want to call it... Something changed. And from the day I said that first prayer, I haven't drank any alcohol or taken a drug since."

A few inmates begin to clap, and I notice the black male guard look up from within the bulletproof office.

I look around the room solemnly, knowing I was one drunk-driving accident away from being one of them.

One missed stoplight.

One lane on the highway crossed without looking.

One dark winter road where I could have forgotten to turn on my headlights.

So many ways in which I could have killed somebody through my reckless decisions back then, and yet... none of them happened.

But here's a room full of women where, in some variation, it did.

"I believe we're all on a collision course with God. And often that divine collision occurs in a crisis. Or at least, it did for me."

I tell them.

"But as soon as I called out to Him with my whole heart, He showed up in my life and has been ever since."

More nods.

"It's easy for me to look around and think I'm too broken to be a Christian... that I've done too much wrong and not enough right. But He meets us all in different places, and I've come to learn that none of them are more sacred than any other. Because where God is, is where sacredness is. And God goes anywhere. Especially prisons, no matter what kind."

The last speaker wraps up and the hands of inmates raise almost immediately.

Carey calls on the old black woman, the one who's been glaring at me every time I glance up at her to see if she's still glaring at me.

"My name is Lisa," her gravelly voice introduces with a slight, misplaced Southern accent, "And as soon as you all walked in, I liked *you* the least."

She points a dark, crooked finger between my eyes and my face twists to horror.

What?

"I hated you when you all walked in..."

I chuckle nervously, glancing over at Carey to *do something*.

"But then you told my story," she finished her thought.

I turn my slightly softened, but confused, eyes back to her.

She has coarse, frizzy hair. Short enough that it forms a tiny, round puff at the top of her head.

Her eyes look tired, even though seemingly all four of her limbs are twitching or at least moving in some way.

She's skinny. *Too skinny.*

Depending on how long she's been in, that fact tells some of her story for her...

"I was sober for seven years," my thoughts snap back to her and my eyes focus on her face like a hawk, "I was just like you, happy, productive, and useful."

I squint, *What happened?*

"Then one day, I told myself I could drink again. I thought it had been so long, that maybe I was healed. I had stopped praying about a month before that. My life had gotten so big and good," she shrugs her boney shoulders, "I got busy."

I blink hard, and the room is so silent, no one is even breathing.

"So I drank, 'cuz I thought I could," she looks down, shaking her head with palpable regret, "I couldn't."

The whole room watches her.

"Within three weeks, I was worse than ever before. Started doing drugs again, which I swore I'd never do," I nod to the sound of her voice, knowing I've made a similar vow to myself, "And then I became a prostitute to support the habit."

She looks up and directly into my eyes.

"One night in a blackout, I stabbed a man to death in a gas station parking lot."

My heart skips and jaw drops.

"I didn't even know him. I don't know what he did. All I know is that I came to the next morning in a jail cell and handcuffs."

I cannot take my eyes off her.

"Aggravated murder is what they call it," she smirks knowingly into my eyes, "and I'm going to be here for the rest of my life as a result."

I swallow hard, unable to look away.

"I was just like you before I relapsed," her gaze turns soft, "Go figure, I judged you from the jump."

She shakes her tiny puff of black hair, humbly.

"You helped me a lot today. You showed me what I once was. And if I was all that once, then maybe I can be it again, in here..."

I blink hard, feeling my body begin to breathe again.

"With God's help," the hoarse black woman adds. And I nod.

She didn't know she had my story, and neither did I.

So we judged each other, because we didn't know each other.

Dear God, Even when I'm here doing Your work, I still judge. I still separate. I still... fail.

Help me. Oh God, please. Help me to be a better Christian and grow in Your love.

I look up into her eyes with a modest yet knowing smile.

Amen.

"I'm going to say a prayer tonight that you never take your sobriety for granted, like I did," she offers to me, in conclusion.

And I nod into her eyes with conviction, knowing she helped me more here tonight than I could have ever helped her.

Later, as the bus drives us back to the front office where we will check out and leave, I watch the airplanes depart on the other side of the water and think about the old black woman.

I wonder where she might have traveled to, had she been allowed. Had she not stopped praying...

And I wonder how long it would have taken for me to stop praying, grow complacent and relapse, had I not heard her tonight.

We hated each other and judged one another.

And, in the end, we learned we are the same.

And, no matter which side of the bars we're on, we all need God... desperately.

"I love how the snow looks while it's falling," the black woman in the passenger's seat tells me one month later.

I stare out the backseat window, at the colossal amount of snow the sky above dumps on the world all around us.

Hours before, Wanda and I were sitting in the Hoboken train station when Light Rail service was suddenly suspended due to the increasingly severe winter storm.

That had never happened before.

I didn't have money for an Uber.

As we sat on what looked like wooden church pews in the stained-glass windowed station, she and I struck up a conversation while stranded.

She told me how her name was Wanda Lamb and she worked at what may well be the largest publishing house in the world.

I told her how I used to write.

She told me about her two daughters.

I told her I wasn't sure how I was going to make it home to Bayonne.

She told me her husband was coming to pick her up and offered me a ride, if I was willing to wait an hour with her, until he arrived from work.

So here we sit, with her white husband driving us all to Bayonne.

I stare at the back of his blonde head.

I think about how my mother takes such pride that our family is all blondes... that her grandchildren are all blondes...

I think about how, at sixteen, I dyed my hair brown and she referred to me almost-exclusively as "Rosita" around the house, as well as in public, until I dyed it back.

I stare at the back of his blonde head.

"I love how the snow looks as it's falling," she repeats in the dark car, and I lean over to the window to watch it with her.

"I don't like it once it's fallen," she clarifies, wistfully, "but I like the way it looks *when* it's falling."

And I watch each flake float and fall.

Early Winter 2016
In memory of Gregory Gunn
Montgomery, AL

My ex-boyfriend Oliver used to have a saying: "It's good to feel nervous. It means you're doing something."

By that logic and the massive pit I feel in my stomach as I walk to my first class, I am about to do something *big*.

I fidget with the headphone in my right ear on the unseasonably warm Manhattan day and glance again at the walking directions on my phone, while Kanye West serenades me in the background.

Breathing in and out, I look up at the blue sky peppered with cold, white clouds, then down at the black combat boots which I occasionally wear to work when I'm running *very* late.

I review the directions on my phone again in case I missed a turn in the last five steps. Then I gaze back out to the sky, out of suspicion its clouds may have heard and heeded my inner dialogue's call to run away.

All around me are signs for Columbia University, the campus of which I'm, evidently, smack in the middle.

A rising sense of inferiority looms before me like a towering tsunami wave.

I never graduated college, the thought keeps reminding me.

My chin and gaze raise toward the sky, as my feet keep walking.

God, I know You brought me this far. And I believe You won't drop me now.

My eyes stare twenty yards in front of me, to 120th Street, at a sign which reminds me where I'm *not* going: Union Theological Seminary.

Their students are about as white as NYTS' students are black.

It's time for me to turn.

My class is at the Riverside Church. I've never been there before, but evidently I'm supposed to head to a classroom on the second floor.

I pick up the pace of my walk, as I glance at the clock and see that class is a mere ten minutes from starting. I feel the physical presence of the church growing closer, although I can't see it and the gnawing hole in my stomach expands, nearly swallowing me whole.

What am I even doing?

I've been avoiding the thoughts in my head as much as I could, but as Google Maps brings me closer to my destination, my mind is now screaming.

Go back.

It's all black people.

You don't belong here.

You're not Christian enough.

You're white. They're not going to welcome you.

They don't want you here.

Go back.

Go home!

I blink hard and continue walking toward the church.

Suddenly I look up and see a tall white building in front of me. According to Maps, I'm supposed to turn right before I reach it. It looks like a school building.

It looks reputable.

What if my school isn't?

(Even though it is.)

Would I even <u>think</u> that if it were a predominantly white school?

And I already know the answer.

God, please help me. Please help me. Redirect my thoughts. More importantly, guide my feet.

Stacey always says: "We can't always think our way into taking the right action. So we must act our way into right thinking."

God, help my actions change my thoughts. Guide my career. God, I know you are the Guide on this path

You've laid out for me. Please give me the courage to walk it and the humility to lay down my prejudices.

My feet follow the direction of my prayers and as a powerful bassline begins thumping in my ears, I turn right and see steeples so tall, they are grazing the clouds which dot the New York City sky.

I stop dead in my tracks.

My jaw falls as my eyes keep looking up, and the church's presence soars higher than Heaven and feels so large that God, Himself, might fit inside.

After a stunned moment...

I begin to walk again, this time faster toward the colossal grey building. The ornate details of countless steeples and the massive belltower keep my eyes fixed on it.

I am going to class here.

As I stroll up to the front gate, I see a black man walking through a set of double doors.

The words "NYTS Students Enter Here" accompany an arrow on a sheet of white printer paper.

I doubt whoever printed the sign stole their paper and ink like I had.

Yet I follow the black man who disappeared inside.

Gripping my fake leather tote bag which I purchased on clearance at Macy's last time I was home visiting my parents, I feel the obscene weight from all of my course's books inside.

Here we go.

I pause.

God, here we go…

At this point, I'm not sure if I'm praying or using His Name in vain.

And I push open the unwieldy glass and gold swinging door to enter.

Ten feet inside, I see a black and glass revolving door waiting to bring me into the belly of the cathedral.

I move toward it, and enter.

My cheap boot hits the marble floor, as the air scatters from my lungs.

Everything my eyes see is made of stone and marble.

The floor, the walls, the ceiling, *everything…*

Everything feels heavy, luxurious, massive, and timeless.

My five-foot frame wanders inside a bit further.

Not a person in sight.

Where'd that guy go?

A few ornate metal benches pepper the grand space that I slowly piece together is a foyer of sorts and smells soothingly like a potpourri of stone, dust, and incense.

Warm yellow lights illuminate the area.

I walk further inside as a white man emerges from a door I hadn't noticed up ahead to my left.

His bottom half is hidden behind a giant piece of stone, which is clearly a desk for a church doorman of sorts.

I pause Kanye, as my eyes catch what is across from the desk: a bulletin board peppered with colorful flyers of church events, as well as at least a half dozen lit-up shadow boxes filled with what appears to be historical content.

"Can I help you?" a voice offers.

It's the man whose legs are hidden by stone.

"Oh," I turn toward the old white man in a well-worn navy suit, laughing lightly, "Yes, sorry! I'm a student of the New York Theological Seminary, and..."

"Turn here," he points to the door at his right (my left) that, again, I hadn't noticed, "It'll open up into the school building area. Take the elevator to the second floor."

I smile at the old man.

"Thank you," I nod, making my way in that direction.

"Are you a new student?"

"Yes," I push on the metal bar with the forearm of my sweater to open the door, turning back toward him.

"Good luck," he nods with a smile.

I smile and walk into the fluorescent-lit space, leaving him— the last white person I'd see for several hours— behind.

Ding!

The elevator arrives and I step in, pressing the number 2 with my knuckle.

As the doors close and I move upward, I pluck my phone from the open mouth of my totebag.

Lighting it up, I see my music is accidentally still playing and that my phone battery is at a mere twenty percent as a result.

There's no way that will last me through class and my three-hour commute home to Bayonne.

I hit pause on the music and as the elevator door opens up onto the second floor, I walk out with a sigh and hold the button to shut my phone off.

Power down?

I swipe my finger, immediately realizing I would have been wiser to shut it down after I found my classroom without incident.

What number was the classroom again? I know I had it in an email.

But to restart it, find my class details, then shut it down again would steal even more precious battery life.

Looking around, I see a few vending machines off to my right, along with double doors which are dark beyond their windows.

I don't think my class is through there.

So I turn left and begin wandering the hallways, hoping to hear something promising.

Sure enough, as I walk the beige and black checkered tiled floor, I hear a woman's voice. As I move toward the room containing it, I wander up to the open doorway and gaze in.

The black woman speaking at the head of the table looks up at me, as do eight other black people.

My eyebrows raise and my heartbeat quickens.

"Excuse me. I'm sorry. Biblical Storytelling?" I hear myself ask.

She smiles sweetly, but also understandably a bit annoyed by my interruption.

"All the way down the hall to the right, in the chapel."

"Thank you, ma'am," I look into her brown eyes, nodding, "Sorry again for the interruption."

I wave and she smiles again as I exit.

I begin moving down the long corridor of classrooms and bulletin boards.

Again, I hear muffled voices.

I see the word "Chapel" on a black sign with white lettering and move toward the room. It looks very different from the other standard classroom doorways.

For one thing, it's not a door that's flush with the main hallway. It's dark and tucked inside a shadowy corner all its own at the end of the hall. And the whole entryway is lined with tiny navy and gold shimmering tiles, each about one inch by one inch.

The excited hum of voices within lures me and I step through the dreamy, constellation-like entryway, in awe, staring at each tile as I walk past.

The room opens up and is less impressive than I had envisioned given its entrance, but...

Shit.

It's all black people.

My body tenses and I give a weak, half-smile to those few who glanced my way, as they laugh and converse with one another.

This is no joke, I realize.

I'm <u>here</u> now.

293

The room feels warm, with wood-paneled walls, like a living room from the seventies. It has several windows on the far wall. And the back wall is simply rows of large white cinder block bricks.

There are two levels to the room, separated by a step and then sloped seating upward, like a college lecture hall but not nearly as large.

At the front of the room is a massive wooden cross hung above a petite stage. The entire wall behind the cross is lined with tiny gold, silver, and green reflective tiles.

I usually sat in the back during my college courses, and my grades reflected it. This time, I will try something different. I want to be a different kind of student here.

Noticing the professor is not here yet, I make my way up to the first few rows.

As I walk the aisle, a few of the convivial voices lower and quiet. Some of the laughter falls still.

I scan all the empty metal folding chairs, looking for one that feels welcoming, like a transfer student at their first lunch in a high school cafeteria.

Out of the corner of my left eye, I notice one black woman in her late forties or so who is turned around in her seat speaking to another black woman. She does a rather indiscreet double-take towards me as her words drift slowly into what I can only imagine is surprised silence by my presence here.

The left doesn't feel very welcoming, so I turn my head to the right and see several empty chairs, as well as an approachable-looking black man in his late sixties or so.

Everyone in the class looks to be at least ten years my senior.

I step into his row and, gesturing toward a seat two chairs away from him, I muster the words: "Hi, is anyone sitting here?"

He looks at it, then back at me.

"Looks like it's all yours," he offers in a cheerful tone, pointing at me playfully.

"Thank you," I tell him, for more than just the chair.

I heave my heavy bag off of my shoulder and allow it to plunk down onto the floor, grateful, also, for the break my aching shoulder is finally receiving.

"Have you taken any of Dr. Shepherd's classes before?" the old man asks me, as I instinctively pick up my turned off phone.

I shake my head, tossing the useless brick back into the mouth of my bag.

"This is my first class *ever,* actually."

I watch the brown eyes behind his glasses widen, as he smiles an imperfect, genuine smile at me.

"Oh, you're in for a treat," he promises, shaking his head, "Dr. Shepherd is a legend here."

My eyes widen as my new friend continues to educate me.

"You're going to be real spoiled having him for your first class. No other professor will measure up!"

He laughs lightly and I follow suit, already nervous and impressed by our absent professor.

"Do you know what time it is? Doesn't class go from six to eight?"

My friend nods, looking at the digital watch on his wrist.

"6:02," he reads, looking back toward the tiled entrance, "Dr. Shepherd should be here by now."

I nod, as I pull my blank notebook out of my bag, along with a printed syllabus, pen, and two highlighters I'm, uh, *borrowing* from my desk at work.

God, please forgive me.

I briefly wonder if I should take out all of the required books and put them on the seat beside me since none of the seats have desks.

The hum of voices and laughter lower to near silence, and I look up, startled by the sudden shift.

Turning backward, I see him.

I don't even need to hear him introduce himself. This man is not a student.

I watch him.

Short.

Older.

Obviously, black.

Glasses.

A grey homburg hat.

Tan trench coat.

Three-piece grey suit underneath and a matching briefcase.

Despite his cane and obvious limp, this man walks as though he carries a legacy on his shoulders.

His presence, at once, fills all the gaps in the room our hushed silence left vacant.

His strong aura, like a vacuum sucking out all ancillary conversation and scattered focus.

I stare, along with the other students.

He makes his way up the aisle, pressing his weight onto the heavy wooden cane in his right hand, and staring at the cross the whole way.

When he arrives at the front of the room, he removes his hat to reveal a perfectly bald— and perfectly *round*— head.

And with no sense of rushing, he silently lays down his cane, leather briefcase, and coat onto the front row seats beside his hat.

I stare at his purple and grey bow-tie and serious expression.

Dr. Shepherd looks up at us from almond-shaped eyes beneath silver wire-rimmed frames, staring at each one of us.

I can't help but feel him stare at me for the slightest moment longer than the rest.

Before Dr. Shepherd had arrived, a few more students trickled in, including one man with paler skin. Not white. But not black, either. Also, the only other student who looks about my age.

I glance over at him to break the gaze between me and the intimidating Doctor.

The somewhat pale-skinned student is grinning and nodding.

I look back at our professor, but he has moved his sights to other students.

Short, but unquestioningly sturdy.

Vulnerable with his cane, but also intimidating and unwavering.

He stares at us silently and then...

"Good evening, Beloveds..."

Although just "meeting" him for the first time, the only way I can describe his voice is: unforgettable.

Immediately, I know if a movie were ever made about this man, Denzel Washington would *have* to play him. No one else would do, because his entire comportment conveys: *I expect the best, and I receive it.*

And everyone knows Denzel's the best.

"We will begin with a prayer."

I glance around and see everyone else bow their heads, so I follow suit.

Joining my sweaty palms together and folding my fingers down, I close my eyes and listen to his unmistakable voice.

"Our Loving Father, we humbly thank You for bringing us to this classroom to learn this evening. The time— *this* time— is for *Your* glory, in furtherance of *Your* Name."

A handful of students emit small hums.

"So that, Lord, we may become ever-closer to You, we ask that You open our eyes to the ways in which we can spread Your love into this world, as story-tellers, as intercessors, as pastors, and, like Jesus, as *servants* to our fellow children."

I shift in my seat a bit, always impressed with the way some people can pray.

My mind turns to Stacey, but is interrupted by his strong voice.

"Our Dear Father, we know You love us, having made each of us in Your divine image. And we love You."

Hums ring out in the room.

I've never been in a room where people hum when someone prays before.

"Help us to serve You in *all* things, at such a pivotal moment in history. At this time..."

He pauses.

"This *advent* of the Black Lives Matter Movement..."

My joined fingers seize, the same way they did when I was six and heard my grandmother say what she said in her all-white kitchen.

"We ask You to bless this awakening, Lord..."

More hums.

"And we ask You to bless the victims of racism of all kinds..."

Louder hums.

"We ask You to lift up all of us who have survived racism in some way..."

300

Several students sigh "amen," and I keep focusing on his words, praying with him.

"And we ask You, in Your boundless, endless love to lift up those who hold racism in their hearts."

My eyes shoot open... and up.

At him.

I watch him with his eyes pinched closed, continue leading us in prayer, as a hush falls over the room.

"We know to be far away from You is the ultimate sickness. And to hold hatred in one's heart, the most terminal distance."

More hums.

"Today we lift up this movement."

Louder hums.

"We lift up the survivors."

The man beside me raises his arm toward the Reverend Doctor.

"We lift up *all* racism's victims, in *every* shade."

Two students proclaim "yes" and "Jesus."

"And the perpetrators of this hate and evil and darkness..."

I close my eyes, humbled and incredulous.

"We pray for them, Lord."

I feel burning beneath my closed eyes.

"In Jesus' Great Name, Amen."

I whisper "Amen," as other students nearly shout it.

I try to hide the tears as my eyes open.

They blur my vision.

And I can scarcely see.

All this time I'd been praying for them, I never imagined they've been praying for me.

PART III: PRACTICING LOVE

"Little children, let us not love in word or talk, but in
deed and in truth."
1 John 3:18

The next evening, as my feet pick up the pace on the treadmill, Bishop T.D. Jakes preaches to me about blind spots.

I look around and see more black people in the gym than white, which is normal.

He asks me if there are any places in my life where I refuse to let God change me.

I stare down at my running feet.

He asks me, if I *really* looked inward, if I would find hate hidden anywhere.

I raise the speed of the tread.

He asks me who is suffering because of my inability to look at certain parts of myself.

I look again at each of the black people in the gym.

He asks me how I could honestly say that I love God if I have hate for any of His children.

I blink hard and raise the speed again until I am panting.

He asks me how I am treating the people in my life.

I glance down at my water and keep running.

He asks me how deep my faith *truly* is.

I hit the Up arrow again to add even more speed.

He talks to me about mercy.

I think of my sobriety and the woman at Rikers, who I very easily could have been.

He tells me that God wants me to become a sanctuary.

The word echoes in my soul.

He tells me that it's not about "them," but that it's about me.

I look up again, at the black people.

He tells me that God wants *me* to be free.

I exhale hard, sprinting, but still unable to outrun my failings.

The Bishop's booming voice chases me:

"What's in your blind spot?"

A week later, I am on a phone call with a young woman named Keisha.

By her name and her voice, I assume she is black.

She's helping me with a fraudulent charge on my bank card.

She has reversed it, laughed sweetly at my joke about how dumb the person was for choosing my modest bank account to steal from, opened an investigation, and mailed me out a new card with a new number.

I ask to speak to her manager... and her voice tenses as she agrees.

"You've just done such a great job helping me today," I tell her, reassuringly, "I want them to know what an asset you are as an employee."

Her tone brightens and I can hear her smile.

"Really?"

"Yeah, you really calmed me down and set my mind at ease. I'm very grateful."

"No one ever does that," she laughs, awkwardly, "Hang on, let me see if she's available."

"Okay, no worries."

After a moment, Keisha picks up the line and tells me her manager is on another call at the moment.

I tell her I'll hold. I tell her I want to be sure her manager knows.

After two minutes holding, I tell Keisha's manager what a terrific employee she is. Her manager's tone is as shocked as hers.

"I can't tell you how refreshing this is," the manager's voice sounds like it belongs to a white woman, "I usually only hear complaints about employees."

"Keisha's awesome. You guys are very fortunate to have her."

As I hang up the phone, I think about the kind, light-skinned black woman who used food stamps in the grocery store last fall.

I wonder where she is now, and if she's doing any better financially.

I wonder if Keisha has ever been subjected to racism when it came to finding or keeping work. I glance down at my phone.

I don't think my simple compliment to her manager can reverse any of what has happened to her before this moment, nor reconcile all of what I've, personally, done either.

But I hope it can build her up from here, build her up as valuable in her manager's eyes, build her up as exceptional in her own.

It is a small act, but so is laying a brick. And small acts repeated, like laying individual bricks one-by-one, build sanctuaries.

Dear God, Thank you for this new day. Please be with me and deliver me from anxiety so I can be more useful to those around me. Please help me to be kind, especially to people of color today. Please be with them. Help them to feel Your presence in a new way. Lift them up financially. Help them to have great relationships. Help me to do my part, whatever part You want that to be.

"Good morning, Isaiah!" I smile at my building's black doorman an hour and a half later. He's my age and originally from Haiti.

"Hello, Trisha," he greets me in his distinct accent, neatly-ironed blazer and tie.

"How was your weekend?" I ask him.

"Good."

I slow to a stop in front of his desk, like usual, and listen to his melodic voice.

"Some friends and I went to a great little Jamaican restaurant that opened in our neighborhood."

"Ooh!" I coo with sincerity, glancing down at the "John 3:16"-stamped leather bracelet he wears every day, "I've never had Jamaican food before! How was it?"

"Oh, it was delicious! You have to try it!"

I had never really thought about Jamaican food before.

I laugh and promise him I will. Then I excuse myself to head upstairs, as I am late, per usual.

My smile never fades until I reach my floor, which means most mornings I'm smiling because of Isaiah the entire walk to the elevator bank and the whole elevator ride up, including any stops for other people on lower floors, too.

When I first started speaking to Isaiah, I imagined I was showing him that these people who walk past him each day see him as a human, as a fellow, as a *person*. I imagined I'd be helping make his life better.

Now I can chuckle at that ignorance.

I'm making my own life better.

Being kind and befriending him turned out to be one of the most selfish things I've done.

True to form, still grinning, I hit the "Up" arrow to head upstairs and begin my workweek.

Later that night, again, the Bishop preaches while I run.

He tells me that the passage of time does not, by itself, give somebody a new life, but rather the newness of our thinking does.

I adjust my right headphone and look up at my neighbors exercising. As usual, most don't look like me.

He promises that the enemies fighting my spirit today won't last forever.

God, please don't let this racism and ignorance last forever.

He quotes the Bible that those weapons formed against me will not prosper.

God, I know that racism is the enemy's weapon of false pride and division against my soul and Your children. I know it will not prosper. I know with Your help that it <u>cannot</u> prosper.

I raise the speed on the treadmill like I usually do.

He tells me that God will condemn the tongues of those who speak against me.

I recall all the times my tongue has risen against someone of another race, or laughed at a racist joke, or stayed silent when I should have spoken up.

All the sins of both my tongue's action and inaction...

The memory of that dingy white concrete stairwell at Luke's fraternity house haunts me all over again.

And I feel the shame all over again. The regret, all over again. The moral failure, all over again.

He tells me that everyone is fighting a battle and we don't need to feel shame about what our battles are. He tells me that *right now* can be my time for healing.

I lift my head and pick up the pace.

He tells me that we, each, are on a journey to become the best versions of ourselves.

I close my eyes and align my spirit with his words.

He prays over me that my past habits won't hinder this growth.

Amen. Amen.

I shake my head and, again, raise the speed while I listen.

"...the real battleground," Bishop Jakes tells me, "is in your mind. That's where the fight is."

He tells me that we usually fall asleep with these demons.

And I think about my nightly prayer for God to forgive my racism.

He tells me that, in the morning, we wake up with them.

And I think about my morning prayer for God to deliver me from racism.

He tells me that we take them to work with us.

And I think about Isaiah.

As I glance up, I see a white woman and a black man walk in through the front doors holding hands and immediately feel a familiar irritation rise into my mind, as something in my chest tightens and grows hot.

He tells me that it's the silent war going on inside of us that God wants to heal.

That's it, God.

That irritation, that tightening.

Deliver me from that reaction.

I shake my head, hoping against all experience to literally shake the hate loose, as my finger presses the "Up" arrow to increase the speed.

God, take it away. Take it away. Take it away.

I want to follow You. I don't want to be racist. Take these thoughts and these reactions away. Take it away.

Make me a new me, God. I can't do it, but You can. Make me a new me. Please.

Stacey often tells me that we never have to beg in prayer, but I've come to learn that sometimes begging is all that comes out.

India.Arie's melodic voice rings out like church bells in my apartment, as I lower to my knees on my prayer rug. I can still feel a strange tightness in my chest from my run an hour ago.

I close my eyes and meditate on her wise words.

And I keep my eyes closed.

God, please help me to be my brothers' and sisters'
keeper and protect their hearts and bodies from
hatred. Help me to hear them. Help me to lift them
up, respect them, love them, and support them the
way You would have me do.

I open my eyes and stare up at the night sky through a
recently Windexed window.

I know when I take care of others, You'll always take
care of me. Help me to think of myself less often and
think of how I can help others more.

"Is there anything else I can help you with today?" she
asks me, as I pace my office hallway, holding the cell
phone to my ear.

"Yeah, uh, can I speak to your manager?"

Realizing I must sound like countless white women
before me, I follow it up immediately to mitigate her
certain anxiety, "I just want to tell them how great you
were today."

"Oh, wow!" the young presumably black woman
responds, "Well thank you very much... Let me
check!"

"Thanks so much," I smile, glancing at the office door.

She returns a moment later.

"So, she isn't in today, but I can transfer you to her voicemail and you can leave her a message...?"

"That'd be great," I tell her. Still uncomfortable with my own existence most points in a given day, I love when that's the case.

"Well thank you very much," she tells me in a friendly tone, "You have yourself a great weekend!"

"You too, Jesinika! Thanks again for your help!"

"Of course! Please hold for my manager's voicemail..."

"I was the prison chaplain at Rikers Island back in the day," Dr. Shepherd recalls while seated on a folding chair at the front of the chapel.

My eyes move downward from the giant wooden cross behind him.

There is something almost mythic about his presence as he teaches us against the backdrop of bejeweled tiling.

I'm not idolizing him or anything. I'm just saying... it's sort of unavoidable.

I stare at his navy and yellow paisley bow tie.

"Back in those days, I was the only black man *working* at the prison."

He glances around the room in his immaculate three-piece navy suit and looks my way no longer than he looks any of the other students'.

"And some of the white guards didn't like that fact too much," he shakes his head, with a knowing look, as a few hums of shared experience sing like a quiet lullaby from the back of the room.

"Well," he continues, "they had paid a young white inmate to rough me up as I was transporting him to another section of the prison."

My eyes widen.

"They paid him with a pack of cigarettes."

That's it?!

He glances my way again and catches me wide-eyed, in shock.

His mouth breaks into the slightest possible smile, clearly amused by my naivete.

He continues.

"The white inmate... a big guy.... around six feet," the five-foot-six-inch Doctor recalls, "He paused right before we were set to go through a gate and turned to me, saying 'You know this ain't personal, Reverend. It's just business.'"

The Reverend Doctor takes off his glasses and begins to clean them.

"Well, they were all unaware of my military history."

He starts laughing in a low tone.

"Unfortunately for the inmate."

A few of us laugh.

"After about fifteen seconds, he was on the ground and I called for backup, and after a long while," he replaces his glasses over his eyes, "the guards who had paid him finally arrived, expecting me to be beaten badly."

A few more knowing hums.

And he laughs some more.

"When those guards got there, ooh!" the old man calls out, smiling, "They were in *shock*."

He nods more and looks down, with a smirk.

"I had my foot on the inmate's throat and that big guy was terrified. They didn't know I had served in the special forces and spent time as a POW in enemy territory."

My eyes widen somehow even more, and I lean forward, riveted.

How is this man's life not a movie?!

"I tell you all that story because you will experience hostility as you go out and share the Gospel with people."

I nod and write that sentence down.

"While your intentions may be pure, others' intentions may not be. And the enemy is *always* looking for ways to knock you off your game."

We all nod now, and I hear the not-white, not-black student hum.

The Doctor glances this way.

"However, like God prepared me in my past for that moment at the gate with the inmate, He, too, has prepared *you* in *your* past for your own struggles with the enemy."

I nod in agreement.

"You were called to tell the story of the Gospel," he looks out at the room, "for such a time as this."

Mid-Spring 2016
In honor of Charles Kinsey
North Miami, FL

My feet jump on the treadmill after a long day at work, and I start running.

Bishop Jakes' voice commands my attention, as my pale finger pushes on the equipment's arrow, raising the speed, and I close my eyes, listening to the black preacher.

He tells me that I might own territory, in the spiritual realm, that I don't realize.

But he tells me I may need to fight for it.

God, I'm ready to fight for peace in my mind, to eradicate hatred of all kinds from my soul.

He tells me I may need to wait for the victory.

I'm running.

He tells me I may get tired while I'm waiting.

My finger pushes the up button twice, and my feet pick up the pace.

He asks me if I know what it's like to feel tired.

God, I'm tired of the ignorant thoughts. I'm tired of the thoughts of pride. I'm tired of feeling separate from and divided.

I raise the speed again.

"Trying to hold your head up, but you're tired," he says, "Trying to be tough, but you're tired."

God, I'm tired. Please give me the strength and endurance that I need to be Your love out in the world.

I'm so tired.

"By the way," I turn back to my new client as we're almost to the door leading out of his swanky office, "your receptionist Brittany..."

His eyebrows raise and his posture stiffens, as though bracing for bad news.

"She's awesome," I grin, nodding to the man I've been trying to earn as a client for weeks, "I can't tell you how many receptionists I talk to in my day-to-day at this job."

He loosens and laughs a bit.

"She is, by far, the nicest receptionist I've come across," I shake my head at him, continuing with a smile, "I actually look *forward* to talking to her, which says a lot because most receptionists are miserable."

We share a laugh. He doesn't know I once was one.

"Yeah, she's the best I've ever had in that role," he responds, chuckling, "I'm terrified she's going to find a better job than here."

"I know you mentioned expanding your sales team," I offer up, "As someone who works in sales, I can tell she'd be a great salesperson."

He looks at me in a funny sort of way, with a smile.

"Anyway, I'll let you go," I smile, reaching for his hand, shaking it, "Thank you so much again for your business. I can't wait to exceed your expectations."

On my way out, I offer a smile to Brittany, who is black.

And on my way down the elevator, I remember the CEO of the mutual fund, all those years ago, who evidently believed a black girl would not make a good impression behind a front desk.

What an absolute fool.

India.Arie's voice wafts through the dark room, as I watch the flames on the four candles in front of me.

I close my eyes.

God, please replace any darkness and any hatred inside me with Your love and Your light. Help me to lift up people who need it, especially people of color. Amen.

"The story behind the hymn 'Amazing Grace,'" Dr. Shepherd proclaimed to the room, "Does anyone know it?"

I shake my head and, out of my periphery, I see other students doing the same.

It had been a normal Tuesday in class up to now.

He looks down at the ground, then out at the class.

"It was written by a slavetrader."

A jolt shoots down my spine, and my eyes instinctively lower to the floor.

Shit.

"What?" a black woman across the aisle asks, clearly as astonished as I am by the news.

"Yes," our professor confirms to her.

"Wowww," a black man sings out a few rows behind me.

"He was an Englishman, a white man, named John Newton," Dr. Shepherd tells the class, the rest of which, I assume, is looking up at him.

And even though I know they're looking at him, a small part of me can't help but feel they are glancing over at me. The lone white person in the room. To see how I am responding.

Shit.

Shit!

Just sit here and don't move.

I look down and begin to pick at the skin around my fingers, but am still listening.

"He was an active slavetrader, having traveled to Africa many, many times to transport kidnapped Africans and force them into slavery. Here was a man propagating the most horrific spiritual crime imaginable..."

I feel every inch of white skin on my body crawling.

And tears well up in my eyes.

I was selfish to come here.

I was selfish to come into this space and occupy a seat...

God, why did You call me here?

Why did You call me here of all places?

I shouldn't be here.

Frantic, my pale eyes dart around the floor and then up at Dr. Shepherd. His wise brown eyes are looking directly at me.

My mind... and time... freeze.

For a moment, he and I stare into one another's eyes.

Mine: green, hot, and brimming with regret, horror, and confusion.

His: with only conviction and compassion.

322

He draws in his lower lip and gives me a confident, encouraging nod.

And I somehow *feel* what his soul is trying to tell me.

"Come along with us," his certain eyes silently whisper to my uncertain soul, "This message is for everybody in the room."

I stare at him, pleadingly.

"You're here," I feel his spirit tell mine, "You're with us, and you're safe here. Come with us in this story. You're with us."

Clarity overtakes my besetting thoughts, and I swallow hard.

My lips tuck in and I nod, ever so slightly back to him, as his mouth breaks into a soft, subtle smile.

He looks down, then back up at everybody else.

"And one night, a storm set in over his slaveship," he tells us, as I lean forward, learning, "And the boat rocked so violently everyone on-board thought they were sure to die."

My fingers stop fidgeting, and I'm with him in this story, the way he asked me to be.

"And this slavetrader looked up desperately at a sky filled with gleaming stars over a roiling sea, and began to pray for mercy. About that time, the waters calmed, and he realized that there was, in fact, a God."

323

He pauses, standing tall and strong, as usual.

"And he realized that because there was a God, it meant every person on earth was His child."

Tears pool my eyes and, alone, I utter a low hum in agreement.

Dr. Shepherd's tone brightens.

"He converted to Christianity after that experience and, despite remaining in the slave trade for a little while longer, he eventually became an abolitionist against slavery altogether."

I look up, as other students hum and say "wow" around me.

"Amazing grace," he recites to us, then beginning to sing, "How sweet the sound, that saved a wretch like me."

The room, then I join in.

"I once was lost, but now I'm found."

I close my eyes in prayer.

"Was blind, but now I see."

The Reverend Doctor continues his sermon.

"No one is too far gone for the grace of God... no one."

I nod, recalling all the grace God has given me in my life.

Where I once was... *drunk.*

Where I am now... *sober.*

Where I once was... *racist.*

Where I am now.... *on my way.*

The Reverend Doctor stares out across his classroom.

I watch him, in awe of the humility and compassion he has extended to me.

How he welcomed me into, instead of ostracizing me out of, his sermon tonight.

Amazing, grace.

Late Spring 2016
In memory of Terence Crutcher
Tulsa, OK

I'd love to tell you my racism was completely "cured" after such a moving experience in class.

...that in one, profound moment, as I sang "Amazing Grace" with a room full of black people, I was entirely delivered.

...that this story, unlike real life, wraps up neatly in a tidy, little bow with no more struggles, no more failings, and no more inconsistencies.

...that if one's emotions are stirred deeply enough, decades of prejudice will simply fall away with ease and without more work.

But I can't.

This is a memoir, not a movie.

And, as a reflection of *real* life, it's often messy. And complicated. And in this case... still, sadly, incomplete.

I leave the gym after another successful workout and, as I walk across the street in the cool spring air, I gaze up at the jet black sky.

Peppered with dozens of stars— which is more than I could ever see in Hoboken— I sit on the concrete stoop outside my apartment building, still panting from the run... but just... looking up.

God, please direct me. Please direct me in my career. Please direct me on my upcoming exam. Please direct me in my thoughts.

I stare down at my new shoes, which I needed to buy, as my old suicide-decision shoes recently wore out and were causing tremendous knee pain.

And thank You for the means to buy new running shoes. Thank You for using my time on the treadmill so I can grow closer to You. I love You. Thank You.

The memory of the night Brad dumped me wells up in my mind, sometimes knocked loose when I thank God.

And, even though I am not reeling in emotional pain like I was that night, I stare up at the sky and whisper for old time's sake:

"Thank You. Thank You. Thank You…"

The next night, I arrive home again from the gym.

Holding my key fob up to the main entrance and hearing the giant metal lock click open for me, I am often reminded of the giant buzzing lock at Rikers.

It's jarring to remember why such massive locks are needed.

As I enter the building that I call my home and tap the button to the elevator with my knuckle, a tall black man gives a shout behind me and lunges toward the front door. I turn as he grabs it and walks in.

327

My whole body tenses and the elevator dings, sliding open.

I give him a tense half smile, then turn and walk in.

He walks in.

I press my floor. He doesn't move.

My whole body stays rigid.

I watch the doors close and imagine horrific scenarios playing out between here and Floor 4.

The elevator creeps upward.

"You run?"

My head turns to him, terrified.

"Huh?!" I almost plead.

He smiles, either unaware of my panic or, more likely, trying to assuage it.

"Do you run?" he asked, pointing at my shoes, "Your shoes look pretty fresh."

"Oh," I laugh, lightly, "Yeah, the gym across the street."

The door opens to the fourth floor and I finally exhale.

"That's cool. I'm new to the building," he tells me, "I was actually going to go join there tonight, but I got lazy after work."

We both chuckle, exiting and pausing in front of the doors.

"Yeah, it's not bad," I tell him honestly, "sometimes the cardio area gets a little packed, but aside from that, I have no complaints."

I pause for a moment.

"Plus, the price can't be beat."

I pay fifteen dollars a month for unlimited access, as well as unlimited member classes.

"Good to know," he offers up another friendly smile, adding a wave this time, "Maybe I'll see you around."

"You probably will. Nice meeting you!" I smile back this time.

As I turn toward my apartment, the opposite direction of his, I reflect on how exhausted I am with my own bullshit... and how much work I still have to do. But I, also, can't help feel frustrated that God still has not removed this completely.

When, God? I'm here... I'm trying so hard.

I feel guilty for the rest of the night and into the next morning.

Intellectually, I know there are no "lost causes" too far gone for God. After all, he delivered me from alcohol addiction. But, in my heart, I can't help but doubt...

Will my racism <u>ever</u> go away?

Why is it so hard to be decent?

That next Thursday, Dr. Shepherd calls upon the non-white, non-black student to present.

I heard the young man mention his Puerto Rican descent to another student last week after class.

That's the most I've heard him speak, aside from occasional whispers to the two black women who always sit in front of him.

I watch him rise out of his plastic chair, in jeans and a black button-down, and move to the front of the room, carrying a few sheets of computer paper containing scribbles.

He exhales loudly with his back to us, then turns dramatically.

"I'm here today," he nearly shouts, "to talk about the glory of GAWD!"

His tone and even volume raises on the last word.

Taken aback, I lean literally as far as I can against my chair.

"Who here *knoooows* about the glory of GAWD?"

It sounds as though he's preaching like a caricature of some stereotypical Southern black preacher.

And I become incredibly uncomfortable.

Through all of these verbal "finals" in our class, other students sometimes hum during the sermons of their peers, or, when truly moved, offer up an "amen!"

The rest of the class is silent.

I barely hear the words he's saying, because I am so unbelievably distracted by the way in which he's saying them.

My mind is flooded with memories of a junior high me, wherein I changed the way I spoke to fit in.

I cringe for us both.

Back then, it only took me a few weeks to realize that changing my vernacular was a fool's errand, completely artificial, and, as more and more poor students shot dirty looks my way, a part of me accepted that by "emulating" them, I was actually offending them.

It seems as though this guy never received the memo.

"And now, oh GAWD!" he shouts while pacing feverishly, as I turn to all of my black peers, who stare up at him with blank, somehow unsurprised, expressions, "Ohh, LAWD!"

I face front again, looking at the back of Dr. Shepherd's head, one row in front of me.

"We turn to YOU!"

Our professor sits, still, as the young preacher's anxious eyes search hungrily for a crumb of positive feedback that he has not and clearly *will* not receive from the room.

If his cartoonish act were not so outlandish, I would feel badly for him.

Maybe I should... after all, I once tried a similar tactic.

But, I can't.

Instead, I feel sympathy.

Not for him.

No...

But for every single black person in the room.

For being subjected to a verbal blackface-equivalent, right to their faces.

The perpetrator of which, even expecting to be *praised* for it.

The audacity. The ego. The *ignorance.*

I hang my head for every time I've ever spoken or behaved in a way other than my indisputably white self.

I hang my head...

Out of shame. Regret. And sadness for those subjected to it.

As the young Puerto Rican man shouts his unintelligible sermon, I watch my fellow students hold their heads high. Some closing their eyes, presumably to pray.

And when he finishes, I finally breathe a sigh of relief into the palpably tense air.

The Reverend Doctor speaks calmly.

"Okay, you can return to your seat now."

The student stands at the front of the room and responds in a bewildered tone: "I'm... I'm surprised no one reacted to my sermon."

"Okay," Dr. Shepherd greets the remark in an I'm-giving-you-grace-right-now tone.

I watch the dejected non-white, non-black man return to his seat and shuffle his sheets of white paper with frustration.

"That's all we have time for this evening," our professor announces, standing, "Let's come together in prayer."

As a tradition after every class, all of us join hands in a circle and Dr. Shepherd asks one student to lead us in prayer.

"Trisha," I hear his baritone voice turn my way.

My eyes widen, as I move toward the forming circle.

"Would you like to lead us in prayer tonight?"

My mouth goes dry.

"Uh," I hear my voice stammer, still attempting to process what I'd just seen, "Oh... Okay."

I blink hard, looking around at everyone joining hands.

God, please give me the words You want me to share. Help me guide our eyes back to You.

I pause, looking down at each black hand in mine.

Dr. Shepherd's in my right and another black man's hand in my left.

I exhale one last time...

"God," I begin, as we all lower and close our eyes, "We thank You for this day. We know it's a gift many did not receive."

I hear two hums.

"We thank you for creating us, equally, in Your image and in Your love."

Another hum.

"We thank You for the *dignity* that being born in Your likeness requires us to hold for ourselves, and we ask You to remind each one of us of who You created us to be, and to give us boldness in *that*."

"Amen," one voice whispers.

"Hallelujah," another offers quietly.

"We thank You for increasing our understanding each and every day, and we thank You for the amazing opportunity in this class to study Your word."

I pause and see what feels right.

"Please help us to grow ever closer to You, and ever closer in love and brotherhood with one another."

"Amen," echoes around the circle.

"In Jesus' name..."

(I only tense a little bit this time.)

"Amen," we all close.

I feel a tug on my right hand and turn to see Dr. Shepherd squeeze my hand and offer a small smile to me, then turn away.

God, thank You for showing me the progress You've made in my life thus far in this journey. And thank You for taking me even farther. I need You, always.

"See," the Puerto Rican man offers sharply to the disbanding group, "That's the reaction *I* was looking for!"

My jaw drops a bit, incredulous, as I turn to see Dr. Shepherd, ever so slightly, roll his eyes as he picks his coat up off the chair.

I close the book on the Light Rail home from work and stare at its cover.

The vibrant blues, reds, and yellows.

The circular shape of its illustration.

Its blue cursive writing.

Maya Angelou, my eyes read.

I pick up my phone, as I do most of the time without thinking, and immediately open Instagram, also, as I do most of the time without thinking.

I briefly scroll my home feed, and a strange realization dawns on me.

It's... all... white people.

I glance up and out the window, at the cold blue sky.

I should follow more black people.

I blink hard, remembering the exchange in the elevator with my new black neighbor.

Maybe that would help normalize seeing black people more, and I'd no longer tense up when I'm in situations with them.

I begin to search for celebrities that I know of.

Oprah. *Follow.*

Bishop T.D. Jakes. *Follow.*

Eric Thomas. *Follow.*

Les Brown. *Follow.*

More women...

Any singers?

India.Arie. *Follow.*

Rebecca Ferguson. *Follow.*

Andra Day. *Follow.*

Hmm...

Tauren Wells. *Follow.*

He's not a woman, but his music is incredible.

Umm, actresses?

Viola Davis. *Follow.*

Octavia Spencer. *Follow.*

I feel a weird blend of confusion and shame at my inability to bring to mind more well-known black people.

I head back to India.Arie's account, then into her Following list.

Using only their thumbnail photos as a guide, I click "Follow" beside any black faces.

Admittedly, not a perfect system.

As I click follow on person after person, easily around a hundred times, I wonder if this experiment will work.

Setting my phone into my bag, I close my eyes and begin to count my breaths.

And watch my thoughts... the way I learned to meditate in Group.

Four days later, I scroll angrily through my Instagram home feed.

Irritation bubbles just under the surface of my pale skin, as my jaw clenches.

Having been on the app much less than usual lately, I roll my eyes to no one in particular.

And suddenly,
realize

I am annoyed.

And *realize*

I feel angry.

As I learned to do with meditation, I begin to ask myself what I was thinking that *caused* these feelings to well up.

As I breeze past black face after black face, I realize that I feel unseen, unvalued, unrepresented. I feel unsuccessful compared to the tens of thousands of Likes each post on my home feed has already garnered.

I feel passed over because of the evident success of these black influencer and celebrity faces.

I feel unattractive next to the glamour shots of afros and mahogany skin.

And I begin to tap "Unfollow" on as many people with dark skin that I can.

Unfollow.

Unfollow.

Unfollow.

As fast as my white fingers can manage... Unfollow.

As my mind races with dissatisfaction... Unfollow.

As my heart rate quickens and I glance around to make sure no one else on the Light Rail is seeing what I'm doing... Unfollow.

On the progress, a mere four days ago, I had optimistically hoped this experiment would bring about... Unfollow.

On every moment of discontentment, competitiveness, and resentment I feel scrolling through these posts... Unfollow.

As I click Unfollow after Unfollow after Unfollow on seemingly happy and kind people, deep within my soul, I know what I'm doing will not help my aim of ridding racism from my heart.

Deep within my soul, I know I should relate to these individuals on a level which transcends mere complexion.

Deep within my soul, I know we're all children of God and equally worthy to be loved, seen, and celebrated.

But my mind shouts at me: I DON'T CARE.

My feelings are driving the car of my consciousness now.

And right now, I don't care if I'm failing or moving backward... all I know is I don't want to feel these ugly emotions one second longer.

Unfollow.

That night after eating dinner alone on my couch again, I scroll Instagram.

As the proportion of faces looking like mine is now almost back to where it was, I feel more comfortable.

I feel safe.

I feel seen and represented.

I'd love to tell you that I will spend the rest of the evening contemplating how I received a precious glimpse of how black people in our country must have felt for so long...

That my mind will drift back to when I was a small girl watching the all-white doll commercials, except for the lone black doll on the right side of the television screen at the very end...

That I will develop empathy for black girls who would watch the white girl brushing the white doll's hair in a way their hair never could be...

I'd love to tell you that I will pray for the success and happiness and contentment of every single black person I so frantically unfollowed...

But I won't.

Because all my flesh wants me to do right now is: keep scrolling.

The next night, I stroll through the twinkling tiles of our classroom's entrance.

It's my turn to present my sermon, and nerves electrify every part of my body.

A thin veil of shame overshadows my spirit from each visit I paid to my white-filled Instagram today. (And I was on Instagram a lot today.)

God, I know I've fallen short. I know I'm called to love and uplift my brothers and sisters. Please, please take away this spirit of judgment... of... vengeance. I know it's not what You want, and I know it doesn't come from You.

My mind darts back to the black woman all those years ago who told me, via Facebook, that my mouth was speaking the devil's words.

She wasn't wrong.

God, use me to speak Your words tonight. I know I'm not healed. I know I'm not fully recovered from this demon of racism, but I'm asking for You to use me anyway. Humbly, I ask you, Lord, to fill my mouth with Your words, tonight and always. Not my own.

I exhale and turn the corner into the buzzing classroom.

Laughter and chatter fill the air, as my nerves loosen a bit.

It's not so much that I am afraid of public speaking. After all, this wouldn't be a terrific career path if I were...

It's not even the fear I'll forget my sermon. I've adopted a memory technique I read about a few years ago to help me...

The hardest part, to be honest, is viewing the entire sermon I've written from the perspective of my black audience.

Will it resonate with them?

Have I made sure not to disrespect them in my attempt to find common ground?

Will I be able to present this sermon as the white girl I am and not drift into elongated syllables or speaking in an almost musical-like tone?

The long and short of it? *Have I done <u>absolutely</u> all I can to prevent a horror similar to that of our Puerto Rican classmate?*

And, more candidly...

Can I stand in a room of people, in a momentary position of leadership, and stay equal to them in my own heart and mind?

I sit down in my usual black, plastic seat, as my cheap thirty-dollar boot starts fidgeting.

I bend over, grabbing my phone at the top of my bag and lighting it up. Not even sitting back up, I click the lock button and let it slide out of my hand back into my bag.

I don't need that right now.

As I straighten my posture, I look down at the well-worn black dress pants I'm wearing and recall how, even three weeks ago, I still couldn't fit in them.

I've had them for at least seven years.

Sighing and thoughts racing, my mind is suddenly interrupted.

"You're up today, right?" I hear Charles ask me.

Charles is the name of the old black man who sits in the same row. He lives in Brooklyn and felt God call him to be here late in life: 'And if God tells me to be somewhere,' he told me a week or two back, before class, 'I learned long ago to listen.'

I laugh anxiously.

"Yep!"

"I'm next week," his black hand points at the leaves of scribbled-on paper sticking out from the top of my bag, "I'm going to be just like that."

We chuckle together, as Dr. Shepherd makes his way up the middle aisle in the room, to the front.

"Good evening, Beloveds," Dr. Shepherd announces, as usual.

I give Charles a closed-lip smile and turn forward, clasping my hands nervously.

"We have some storytellers tonight, yes?"

I tense.

"You up?" Dr. Shepherd points directly at me.

Inhaling deeply, I nod too quickly.

Smiling, he waves me up to the front of the room, then limps toward his usual seat in the front.

I forget to grab the pages of notes from my bag and lunge upward, toward where he had been standing.

I feel the room of brown eyes upon me.

And I turn.

God, please give me the right words and the right heart for this moment.

Looking out across the room, I begin before my mind can convince me not to:

"When I was a little girl, I went to Sunday School every Sunday morning."

A few heads nod.

"We talked a lot about the Ten Commandments," I smirk, "Some more than others."

I begin moving around the front of the room.

"Honor your father and mother," my white hand extends, "Don't lie. Don't steal."

I continue.

"...easy ones for kids. *Relevant* ones for kids.

But I always stared at that First Commandment: Worship no god but Me. And I would always think how that was the easiest one."

I notice a small smile creep across Dr. Shepherd's face in the front row.

"You see, I didn't know too much about other religious beliefs back then. I knew one faith worshipped a guy who was blue."

A few peers chuckle lightly, while I shrug.

"And I just figured, as long as I don't worship the blue guy... or some other... *unfamiliar* deity... I'd be fine."

My eyes turn from playful to serious.

"I never knew the First Commandment was actually the hardest one."

I hear a woman in front hum.

"You see, I thought it only meant what other people *call* 'gods.' I never thought it meant: anything other than God that we seek after, and take safety and refuge in."

I begin looking around the room.

"Money."

Then I intentionally turn to a woman so I'm not looking at a man.

"Sex."

I turn back to a man.

"Vanity."

I keep turning.

"Self-righteousness...

        Pride.

     Shame.

Drugs.

     Alcohol."

I look down, humbly.

"Other people, their opinions."

Hums ring out as my sermon builds momentum.

"Anything we place above the will of God is a false god, and it certainly isn't just other entities we get down on our knees and pray to.

When we are threatened, where do we go and what do we do to feel safe? That's a *god* we seek.

When we forget that we are *fearfully* and *wonderfully* made, where do we go to find our confidence, value, and strength?

When we receive God's call, where do we go or to *whom* to sustain us in that mission?"

I nod, looking down again.

"I'll make it real."

My green eyes look up over a small sea of classmates watching me.

"When I received the call to come *here*, to attend seminary, I went to the wrong god."

My feet begin walking nervously, as my body sails back and forth in front of the giant cross.

"I was seeing a guy at the time..."

A few hums.

And I laugh.

"It seems some of you already know my sins..."

Some of my peers chuckle lightly.

"And I told him I was called," my head shakes, "And he told me that I wasn't."

I point up to the ceiling as the pace of my voice quickens.

"And instead of seeking my God, the *real* God, the One Who called me, Who put the dream in my heart and anointed me to be here..."

I pause.

"I just... quit."

A hush falls over the room.

"I quit pursuing this path altogether."

I shake my head, as a few other students do, too.

"But thank *God,* weeks prior, I had prayed to the *real* God, saying: 'Lord, please remove anything from my life that is not in service to You and Your purpose for me."

My head nods, confirming His goodness.

"And not long after I trusted that false god, not long after that false god got its way in my life and I quit, that false god left me."

My voice unexpectedly breaks and hot tears suddenly fill my eyes.

"The way my One True God never has."

I suck air in and look up, trying to gain my composure.

"And I learned well..."

I look at Dr. Shepherd who stares up at me.

"That while God may be a man, a man can *never* be my god."

His lips break into another small smile, while my classmates hum.

The two black women in front whisper "hallelujah."

A man in the back nearly shouts to me "Amen, sister!"

And my eyes glance back to our professor, whose eyes are full of conviction and, somehow, *confidence...* in *me.*

349

"As I look at my own life," I continue, drawing my eyes downward to align my heart once more with God instead of finding momentum in the approval being generously lobbed my way, "I think of all the ways in which this *threat* of other people's opinions haunts me, taunts me, and tempts me to bow down and worship *it*, instead of doing and being what God wants me to do and be."

I think silently about racism.

"I think about how the false god of pride tempts me to behave in ways that curry earthly favor, so I can," and I air-quote, "'get ahead.'"

I pause, now preaching more to myself than anyone else in the room.

"Get ahead of *who*?"

My head shakes.

"This delusion that I need *people's* approval and *people's* advancement instead of God and His is a false god that's got to go. This false god of superiority has got to go. This false god of *inferiority* has got to go."

One woman raises her hand briefly, as I rest mine onto my own sweatered chest.

"I am made in the image and likeness of The Most High God," my finger points out, "and so are you! And *anything* that tries to come between me and being the living embodiment of those two facts..."

My head shakes and tone quiets.

"...has got to go."

I sniff from the previous tears.

"Imagine working your whole life earning money, saving money and valuing money, only to find out one day that money doesn't even exist.

What's the currency I'm working to get in my life? *Is* it money? Is it followers on social media? Is it the envy of my friends?"

I pause.

"Is it approval from men?" I look around the room, "Or women? I'm not letting you *guys* off the hook here."

The room laughs with me.

"See when I was a child, I thought like a child, I spoke like a child, and I behaved like a child.

But now that I've grown up, now that I'm an adult and have put away that childish understanding of God's very *first* Commandment, I can look myself in the mirror today and ask: *Who* is my God?"

I pause and stare at my classmates who are staring back at me.

"And if I sort that question out, all the others somehow take care of themselves."

Dr. Shepherd grins and nods at me.

A few of my fellow students clap.

And I nod silently, returning to my seat, silently thanking God for giving me the right words.

"You preached like a black woman up there," Dr. Shepherd exclaimed, as he stands back up.

My eyes widen.

"You put your *soul* into that!"

I feel a few students staring at me, as the clapping continues, and I smile back at the Reverend Doctor.

Forty-five minutes later, after the closing prayer is over and I'm gathering my belongings, Dr. Shepherd walks up to me.

"When I remarked that you preached like a black woman," he begins in a low tone, "I hope you didn't take offense to that. I meant that as a *compliment*."

I look up from my bag and smile broadly into his uncharacteristically uncertain eyes.

"I know you did," I nod, "That's how I took it."

Two black women and I stand on the subway platform laughing together one week later.

"No way," I shake my head, responding to DaVonna's story.

They are both at least fifteen years my senior and classmates of mine.

Sandra lives in Newark, and DaVonna lives in Bedstuy.

Most of our class is male, but there are seven women, including myself.

The train pulls up and the three of us step inside the crowded car.

DaVonna's Haitian accent continues the story about her husband, "So I told him to get up off his chair and get his own butt a Pepsi."

Sandra and I cackle, all three grabbing poles in the car.

(Don't get your hopes up. I have four bottles of Purell in my bag.)

My pinched eyes open to see several people in the car glancing our way.

As the train lurches from side to side between the next four stops, where DaVonna will leave us for her night shift at work, I watch eyes of every color, belonging to seemingly every race, eye our trio with curiosity.

As we continue laughing and storytelling, I watch members of each gender glance at us, attempting to weave a common thread between us in their minds, explaining why we are together.

I watch them, because I know those stares. I know those sideways glances. They were mine. And still are, from time to time.

They are the glances of subconscious minds which tell their hosts that "there must be some explanation" when people of such different backgrounds are together.

The next week, on our commute from class, a black woman walks up to us on the subway platform, holding stickers with a red circle and line through the words "Stop and Frisk."

We each take one and thank her, as she leaves us to approach the next group of commuters.

"You know," I turn to the two black women who have become my friends, "Awhile back, I once asked for a pamphlet on Stop and Frisk from an NAACP group handing them out on the subways."

They both look at me as I go on.

"I got yelled at for being white," my voice pauses, "by a *white* lady!"

DaVonna laughs and rolls her eyes, as Sandra laughs and shakes her head.

"I don't know if she was, like, a spokesperson or what," my blonde ponytail shakes, remembering, "she certainly was bossing everyone around like she was in charge."

The two black women exchange a look I can't translate.

"I was so confused! I mean, I'm sure the pamphlet would have been better-served in the hands of a young man who might have been targeted," I can now relent, but pressing on with a valid point, too, "but I just feel like, with something as big as racism, don't we need all hands on deck to turn the boat around?"

They nod at me.

"I wanted to learn and help," I shrug, "but she, like, didn't *want* me to."

Sandra shakes her head of short, coarse hair.

"I'm a member of the NAACP," she announces, "and I just want to say I'm sorry for that experience. That was wrong of her."

I shake my hands and head frantically, reassuring her.

"Oh my God, that's definitely not why I said something! You certainly don't have anything to apologize for. *You* didn't say it!"

I immediately feel self-conscious for having said 'oh my God' to my fellow seminary students.

She smiles warmly.

"I know," her soothing voice confirms, "but somebody needs to. Doesn't matter if it's me. You tried, and someone representing a movement I work with shut you out."

Her brown eyes stare into my pale ones, and she continues with firmness.

"That was wrong. If you're willing to do the work to learn about something, you deserve to learn about that thing."

I look at her, wondering at what point I could be so spiritually evolved as to apologize for stuff I've had no part in.

I can barely muster apologies for things I have.

The train pulls up.

And the three of us walk on it, together.

Summer 2016
In memory of Peter Gaines
Houston, TX

A few weeks later, I sit in the wooden pew, one of only
two white people in the entire church.

An old anxiety grips me.

I haven't been the racial minority since our last class,
which was months ago.

(...aside from occasional moments on my commute
where it's easy to wear headphones, scroll my phone,
and read as ways to temper my still palpable social
discomfort.)

I look around the church of about sixty black people.

*Something tells me that would be considered rude
here.*

Dr. Shepherd does not know I'm here today.

I didn't think to reach out and let him know.

Frankly, I'm excited to see him in action, in his
element. On his home turf.

I laugh under my breath.

Something tells me anywhere is his home turf.

I think back to the story of an inmate trying to beat
him up in exchange for some cigarettes from racist
guards.

357

And I look around the church.

I look at the old black men, and the even older black women. I look at the couples, the children. Everyone.

And I wonder what horrors the people around me have seen as a result of their skin color.

God, help me to see everyone here as my brothers and sisters.

Later that night, I kneel down and continue my nightly devotional study of the book "'Thou, Dear God:' Prayers That Open Hearts and Spirits," a book of stories about and prayers from the Reverend Doctor Martin Luther King, Jr.

The next evening after work, I stand on the platform, waiting for the train.

My headphones died earlier in the day, but I still wear them so nobody will bother me.

I can hear the conversation of the two white guys behind me.

"So how's your cousin doing with everything?"

"He's alright, I mean, it's just a really shitty time to be a cop right now."

I think of Alex Fallen— my half black former classmate— at whom's thirteenth birthday party, I

358

held hands with Terrell Jackson. Alex had become a police officer in our hometown a few years back and recently posted on Facebook, telling everybody that most police officers are good, moral people who are just trying their best.

I Liked it.

"Yeah, I can't imagine."

"He said, evidently, there's a new app out there circulating, which allows people to hit record on their phones during traffic stops through a verbal prompt or something. So they don't even need to reach for their phone to start recording," the cop's cousin pauses, "He said their captain sent out an email or memo or something about it, warning them about it and telling them to really watch what they say at traffic stops now."

I watch the train pull up in front of us, as the two voices behind me grow closer.

"That's crazy," the other guy answers, "But I guess it was probably only a matter of time before something like that came out."

"Yeah, so it's definitely making his job harder."

As the doors open, I casually turn to see the two faces belonging to the conversation I've been eavesdropping.

Why would they need to watch what they say at traffic stops?

What on earth have they been saying at traffic stops up until now?

A week later, my friend from Group Sasha and I are sitting in her apartment, on the weathered leather sofa her parents gave her.

We are both wearing yoga pants and sipping hot tea, with the TV on in the background.

It's on the show "Lockup."

I briefly think of the old black woman at Rikers.

"I just love how shamelessly white trash these inmates are," she turns to me, chuckling a bit.

I stare at the screen where a scrawny white man with a twang in his voice dons a "White Power" tattoo across his neck.

I blink, thoughtfully, reminded of the kids I went to school with who could be— and often *were*— referred to as "white trash."

My soul still cringes every time I hear the term.

"Like, who gets a tattoo like that?" she laughs.

I think about Keith Moore, the kid with no plans after high school who called Terrell's cousin that word in the hallway.

I think of the pedophile fathers to the girls in my junior high who often joked about being "white trash," themselves.

I think about my own father's behavior over the years, as well as the disrespectful comments I often heard him make about women.

I think about my own hateful comments, back when I was drinking and trolling social media for significance or, at the very least, attention.

And I ponder her question.

Who gets a tattoo like that?

I stare at the screen and answer on behalf of myself and maybe others.

"I suppose when you don't have anything in your life that you can actually feel proud of, white pride is easy. It makes you feel good about yourself without actually having to do anything to earn it."

I feel her turn toward me. But I stare at the TV.

"It's probably the same with being sexist, too," I wager, "When you're not doing anything worth being proud of, and still desperately want to feel good about yourself, you start to believe the devil's lie that you're somehow more valuable," I squint my eyes, "inherently."

"She asked me why Daddy doesn't like brown people."

My eyes widen and jaw drops.

"What?!" I exclaim into the phone.

"Yeah," my old friend Jenna chirps.

"What did you *say?*"

"I mean, I told her he *does.*"

"And what did *she* say?"

I hear a sigh on the other end of the phone.

"She asked 'Why does he say not nice things about them then?'"

Her daughter is six.

(And her husband is a teacher in the local school district.)

"What?!"

Then there's silence.

And I inhale, seemingly the only one on the call still breathing.

"Kids are very perceptive," my tone is relenting, as my mind surrenders to the truth.

Though I only see him a couple times a year, I have heard her husband make racist remarks.

And, clearly, so has their daughter.

So I continue, trying to help the situation.

"Did you tell her that it's wrong to judge people based on the color of their skin?"

"No," Jenna admits, "I just told her that Daddy loves everyone."

And, for the rest of the call, I silently wonder what that response taught their daughter about "love."

We've only been dating three weeks.

Connor is a few years younger than me and, as always, I am convinced he is The One.

(And, as always, *everything* points toward the opposite.)

He kisses me too hungrily. He is flighty. He is in recovery for hard drugs, but still speaks romantically about them too often for someone who is truly grateful to be sober.

But, as always, none of those things matter: I met him in Group and have convinced myself that he's my soulmate.

There are three of us in the car: Connor, myself, and our mutual friend, also from Group, Alex.

Alex doesn't know Connor and I have been seeing each other. I've insisted to Connor we keep it a secret from everybody.

I'm not proud to admit that, on some level, I believed this would increase his desire for me and make me his "forbidden fruit," so to speak.

But on another, slightly-subconscious level, I, also, knew I'd be embarrassed for the other Group members to see me dating him.

Had Stacey not moved away in the middle of my spring semester and had we not lost touch, I know *exactly* what she'd say about him...

If Brad wasn't "on the spiritual beam," Connor isn't even in the gymnasium.

As we pull up to the parking lot for the Dave Matthews Band concert, I watch from the backseat of Connor's Suburu as he rolls down his window to the black parking lot attendant.

I watch the young black man and his bright yellow reflective vest step over to our car.

"Pull over to Section 30," he instructs Connor, pointing to his left.

"Awwee yeaahhh," I hear Connor's voice turn unfamiliar, "that *derrrrrty therrrrrty...*"

I shrink, humiliated, into the cloth-interior backseat.

Connor, true to his name, had never been anything other than obscenely white in all of his mannerisms up to that moment.

As the parking lot attendant silently steps back, letting our car move through, I blink hard, humiliated for *all* of us.

And angry at Connor.

Why would he talk like that?

Why would he be so offensive?

And why are he and Alex just continuing their conversation as though such a ridiculous thing didn't just happen?!

The car inches toward Section 30, and my sober mind reels for an explanation.

Did he know that guy and it was a joke?

I played the scene back in my mind.

No.

It was clear they'd never seen each other before.

Was he trying to somehow gain the approval of this guy?

I am reminded of the Puerto Rican guy in class, and myself, back in junior high.

I grimace.

Was he trying to gain those invisible points black people sometimes award cool, "accepted" white people that we then use as white social currency to impress one another?

My mind churns all of the possibilities.

Was he outright... <u>mocking</u> him?!

I hastily unbuckle my seatbelt as my thoughts debate each other.

Furthermore, the parking lot attendant didn't even <u>have</u> the accent Connor used!

Connor slowly pulls his car into the spot and the three of us step out, beginning the long trek to the concert venue.

My mind twists and turns the entire walk, as Alex and Connor blather.

I don't know what I just witnessed, but I know that it was racist.

And I strongly suspect it left that parking lot attendant feeling... *a certain way.*

I didn't know it as I slowly forgot about the parking lot attendant that evening and began dancing in the field with my entirely white group of friends, but I would break things off with Connor within a week.

I'd love to tell you I called out the racism I saw in the parking lot that evening as I did it.

But I didn't.

There were a lot of reasons to break up with Connor.

That one wasn't the only one.

That one wasn't even the *main* one.

But, that one *was* one.

Because there were many moments before that— as he made crass jokes in mixed company or wistfully referenced the time he'd overdosed— when I could have lost respect or that naive newly-dating glow through which I viewed him.

But it wasn't any of those moments that broke the illusion...

That revealed to me that Connor was not an honorable man.

That shook me by the shoulders, screaming, "THIS IS NOT THE PERSON GOD HAS FOR YOU!"

It was the indignity in the parking lot that night.

And while the final straw that broke the camel's back was that he had promised to call and set up plans for Saturday night and, at 5pm on Saturday, I had still only received a 2:41pm time-stamped text from him saying "I'll hit you up in a bit and we'll make plans..."

While it was ultimately his unreliability, his immaturity, and my revelatory unwillingness from that Saturday evening forward to "wait on some guy," that caused me to call *him* and inform him he wouldn't be seeing me anymore...

I can't help but wonder if that conversation would have ever taken place had I not lost respect (and patience) for him in the parking lot in Camden, New Jersey that night.

Maybe his grotesque *"derrrrrty therrrrrty"* remark was, in some twisted path, the linchpin to why I broke it off with him.

Or maybe that's just residual guilt trying to console a self that in the moment, as usual, did nothing.

Maybe instead of inner dialogue condemning my silence, it's trying to paint me as some retroactive social justice champion so I can sleep at night.

Or maybe... just maybe... what I'm saying is true.

And despite a nearly week-long delayed reaction processing what I had seen, maybe something inside me *has* started to shift.

Maybe I'm now shaping my life and making decisions accordingly.

Maybe I've always been "tolerant."

Maybe I've just been tolerating all the wrong things.

Fall 2016
In honor of all the women of color who survived
sexual assault and rape in Baltimore
and bravely reported their subsequent gross
mistreatment by Baltimore PD
to the U.S. Department of Justice
Baltimore, MD

"I've *always* wanted to have a black guy," Ingrid
giggles on our IKEA living room couch while
something about the upcoming Presidential race plays
in the background.

My jaw drops a bit at my new roommate.

I had only moved out of Bayonne and into this
apartment two months ago.

I blink hard at her, awkwardly half-laughing.

"Yeah, I've heard they are," her pale eyes race with
excitement, leaning toward me, "*bigger,* you know. Do
you think that's true?"

She doesn't wait for an answer I wasn't going to give.

"I've had a Mexican guy once and a lot of Brazilian
guys," she squeals breathlessly in her thick European
accent, "but never a black guy. That's my goal!"

I continue to sip my steaming herbal tea, listening
curiously as the young woman continues to sexualize
the idea of "a black guy."

And while I'm clearly no racial guru, I know that's *a thing*.

Over the years I've learned that black people, both men and women, are often objectified and referred to in a very unsubtly "animal" type of way when it comes to sex.

It's dehumanizing and wrong.

And I *know* that.

But I'm still somehow painfully unable to do much more than laugh awkwardly.

So I chuckle... so viscerally uncomfortable, I feel incapable of anything else.

I don't like talking about sex with strangers.

And I like talking about objectifying entire groups of people with strangers-I-now-live-with even less.

How does one go about saying something in this scenario?

What do you say to another white person making racist remarks to you?

And *how* do you say it?

Do I just blurt out "That's racist!" and then casually remind her about her unwashed plates in the sink?

Do I treat it like a work project and ask if she's open to hearing feedback about her ideas?

Do I forcibly tie her to a kitchen chair and play YouTube videos at her like some dictatorial "re-education" camp?

Should I appeal to her spirit and ask her to come with me to my all-white Christian Group which doesn't discuss race or racism, but might give *me* the feeling that, hey, I'm "doing *something?*"

And the question looming over all of them...

Am I even *qualified* to say or do anything considering my own glaring shortcomings on the matter?

I have no idea.

Literally no person, no institution, and no after-school special has prepared me for these moments.

I learned a million ways to say "no" to drugs. (Granted, little good those did...)

But I never once learned how to say "no" to *this* moment.

And my recent late-night Google searches have yielded little to nothing, as well.

There are no videos.

There are no listicles.

We're on our own, evidently, in uncharted waters.

Three days later, early Sunday morning, I would be washing dishes at our kitchen sink.

And our bathroom door would open fifteen feet to my right.

And out would walk a black guy wrapped in Ingrid's pink towel, dripping wet from our shower.

And my eyebrows would raise.

And I would *almost* drop a plate out of shock, like my mother did all those years ago.

And I would try not to feel fear as my initial, habituated response to seeing a black man.

And I would try not to register the *actual* facial expression my face wanted to make.

And, instead, I would smile, setting the plate down calmly, and introduce myself from afar to the basically naked man.

And, as I resumed washing my white coffee mug, I would think to myself: "Looks like Ingrid got her wish."

And one week after *that*, I would walk into our apartment to find the two of them curled up on that very same couch where she proclaimed her goal to bed... well, "one of" *him*... watching the documentary "13th," which I had watched alone in my room two weeks prior.

And I would listen from the kitchen, making the nightly herbal tea which quells my urge to binge on desserts, as she lamented: "It's horrible how Americans view black men."

And I would shake my head with resentment, wishing to tell him the truth about her, but staying silent because to tell him the truth would surely hurt his feelings.

Summer 2017
In memory of Jordan Edwards
Balch Springs, TX

She just talked shit about him.

Right to my face.

The most incredible, noble, honorable guy I've ever dated...

The best man I have ever met...

> (...who I didn't know would become my fiancé later that very week...)

And my own mother: just talked *shit* about him.

Alone with her in a car again, I sit stunned, again.

I feel the cool air conditioning blow faintly against my cheeks and can't even hear the radio this time over the hum of my angry thoughts.

How dare she?

She doesn't even know him.

My face twists in defiance and revulsion at the windshield as we approach their beach house.

I love this man.

I love him so much.

What do I <u>say</u> here?

A calm descends upon my shoulders, unexpectedly loosening them.

"I don't appreciate you saying things like that about him," a clear voice evidently my own concludes, "I don't think you'd say that if he were in here in the car with us."

I look down, a foreign clarity leading me.

"What you said is *so* inappropriate and I don't want you saying anything like that about him again, especially not around me."

She turns into their driveway and, as the rage continues to simmer beneath my calm, it dawns on me: if you truly love someone, you can't sit idly by while someone talks shit about them.

You just can't.

"Uhh, Trisha," my fiancé's voice calls to me from our living room two weeks later.

(Yes, we live together. As previously mentioned, I'm a Christian, not a saint...)

"What's up?" I emerge barefoot from the bedroom, towel-drying my long blonde hair above jean shorts and a white tshirt.

"We have to cross Charlottesville off our list."

Last night, we made a written list of potential locations for a destination wedding.

"Why?!" I nearly shout.

Charlottesville, Virginia was the first city's name I wrote down.

It's my top choice, and he knows it.

I watch his finger point at the mounted television on our wall.

The giant black letters beside the news channel's logo are surreal: "WHITE SUPREMACY RALLY IN CHARLOTTESVILLE"

My jaw drops and my eyes widen, trying to make sense of what I am seeing.

"WHAT?!"

"Yeah," he stands, staring at the TV, "so we're clearly not getting married there."

I shake my head, in genuine shock.

"Obviously," I blink hard.

I walk over to the kitchen counter where the list sits, damp towel still in-hand.

He silently hands me a pen, and I draw a line through "Charlottesville, VA."

"I'm sorry, baby," he tells me, resting a strong, gentle hand on my shoulder.

"It's okay."

And I know that it will be.

There are bigger things in life than the location of a wedding. Clearly.

And, doing what we can, we both understand we need to take our business elsewhere.

Fall 2017
In honor of Théodore Luhaka
Paris, France

After a significant amount of research, I finally have gained enough courage to do it.

"I think we should begin a new marketing campaign," I blurt out to the owner of the mobile technology company on the other end of my phone.

Recently promoted to Director of Marketing, an epiphany struck me the other day for how the mortgage application portion of our mobile app might be able to attract new users as an oasis from racial discrimination in the space.

Through feverish Google hunts, I had discovered nearly every large national bank had ongoing racial discrimination lawsuits from the last few years, where black people were being denied mortgages while white people with the same credit score and credentials were being approved.

After picking my naive white jaw up off the floor, I remembered the "joke" my father told his banker friend that day when the black guy in the waiting area of his office overheard.

Today, I decided to grow a pair and finally pitch my idea to my boss.

"Our new marketing campaign can be that, unlike the Big Guys, we don't participate in racial discrimination in housing. In fact, our blind technology actually prevents it."

There's silence.

"We could reference the ongoing cases involving our big competitors and point out where we're different. Some of these cases have moved forward because the loan officer could assume the applicant's race based off their name, for example, but our technology removes that function. This positioning, I think, would gain a lot of media attention and drive a lot of new users to the app."

More silence.

"And, the best news is: we don't even have to change the functionality of our app! It already does all this!"

"Well," my foreign white employer begins.

I listen for a jubilant response, but receive its opposite.

"We want really good borrowers," he tells me in a thinly-veiled monotone accent, "I don't think that kind of messaging would attract the kind of quality borrowers we're looking for."

"I disagree," I protest, emboldened momentarily by my copious off-the-clock research, "There are a lot of great borrowers out there who are unable to secure loans from the big banks due to this kind of discrimination and the *human* aspect of loan approvals. Our platform could be a net for those individuals, as well as for all the white people who don't want to do business with institutions who engage in racist practices."

More silence.

"I feel like the media would get behind this, and it could really snowball into something!"

"You can put something together if you want, and see if anyone in the media bites," he relents unenthusiastically, "I guess it's worth a shot."

Two weeks later, that same owner would inform me I was no longer needed at his company.

Spring 2018
In memory of Danny Thomas
Greenspoint, TX

"Oh, I hate Beyoncé."

I stare at the blonde woman who is my new boss at a new job.

Her name is Brenda.

She shakes her head across the wooden restaurant table, shoveling a bite of Cobb salad into her mouth as my coworker, Dale, and I listen.

"Have you ever seen footage of her concerts?"

I sip water with little melted ice chips out of my condensating glass and shake my head.

Aside from Destiny's Child and a solo song here or there, I've never listened to her music much.

Dale audibly answers "No."

"Ugh," Brenda groans to us, her subordinates, "I hate it. All the black people there..."

She waves her left hand, still chewing, and stabs at a tomato with the fork in her right.

I squint at her neon blue-painted fingernails, which are only a fraction as unprofessional and inappropriate as where this conversation seems to be heading.

"They're too wild, too empowered."

"Too *empowered?*"

My shock at her phrasing escapes in the question, along with eyebrows raised even higher than I knew they were able.

She rolls her piercing blue eyes.

"Yeah, have you seen it?"

Then she stares at me with them.

"No, I..."

Dale stays silent, while she interrupts me.

"They're out of control, and all that pro-black messaging," she trails off before concluding, "It's evil."

I frantically glance around at the sparsely-populated tables surrounding us, to ensure no one is looking at us. They aren't.

Thank God.

Then I stare at the cross necklace around Brenda's neck, growing disgusted by its defilement.

I take another sip of water, recalling the book about Dr. Martin Luther King Jr. that I have been working my way through— two pages at a time— each night before bed.

In it, it describes in details I can't recall how the famous Reverend Billy Graham either gave a sermon on or attended a sermon or event or something by King.

The backlash, angry letters, and threats that Graham received from white Christians as a result was such that he never came out in favor of the civil rights movement again or something.

He didn't even attend King's funeral.

I remember reading it with harsh judgment toward Graham.

I stare at Brenda. And her frizzy blonde hair.

She would have written an angry letter or threatened him.

I watch her stab at pieces of lettuce drenched in blue cheese dressing.

She's definitely the type.

Ultimately, the parishioners who bullied Graham into submission paid his salary.

I stare at who, basically, pays mine.

And I'd love to tell you I did something... or *said* something...

But instead, I was humbled by how alike I was to the person who—just nights before— I had judged so harshly.

I did nothing.

Neither did Dale.

But, this isn't a story about Dale's sins... it's a story about mine.

Summer 2018
In memory of Arthur McAfee Jr.
Longview, TX

I scamper between puddles, already half-soaked, up the sidewalk toward the massive building.

I made it.

I'm here.

I finally paid off all of my credit card debt and, as a reward to myself, decided to extend my recent business trip to Dallas by a day in order to attend Bishop T.D. Jakes' church.

As water squishes between the toes within my dress shoes and relentless raindrops pellet my once-curled blonde hair, I try to simultaneously run and avoid the inevitable drenching.

I never remember umbrellas.

I watch a tall white cowboy in jeans and a full-blown cowboy hat saunter his way inside with a giant brown umbrella about ten yards in front of me.

I blink hard, trying to compute the stereotype I hold of a racist southern cowboy type, as well as the fact that he's walking into a predominantly black church.

Shaking the raindrops and stereotypes from my head, I run past him, slowing slightly as the rain lets up equally as slightly.

"You want under an umbrella?" I hear a deep southern voice behind me call out.

I turn.

It's him.

I laugh, pausing in the rain.

"Sure," my eyebrows give way to the helplessness of my situation, but also leaning shamelessly into the idea of some old, weathered cowboy coming to my damsel-in-distress aid.

He's almost old enough to be my father, and we are about twenty yards from the building anyway.

As he covers me with his massive umbrella, he asks if I'm from around here and if I've ever been to this church before.

I tell him "no" on both counts, but vaguely share how impactful the Bishop's teachings have been to me.

He smiles, looking forward, as we close in on the arena-style doors.

"I been comin' here for a few years now," he clears his gravelly throat, "Best church around if you ask me. Everyone's so kind and welcoming."

I stare down at his walking cowboy boots and wonder about his story.

His hardened hand reaches for the door.

"You go on in and get yourself a good seat. Enjoy!"

I look back at him and smile, thankful for the strange sense of community I feel with him as an outnumbered white person in this setting where black people filter in around us.

"Thank you!" I grin, "Enjoy the service!"

"I always do," he shakes the rain from his umbrella.

And I turn to see a line of black people facing the front doors. They're greeters.

"Welcome sister!" many of them smile at and greet me.

I grin.

Dear God, please help me to be a good guest here today.

The usher keeps walking me down, closer and closer to the stage.

"Are you under thirty years old?" the tall, well-dressed black man asks.

"I *am* thirty," I answer, a hint of confusion escaping my tone.

"Okay," he nods, "I'm going to sit you in the Brickhouse section. It's for our young people under thirty."

I swallow hard at the thought of being surrounded by young black people.

Somehow sitting with black peers is more intimidating than sitting amongst older black people, like I did at seminary.

"Okay," I agree, as we walk up to a section about ten rows from the stage.

My eyes are as wide as they've ever been.

I'm going to be this close to Bishop Jakes?

I blink hard, feeling blessed, despite dripping rainwater all over the amphitheater's carpet.

"Here you go," he motions me into a row, "What's your name?"

"Uh," I stammer, unable to tear my eyes from the massive stage and bright screens, "Trisha?"

I'm so distracted, my tone just answered my own name as a question.

"Guys," the usher commands the attention of the group of about fifteen young black people, "This is Trisha. It's her first time here. Let's make her feel welcome!"

I turn to see thirty brown eyes of varying shades staring at me.

I offer a hesitant, overwhelmed half-smile.

"Welcome!" two young black women exclaim, one holding a tambourine for reasons I do not know.

I stare at it.

Then smile up at them.

"Hi!"

A few men mutter low hellos and then go back to ignoring me, as I find an empty seat surrounded by empty seats.

I chose the front row of the section, in part to be even closer to the stage I've watched on YouTube so many times, but mostly because no one is sitting there.

My eyes dart around the almost exclusively black space.

One man catches my eye.

He's short, round, and brown.

He wears glasses and a silvery-blue shiny three-piece leisure suit that is about four sizes too large.

The outlandishness of his wardrobe amuses me, though I try to hide my smile.

I wonder what my college friends would think of him.

They would certainly find him an amusing caricature of black culture.

Bemused, I can't stop watching this man laugh and carry on about forty feet away from me.

He certainly embodies a certain... stereotype, I quip to myself, as I'm the only one likely to find it funny.

And then I catch myself.

I asked God to make me a good guest.

That doesn't mean teasing or poking fun at anyone.

I hang my head, smile shrinking to nothing.

He's here like me, to worship God.

He's my brother.

Out of the corner of my eye, I see the silvery-blue orb growing larger.

I look to my left, to see him and two other men making their way down my row.

I happen to catch eyes with him from under his glasses.

"Is this seat taken, sister?" he points to the seat to my left.

"No," I answer sweetly.

God...

You never cease to amaze me in the ways You humble my pride.

I'm sorry for judging him.

I'm sorry for thinking unkind thoughts about Your child.

Help me to be kind to him. Help me and deliver me from my prejudice.

My prayer is interrupted.

"Let's get on our feet!" a stunning Afro-donning woman in a striped jumpsuit and trendy leather jacket announces as the band comes to life and other impeccably dressed choir members energetically skip onto the stage.

I hear the tambourine shake behind me and I suddenly realize that this service will be *nothing* like my childhood Catholic masses.

"Greet your neighbors, shake their hands, and tell them the Lord has *great* things in store for them!"

I turn to Leisure Suit Man, who I watch turn toward me before his friend to his left.

With earnest eyes, he looks into mine and tells me emphatically, "The Lord has *great* things in store for you!"

And I can feel the hope and love behind his words.

I reach out with my white hand and watch it be enveloped by his black one, shaking each other's.

"The Lord has *great* things in store for you, too," I muster to him.

God, it never ceases to amaze me how absolutely You can humble me...

I stare up at the black man preaching. It isn't the Bishop.

Despite my checking the website before attending this week, it's clear I should have called.

The Bishop is on a mission trip in Niger.

The announcement of which brought on incredible disappointment, as well as old memories of a fourth grade Reed Jacobs.

I don't know this man.

"God keeps down those who keep others down," his voice echoes in the microphone.

"He sees the people trying to keep you down!"

He has a tone I feel... *targeted* by.

He's preaching to a large group of black people about how the people keeping them down will be hunted down by God and punished.

"He's going after them!"

I blink hard, wet hair now-ponytailed.

"In the middle of the night, He'll confront them in their beds!"

I stare at him from above ruined mascara, caused by the rain and the tears I shed an hour earlier during the moving praise and worship portion with the choir.

"They won't be able to outrun Him! He will deal with them!"

I feel a familiar feeling well up inside me.

"He will cast them down!"

I watch him on stage, then turn my eyes downward toward my bag.

"And then He'll raise you up to replace them!"

The two young women behind me shout "Hallelujah!"

And the vibe feels hostile to me, I realize.

There's a white girl sitting beside me with her black boyfriend, but we are the only two white people in the young people's "Brickhouse" section where the greeters sat me.

I can't help but feel he's talking about... *white people.*

The usher told me repeatedly not to stand up or walk around during the sermon, that the whole thing was being televised, and that standing and moving around ruins it.

I look at the man preaching about what feels like: *revenge*.

And punishment.

And I feel... unwelcome.

And, for better or worse, attacked.

My thoughts war with each other about being respectful of this place and the people inside it, being grateful for all the Bishop's work and staying seated, as asked... contrasted with my interior feelings which are nearing a boil.

Of anger toward *this* man's message of anger.

Of sadness for wasting my time and money to come see this unknown man preach.

Of judgment as I look at his wife, who is seated on the far side of the stage, wearing outlandish shoes and a long, flowing blonde wig.

My eyes turn back to him and stare accusingly at his shiny shoes, his purple tie and pocket square and well-tailored suit.

During one of our classes, Dr. Shepherd had warned us about preachers who wear a different suit or outfit each week, viewing tithes as their personal shopping budgets.

I wonder if that's this couple.

I wonder if I would even consider that prospect if they were white.

I wonder if it's my own fragility causing the anger inside me.

But... also...

God dealt with me on my racism and still is.

I look at the man pacing like the Puerto Rican guy did in class that day.

How dare he boast to this massive congregation about that pain and shame, as a means to comfort and delight them. No one's suffering should comfort, and even worse, <u>excite</u> a Christian.

I look down at my bag again, then turn my head toward the back doors which are lined with black men who are all ushers.

"The pain they caused you will be returned ten-fold to them!" he declares loudly.

A few people clap, and I hear a few sparse "amens."

I reach for my bag, and clutching the handle, whisper "excuse me" to Leisure Suit Man on my left as I stand up... and walk out.

I stare out the Uber driver's backseat window as we fly down a still-rainy, nearly empty Dallas highway back to my hotel.

396

Sadness that I did not see Bishop Jakes overwhelms me.

Disappointment in myself pervades my spirit.

I watch raindrops race across the glass.

Was it racist of me to walk out?

I wish the raindrops would tell me.

Did I do it out because I felt threatened and fearful that I would lose ten-fold, the way he was prophesying, or did I genuinely believe that the vengeful, cast-them-down message was the opposite of what Jesus preached?

I sigh heavily, turning my eyes to the road in front of us through the windshield.

Could my one action of walking out somehow... be both?

Misty raindrops coat the windshield's glass repeatedly with gusts of wind.

Suddenly I notice police lights up to the left off the highway.

As we near the flashing lights, I notice a tan sedan overturned, on its roof in the median strip.

My jaw hangs and out of the corner of my eye, I see Julio, my South American driver, perform the sign of the cross, a familiar relic of my childhood "faith."

My rubbernecking of the accident now turns into similar staring at him.

Only now do I notice a maroon and silver rosary dangling from his rear-view window and a picture of the Mother Mary on his dashboard, and a peace comes over me.

The kind of peace you only feel when you know the person you're with is a sweet believer of God.

I half-smile at the back of his head and headrest.

God, thank you for giving me this driver. Thank you for helping me to find that peace in You and Your presence once more after this morning.

"You know," Julio begins suddenly in his thick accent, "I pickup a lot of people, from a lot of places, but I've never picked anybody up from church before."

I look at him, hands folded in my lap.

"I take a lot of people to clubs, to hotels when they are married to other people and not each other, and I pick them up the next morning after these rendezvous. But I never pick anybody up from church."

He glances back at me through the rear-view mirror.

"This makes my Sunday," he grins, "I'm so excited. This gives me so much hope about people!"

I smile wearily into his sincere rear-view eyes, as confusion and shame still cast their looming shadows over me.

"I was just thinking the same thing when I saw you do the sign of the cross."

After the trip to church I just had...

Where the pastor was more or less romanticizing an Old Testament God's vengeance...

"You saw that?" he shakes his head, smiling, "I do that with every accident I see. I always say a prayer for whoever was involved in the crash."

"That's amazing," I gaze, hypnotized by the swinging rosary.

"I just think, if my family was involved in an accident, I would hope people would pray for them."

I look back at him, and smile.

"That's a good point. And we're *all* family, right?"

He grins and nods, as we veer off the highway onto an exit ramp.

"But I mean what I tell you, I pick a lot of people up, and many of them are going places not worth going."

He shakes his brunette head.

"It gives me hope to pick you up, to know people are going to church and pursuing God. That people are still trying to be good in a world full of its opposite. I feel like He put you in my car for a reason today, to encourage me."

My eyes turn somberly back to him.

But I rudely walked out of church…

Would he change his mind if he knew?

Would he think I was racist to do so?

Was all of this part of some Plan?

We pull up to my hotel.

"Thank you for riding with me today. I will give you five stars since you were such a nice passenger."

He turns back to me as he slows to a stop.

His brown eyes, brown skin, and brown hair stare at my pale eyes, pale skin, and pale hair.

"And God bless you."

He says I encouraged him…

"You really encouraged me today, too…" I tell him with earnest eyes, "You have no idea. God bless you, too."

"I'm going to be praying for you," he promises with a nod.

I smile and begin praying for him as soon as I shut his backseat door.

As the black doorman opens the lobby door for me, I smile at him, say a silent prayer for him, and decide to go for a run in the hotel gym.

I'm going to listen to Bishop Jakes today no matter what.

I think I'm going to pee my pants.

My fiancé and I pull into a gas station parking lot in
Jersey City, as my right leg fidgets in the passenger's
seat.

"Oh my gosh," I plead with him, as he puts the car in
park, "I hope they have one!"

The last gas station we stopped at had a restroom that
was out of order and unusable.

"Go, go! I'll park," he urges me as I hop out and run
in.

I'm so distracted I don't even notice the graffiti and
litter everywhere around us.

Once inside, the black woman behind the counter
points to the back of the dingy, flickering fluorescent-
lit room.

I practically run through the short aisles of Gatorade,
Chex Mix, and peanut M&Ms.

Once finished, I emerge from the small bathroom,
wiping my drenched hands on my jeans and thinking
about the Purell that is perpetually packed in our
glove compartment for me.

I push the glass door open as the tiny bell atop
chimes.

Hot, smelly air knocks me in my face as I step back outside.

Where is he?

The car is gone.

I begin to panic.

Scanning the parking lot, I see two gas pumps with black people pumping their gas, an old, beat-up green Honda blaring rap music over by the tire fill-up area and...

A giant sigh escapes me as I see our car parked quietly about twenty yards to the right of the green Honda.

As I take my first step in that direction, I see a massive black man emerge from the green Honda's backseat.

He has to be at least 6'4".

I notice a thick chain around his neck and watch him carry the gas station's vacuum to the driver's side door.

The bass of his rap music thumps and the rapper's voice booms so loudly I can't even make out the words.

Without thinking, my left thumb silently reaches across and turns the out-facing diamond of my engagement ring inward so that it rests in the palm of my hand, the same way I once saw done.

I clench my left fist, continuing to walk in the direction of our car.

Why on earth did he park over there by this guy?!

I watch the large black man bend over repeatedly, vacuuming the crevices of his driver's seat.

As I tensely walk, the rapper's voice slowly... becomes... clearer...

Wait.

"There is nothing as powerful as a changed mind."

Wait...

My walk slows, and I stop dead in my tracks about thirty feet away from the man.

The booming voice, now familiar.

The large black man must feel me staring at him, because he stands up and looks over at me.

"Is that Bishop Jakes?" I ask incredulously, pointing at his car, though already knowing the answer.

He nods with a confused expression.

"I love him!" I declare, reaching down and turning my ring outwardly again, feeling ashamed, "God bless!"

I smile at him and wave, and he does the same in return.

As I walk toward the car, guilt and humiliation overtake me.

My false smile shrinks, and I stare down at the diamond on my hand.

Reaching for the handle of the door, I sigh, exhausted by how instinctive these reactions are within me.

He was listening to a pastor. One of my favorite pastors.

I sigh again, hand on the handle but not pulling it yet.

God, Please bless that man mightily. Show Your favor to him in new and abundant ways.

Please remove from me these racist thoughts and behaviors. Please remove the fear of people who look differently than me. Please help me to come up higher in Your love.

Please continue to humble me, to destroy this pride.

Amen.

As I open the door, my fiancé leans over, looking at me with concern.

"What's wrong, baby?"

I climb in the car... and tell him.

Fall 2018
In memory of Botham Jean
In gratitude to Brandt Jean
Dallas, TX

When I thanked Dr. Shepherd for an incredible semester that last night of class, I never imagined it would be the first and only course I took at New York Theological Seminary.

There were so many other classes I had wanted to take, but, alas, God led me in another direction. I simply didn't have the money— or, evidently, the grace— to stay there and take more.

I had even taken it so far as to have another meeting with Ms. Ayanla Brown, the Director of Vocational Discernment, about filing for some financial aid.

She told me, "Where God calls us, He will sustain us."

So I went home that night and got down on my knees to pray about it.

I thought for sure He'd call me to take that next step, but, when the time came, the only thing I felt in my spirit was that one Bible verse, you know the one... something along the lines of: "If you go to offer your gift upon the altar for the Lord but owe a debt to your brother, go and repay that debt, then return and offer your gift."

Well, I didn't owe a debt to a brother, but I did owe a debt to my father. (And the credit card companies, and the IRS, and the bank...)

What I can see now is that I was never called to seminary to actually become a preacher. I was called there for God to work on the racism that I had been praying so hard about.

Funny, I didn't see that at the time though.

(I may have been labeled "gifted," but I'm not always too bright.)

Today, the dead black man du jour is Botham Jean, who was tragically shot in his own apartment by an off-duty police officer who accidentally entered the wrong apartment and assumed he was an intruder, in hers.

So much tragedy in one story, where do we even begin to digest and proactively move forward from it?

As I've been watching the story play out on the news lately, I've related to my usual character.

The shooter was a woman.

The shooter was white.

The shooter was blonde.

The shooter was only a year younger than me.

I don't know anything about Botham Jean other than the fact he was a black man.

Why do I relate to the person in the story who merely looks like me on the outside?

How shallow.

How stupid.

I've grown to resent my mind's simplicity, its involuntary tribalism.

But even if my mind were working out of its own prehistoric wiring, isn't it my responsibility to change the patterning once I see it?

I'm working on it, and I'd love to tell you I'm healed by now.

Believe me.

But I still can't.

As I decide to procrastinate my cold-calls for another five minutes, I reach for my phone and pull up Twitter.

Instinctively, I tap the trending button and see to the headline "Officer Guyger Sentenced to Ten Years."

Immediately I feel bad for her.

For *her*.

Not the black man who was shot in his own apartment while, presumably, unwinding from a day at work.

Not for the black family he left behind.

For *her*.

My mind begins, without my permission and before I can even notice, to build *her* story: She was a woman who lived alone. She was tired. She saw a man in what she thought was *her* apartment. (Don't bury the lead: a *black* man.) ...she defended herself.

As my soul comes to in time to hear my mind's inner workings, I sigh, pissed at how much work there is yet to do after all this time.

I then see another topic trending: "Brandt Jean."

Who's that?

I click into it and see posted videos.

I sneak one headphone into the ear sheltered by my cubicle walls.

I see a young black man with glasses swivel slightly in a courtroom chair in front of a microphone.

And I watch.

I watch this young man, the victim's brother, suggest to the police officer who murdered him that she "go to God."

I watch this young man, who could have very easily stayed numb from the immense pain which has suddenly been thrust upon him, tell the very source of that pain "I forgive you."

And then... I watch this young man adjust his tie and say "I love you just like anybody else."

Through humbled and burning tears, I watch him tell his brother's murderer "I want what's best for you."

I watch him explain to her, intimately, that, to him and his brother, that would mean giving her life to Christ.

I watch him ask the judge if he can give her a hug.

I watch the hair on my arms stand at attention.

And I watch these two bodies move toward one another and embrace.

I watch the black judge cry in the background.

I watch a white woman— the murderer of his family member— cry in his arms.

And I watch teardrops fall onto my desk.

Clicking out of the video and wiping my cheeks, I begin to read all the anger from black photos directed at Brandt Jean.

"How the hell is he going to forgive her?!"

"Typical black forgiveness getting the headline from white media! WE WANT JUSTICE!"

"This sets us back a hundred years!"

I can't tell a black person how to react to a racially-motivated crime.

And I can't tell a black person how to react to how *another* black person reacts to a racially-motivated crime.

All I can tell you is what it's like trying to overcome racism.

All I can tell you is what *I* felt as I watched that video.

I read more comments to learn the Officer had a history of sending racist text messages.

And I reflect back on some of the text messages I used to send.

I can look at the tragedy of Botham Jean and tell you who I most resemble.

And I can look at the tragedy of Botham Jean and tell you who I *wish* I most resembled.

Watching Brandt Jean behave like Christ to a racist white person remains one of the most humbling experiences of my life.

Not since Dr. Shepherd has anyone inspired me to continue confronting my own racism like he did.

That night I try to outrun my thoughts on the treadmill in our new home's remodeled basement.

Staring straight ahead, I hear the voice of famed motivational speaker Eric Thomas commanding my feet forward.

"Practice don't make perfect, ya'll," he informs me, and my pace slows, surprised.

Then he announces:

"Practice makes *permanent.*"

As I keep running, I think about earlier, wondering about where I go from here in this journey to abolish my racism.

And I realize...

It's going to take practice to get this right, to learn how to navigate social situations with other white people, and to unlearn so much of what I've been taught.

It's going to take practice to start actually believing what I already know: my position is the one that is right.

Advocatory love is right.

Because, as I learned in that car ride with my mother, you don't truly love someone if you don't defend them behind their back.

The Bible tells us we are all created in the image of God.

And there is no asterisk on that verse, specifying a skin color that is made slightly *more* in His image.

And if my position is now rooted in the Word, I must become brave enough to act that out in the world, the same world that is always tempting me to veer off God's path.

My finger slows the tread to a stop and I wipe my forehead with a small beige towel, stepping off the equipment.

I adjust my black pants and sports bra, as I walk into the spare bathroom in our basement to shower.

As I cross the threshold of the door, the image "James 4:17" pops up in my mind.

This sometimes happens to me with Bible verses. I have no explanation for it.

With a furrowed brow, I grab my phone out of the thigh pocket on my exercise pants and type it into Google.

Then gasp.

A few weeks later, I am at yet another forced lunch with Brenda.

This time she took six other hostages with us.

"Oh my God," Dale gasps, staring down at his phone while we await the check.

The entirely white table looks over at him.

"What?"

"There's been another mass shooting," he informs us.

413

"Ugh," coughs Brenda beneath particularly wild blonde hair today, "I hope the shooter was someone from Black Lives Matter."

My eyes widen, as I see Diane— my young, brunette coworker— subtly roll hers.

The table is silent, except Brenda.

"I hope they pin it on some BLM psycho, then another one copies them, and the whole movement gets taken down."

How dare she infect us with this poison.

"I don't."

She looks up, and I'm staring directly into her beady blue eyes.

"I don't," I repeat, sternly.

"You *don't?*" she challenges me, eyebrows raising.

"No," I confirm flatly in front of the rest of the table.

God, give me the words.

She stares at me, her subordinate, in front of the rest of her subordinates, except Vivian, who, mercifully, is out with the flu today.

"I hope it was," she repeats.

I feel a strange confidence surge, realizing that in the others' silence and Diane's eyeroll, *some* of these people must agree with me.

That they're sick of her shit, too.

"I hope it was one lone wolf, one psycho," I pitch to the table, "Someone with no ties to any group or party, even the ones I disagree with. I hope it wasn't someone from the left or the right. I hope it was someone from out of the blue."

Brenda has stopped looking at me.

"Why?" she now asks the empty breadbasket of crumbs which sits in front of her.

"Because if it was someone from a movement, you're right," I concede, "there could be copycats. Which would mean *more* death. And *more* violence. And *more* tragedy. And I'm a Christian, so I *obviously* don't want that."

This foreign version of me prods at her, reminded of the cross necklace she wears every day.

I always thought the judgmental, "holier-than-thou" Christians I grew up with were my least favorite Christians. I was wrong, because I didn't know "Christians" like Brenda existed.

So I keep going.

"I hope it wasn't somebody from Black Lives Matter. I hope it was one lone lunatic," I stare at her, "With ideas so crazy, no one else would ever agree with what they're trying to get people on-board with, and that all of the theories, and ideas, and conspiracies they have are ignored completely."

The rest of the table silently fidgets with whatever is left in front of them.

"I don't," she doubles-down, shifting in her chair and gripping her phone as uncomfortably as I did at the march for Eric Garner, "I hope it was Black Lives Matter."

But her tone this time is softer, faster even, as though trying to hurry away the rest of this conversation.

"Nahhh," I grin at Brenda with heavy-handed sarcasm, "Nobody wants *that*."

And I watch Diane cover a smirk with her dirty cloth napkin.

I know I didn't mention anything about racism.

I know my response wasn't perfect.

But, for literally God's sake, at least this time I no longer stayed silent.

Early Winter 2019
In memory of Elijah McClain
Aurora, CO

Is somebody... screaming?

I glance out the windows of my moving vehicle and see no pedestrians, though I hear... *something*... muddying the sound of the Coldplay song I'm listening to.

I slow to a stop at the newly-turned red light on the three-lane one-way road.

From the left-hand lane, I turn to my right and see a black man staring straight ahead in a forest green SUV.

So weird.

I turn down my music as the light turns green and again, hear muffled screaming.

Cruising just above the speed limit, I roll down my passenger-side window and finally hear it.

"THAT WORD!"

My eyes widen.

"THAT WOOOORRRRDDDD!"

I look around and see a black car swerving aggressively behind the green SUV.

"Oh my God," one hand covers my mouth, as the other grips the wheel.

The black man out-paces my driving and the black car is beside me now. I watch, stunned, barely focusing on the road.

I watch his angry red face scream, leaning out his open window.

I look ahead at the green SUV, trying to get away but still trying to drive calmly.

I wonder about the black man inside.

I wonder about the white man I'm witnessing.

I wonder what I should do.

I look down at my cell phone to call the police. *Will they believe me?*

Will the black man report it?

As my mind is warring, the black car and I have to stop at a red light the green SUV narrowly missed.

I stare straight ahead, terrified.

My music is still off, though my window has been safely returned to a closed position.

As I reach inconspicuously for my cell phone, the light turns and I pull ahead.

The black car zips over to the far right lane, turning right at the next turn.

And I wonder, as I watch him swing into a street-side parking spot and my car glides along, if I should turn around, call the cops and get the license plate.

What's the crime? Harassment?

I wonder if I could report it as a hate crime or something.

But is it a hate crime? I ask myself.

I thought hate crimes were only outright violence.

What is a hate crime?

My car keeps moving with the traffic.

And with each yard that I drive away from the shocking and horrifying event, I berate myself for not doing something.

Anything.

That night, I will tell my husband what I witnessed, as the news anchor announces more hazy, increasingly conflicting details from the recent Jussie Smollett allegations.

"It's really tragic," he will remark, "People won't believe the story of the guy you saw tonight because of this guy."

He will point at the TV.

And I will know he's right, because— had I not seen it for myself, with my own eyes— I wouldn't have believed the story, even *before* Jussie Smollett.

That night, I will pray extra hard for the people who live in a jarringly violent world I've had the luxury of being oblivious to.

I will pray for the black man in the green SUV.

I will pray for Jussie Smollett.

And I will recall Stacey's words and donate to an organization which prosecutes and seeks to prevent hate crimes.

Spring 2019
In memory of Michael Dean
Temple, TX

"Well you don't have to be a bitch about it!" the middle-aged five-foot white man fires at me.

"*Excuse me?!* You can't call me a bitch!" I shoot back, disgusted.

"That's it," my husband's voice concludes with authority from the cell phone at my ear, "Tell him to get the hell out of our house. He can't speak to you that way."

I stare at this grisly, weasley little man who, with his young, black coworker, was sent by the company we hired to install a new shower.

"You need to get out of our house and *leave,*" I proclaim.

"I want my money first," he arrogantly tells me.

"You didn't finish the job! I'm not paying you!"

"Tell him you're going to call the cops if he doesn't leave immediately," my husband directs from inside my ear.

"If you don't leave *right now,* I'm going to call the police. Get out of our house!"

"*Call* the police," the white man taunts me from eye-level.

421

I tell my husband I will call him back, then hang up.

As I begin to dial 911, I hear rustling from the bathroom.

"Ma'am, ma'am..."

It's the black guy, stumbling out of the bathroom doorway with pleading eyes.

"Please don't call the police," his eyes dart to his coworker, "Ned, go sit in the car. I'll finish the job myself, and no one needs to call the police."

The white guy and I both stare at him.

The black young man turns back to me.

"Ma'am," he asks me in a desperate tone, "If I finish the job myself and this guy doesn't enter your house again, will that be okay?"

I lean back, realizing he is terrified by the idea of police officers arriving.

And *why*.

I sigh, still seething at the little white man, but heartbroken by this young black man's terror given everything going on in the news (and presumably everything that's gone on before the news filled the rest of us in).

"That's fine," I relent to him then point to Ned, "But he cannot have any part of it. I don't want him in my house."

"Absolutely not," the black man promises me, waving his hands in an emphatic way.

The tiny white man stomps out of our home, and I lock the door behind him.

"Thank you, ma'am," I watch the young black man finally exhale, "He is so disrespectful. You didn't deserve to be treated like that. He never should have said those words. I'm so sorry."

"You don't need to apologize for him," I tell him, my eyes involuntarily tearing up as they often do in moments of confrontation, "That doesn't fall to you. You didn't say the words. I'm just really sorry all the work falls on you now because he was such an asshole."

The young man shakes his head.

"It's fine. There's no need to call law enforcement when we all can figure it out."

I watch him move toward the bathroom. He stops.

"I *will* need to go back out and get the new shower door from the van though in a little bit."

"That's fine. I just locked the door because I was scared for my safety with him."

"I understand. He won't *do* anything; he's all talk. But I understand."

My cell phone rings. It's my husband checking on me and making sure I'm okay.

Ten minutes later I watch the young black man struggle to haul in a heavy, seven foot glass shower door all by himself.

As he finally wraps up the job and is leaving, I apologize again that the labor fell to him to complete alone, while his horrible coworker simply sat in a van scrolling his phone.

I ask for his name and for the white guy's name. And I tell him why.

Within the hour, I call the owner of the shower door company.

I tell the owner for over twenty minutes what a liability the white guy is, how threatening and rude he was to me. And I tell him what an asset Dwayne is.

The owner tries to hurry me off the phone, and I refuse to let him.

"No," I command, "You need to hear this. If it were not for Dwayne calming the situation, you would have a police report filed against a worker of yours right now. Potentially, even a lawsuit against your company. Furthermore, Dwayne did all the work himself while that other guy just sat in the van."

The shower door company owner paused on the other line.

"Ned is a menace," he relents finally, "This isn't the first time I've heard this complaint about him. He's just an angry person."

"Well, I don't even know why you have him on your team then, because until Dwayne entered the room, I was ready to write countless negative reviews of your company online. Dwayne saved *your* ass today, in every sense of the word. You should not only hold onto him, but you should give him a raise or promote him or something, and *never* let him go."

There's silence.

"Alright, thank you for your call. I'm going to credit your bill two-hundred dollars for the trouble, and thank you for letting me know all of this."

We hang up.

And I wonder if Ned will have a job tomorrow.

And I wonder if the roles were reversed, would Dwayne?

And I wonder what it would feel like to fear the idea of law enforcement as much as I saw Dwayne fear it today...

Toni Morrison died.

I don't know who she is... or rather... *was*... but judging by all of the posts by news outlets on social media, along with corresponding quotes of hers, I realize she must be important and Google her.

Clicking into a page of her most "thought-provoking" quotes, according to the title of the site, my eyes scan it.

That one's good.

...Oh, that one's <u>really</u> good.

And then...

My heart skips a beat.

"What are you without racism? Are you still good? Are you still strong? Still smart? Do you still like yourself?"

And I pause, asking myself each question slowly enough to actually answer.

How much of my pride still rests in my unearned complexion?

Not nearly as much there used to be. But undoubtedly still a little... which, if I'm trying to be Christ-like, is definitely too much.

My eyes scan the website and see a page promoted: "1 Year After His Death, The Best Anthony Bourdain Quotes."

And though it feels a little counterintuitive to click into a white guy's page while thinking about racism, I'm drawn to clicking into it.

Again, I scan the page…

Good.

Ooh, really good.

And then…

"Maybe that's enlightenment enough. To know that there is no final resting place of the mind, no moment of smug clarity. Perhaps wisdom… is realizing how small I am, and unwise, and how far I have yet to go."

A jolt of proverbial lightning shoots down my spine.

Maybe I'll never be unracist.

The thought hits me hard.

Maybe God is taking His time with this one in me to remind me that it will take time for us, collectively.

Maybe it's like a drug and its half-life in your body, that no matter how much its presence reduces by half, it never reaches a full zero.

Maybe the best I can hope for is to wake up each day and be less racist than the day before.

And maybe my soul will just grow bigger to take up the space where the ugliness used to live.

But maybe it will never be completely gone.

Thirty minutes down an internet rabbit hole later, a familiar voice begins to play.

"I don't know anyone who understands the power of words more," Oprah pinches her fingers together for emphasis, "than Maya Angelou."

I stare at the screen.

"I've *been* in her home, at a party, with someone telling a homophobic joke or making fun of somebody in a derogatory way and *watched* her invite them to leave."

My eyes widen.

"Or stop them, in mid-sentence and say: 'Not in *my* house you won't.'"

Imagine… that level of confidence, that level of integrity to one's own beliefs…

The screen cuts to fluttering pages of cursive writing, set to delicate piano notes.

And her unmistakable voice begins… *Maya's.*

"Words are *things.* I'm convinced."

"You must be careful about the words you use or the words you *allow* to be used in your house."

"In the Old Testament, we are told, in Genesis, that 'in the beginning was the Word.'"

I close my eyes as my spirit listens to the teacher.

"And the Word was God, and the Word was *with* God."

"That's in Genesis."

"Words are things. You must be careful," her thoughtful voice seems to edit her words even as she goes, so that each sentence is its most impactful upon its hearing.

"Careful about calling people out of their names, using racial pejoratives and sexual pejoratives and all that *ignorance*."

Her voice hits the word hard.

"Don't do that," the wise Doctor instructs.

"Someday we'll be able to measure the *power* of words," she warns, "I think they are *things*. They get on the walls. They get in your wallpaper. They get in your rugs. They get into your upholstery, in your clothes. And finally, into you."

I shake my head.

God, make me that strong. Make me that principled. Make me capable of standing up for what is right the way she did.

And then I think about my father.

I think about his words getting into me, into my spirit.

I think about how, even not aimed in my direction, the use of such words feels... *violent*, somehow.

Hostile to a spirit turned toward God.

I think about Dr. Maya Angelou firmly commanding someone to stop spreading hate or forcing them to leave her home.

Can you imagine?

PART IV: TEACHING (AND STILL PRACTICING)
LOVE

"Without courage, we cannot practice any other virtue
with consistency."
Dr. Maya Angelou

I see a video posted by one of my favorite social media follows: Tabitha Brown.

If ever there was a living embodiment of the words "love" and "joy."

Sometimes she starts her serious talks with something along the lines of: "I don't know who needs to hear this, but God put a Word on my heart for somebody."

Tonight, that somebody is me.

I watch the black woman smile compassionately into the camera.

She begins talking about... *traditions.*

And I listen to her.

She tells me that, one day, I may decide not to participate in certain traditions anymore.

My spirit stirs, already knowing the tradition my soul has outgrown.

She tells me that I may decide to make changes once I start my own family.

I look down at my growing belly, as my mind swirls, envisioning the inevitable shitstorm that will come from changing the way it's always been.

She tells me it'll be okay.

She tells me that just because it's always been done a certain way "doesn't mean it has to continue to be done."

My heart lifts, gaining strength from this stranger.

She promises that I can start my own traditions.

Or I can choose to never take part in traditions again.

She tells me that's my business.

I listen to her wisdom, as emotion surges beneath my skin.

Then she stares into the camera.

"Whoever that's for, you take that. And you *run* with it."

One month later, I rub the side of my stomach where tiny feet are kicking, and I turn the page to a book as my husband drives us down the highway.

I inhale heavily, looking up.

"You okay, babe?" he turns to me attentively.

"I'm okay," I exhale a sigh, staring at the tiny farmhouses peppering the vast green countryside, "I just know this Thanksgiving is going to be different now that we're staying at a hotel and not my parents' house."

He nods, staring ahead at the road.

There's silence.

"I think it's what's best, though," he consoles me, "You know? You said you don't want to shut them out completely."

I consider his words— and the option— for seemingly the millionth time.

"I just can't," my head finally shakes, "Then I squander any opportunity to be helpful, you know? Like what if one day they decide they want to change? Maybe I could help them."

Pausing, I then roll my eyes.

"I mean, I know it's not my job to change people who have expressed *zero* interest in changing," a tired sigh escapes my chapped lips, "But it's also not my job to hate them. Jesus never hated anybody. How can I? I've been praying for them."

I look down at my swollen feet stuffed into worn out grey slippers for the drive.

There's silence again in the car, and I lean against the door, watching the steady white line on the outside of the highway race along.

"God never told me *I* was too far gone," I confide quietly to the white line, "He pursues addicts, criminals, murderers, and racists... So, if my job is to carry His love out into the world, I feel like I have to at least show up and be willing to do the same."

434

"It would be easy to sit on a high horse of judgment and write them off," my husband turns to me briefly, "but that'd be making it about you and your own pride, instead of trying to be helpful. It'd be saying: 'You still have this wound and I've already healed, so screw you. Fend for yourself.' You're not doing that."

He adjusts his grip on the wheel.

"You're a good person, Trisha."

I glance over at him.

"You know I'm not completely over it yet," I tell him dejectedly.

He laughs a bit.

"Honey, that's like someone saying: Sure, I've lost forty pounds, but I still have ten more to lose. I don't have anything of value to offer someone else trying to lose weight. I can't help them."

My husband continues to reassure me.

"You've done a lot of internal work, sweetheart, and now you're trying to bring that outward. Sure, you're not flawless with everything— no one is— but that doesn't mean you can't help someone who *is* where you *were*. That doesn't mean you have nothing to give. That means you're the perfect candidate."

I stay quiet, a skill I know too well.

"So many people today want to point the finger," he reminds me, "and condemn someone else. Not nearly

435

as many are willing to tell that person with humility, 'Hey, I was where you are. And there's a way out.'"

I blink in the direction of some cows out the window.

"Should I have told them the real reason why we're not staying at the house?" gripped with doubt, I turn back to him.

"No," he shakes his head, "you know what the family game night always descends into. Nothing you say will change that, because nothing you've said up to now has changed it."

I can't help but feel it's a cop out.

"Pick your battles," he advises me, soothing my inner debate, "You're protecting your own mental health by removing yourself from the family game night that always turns racist."

We shake our heads.

He's right. I *do* always know what family game night turns into.

"And you're giving them their daughter for Thanksgiving," he continues, "which is a loving and very civil thing to do. But if something gets said while we're there that causes you to feel uncomfortable, you can speak up about it, and I'll *always* have your back."

"I love you," I look over at him earnestly.

"We can always leave, too, if your boundaries are not respected."

My eyes roll involuntarily.

"My boundaries being respected?"

I laugh slightly.

He reaches over a strong hand, laying it on my thigh.

"We can go and bring the light, and if they don't accept us and what we're about, we'll just shake the dust off and keep it moving."

I nod silently, nervously.

God didn't give up on me.

Who am I to give up trying to bring His Love anywhere?

My other leg bounces as I watch more cows whiz by.

I think about the tradition of racism in my family.

How, like so many other people, I grew up seeing a pattern, vowing to never become it, only to wake up one day as another one of its living embodiments.

I think about all the life decisions I've made in silent observance of racist ideas.

Friendships I've missed out on.

Childhood crushes never enjoyed.

Places I've never traveled.

Life experiences I've never seen.

Wisdom I've never gained.

All the time I occupied running parallel to those missed moments, like Dr. Shepherd said, spent so far away from God and being at one with His Love.

I think about certain family members.

The love...

The humor...

The joy...

The spiritual *expansion*...

They've missed out on, too, by insisting on staying apart, staying "superior."

"I'm reading this book by Thich Nhat Hanh," I tell the glass on the window, as my fingers fidget with its softcover binding, "and there's a line I read last night after you fell to sleep."

I feel him glance in my direction.

"'Everyone in the war was a victim.'"

There's silence.

"That's how it is with racism... on a spiritual level. Everyone's a victim. Everyone's a prisoner," I look over at him, telling him the truth I've now learned, "because it takes two people to imprison somebody:

438

the prisoner and the jailer. And the jailer is in prison the whole time, too, making sure the prisoner stays behind the bars they've built."

I think of how my own indoctrination into racist ideas began so tragically early.

I had been handed the keys and told to keep watch.

I think of all the collective energy white people have wasted over the centuries, trying to keep black people apart, quiet, and down...

I let out a sigh.

"We're all prisoners in this, one way or another."

Spring 2020
In memory of George Floyd
Minneapolis, MN

We watch from the couch as thousands protest on TV.

Wide eyes glued to the screen, I nurse our infant son beside my husband.

To see so many people holding signs reading the all-too-familiar-now "I CAN'T BREATHE" while wearing protective masks over their noses and mouths feels surreal.

I stare down at our son and briefly wonder if I would be here, if he were not.

Would I be out in the streets somewhere protesting?

Or would my germophobia amidst a global pandemic win out?

All hypotheticals, I remind myself, as there's nowhere else the three of us could possibly be right now except safe, at home, with a newborn on our couch.

"Did you watch the video?" my husband breaks our silence but not his gaze at the screen.

"No," I shake my head, watching the protesters, "not yet, anyway."

"I did."

My eyes shoot over to him.

"What'd you think?"

"It was really fucked up," he shakes his head quickly, "No one could possibly watch that and side with the police officer. It was unbelievably disturbing."

He doesn't swear often around me. The video must be *that* bad.

"Really?" then I pause, turning back to the broader reaction playing out on the television, "I mean, I guess it *has* to be, to elicit this kind of response."

"Exactly," he nods, "What that guy did to George Floyd..."

He trails off.

"Gives a bad name to all police officers?" I offer.

"Gives a *horrible* name," he corrects me in a low, pained tone.

I think about the protest I attended after Eric Garner's death.

And we sit, silently, watching this moment of history together as a new family.

Later that afternoon, I ask my husband to grab me a book to read to our son.

Moments later, he emerges holding a children's book we'd ordered months prior about the Reverend Doctor Martin Luther King Jr.

"Because we want him to have a good soul," he nods at me with the same stern conviction Dr. Shepherd nodded at me all those years ago.

And I begin to cry.

In awe of this man I married, this child we've brought into the world, for the state of our country, and for the long journey ahead for us all.

And that night, I watch the video of George Floyd being killed. Because I must.

The next day, I sit on the couch watching the news anchor switch between massive protests all around the country, and even internationally now.

Our infant son sleeps in my arms.

I mute the TV.

And I turn my eyes downward, toward him.

Staring at the curve of his little nose...

The pout of his rosebud lips...

The delicate lashes that rim his sweetly closed eyes...

I listen to him breathe.

And suddenly... I am haunted.

Fear grips at my throat as I glance up at the news and wonder how many people in these crowds believe that "white men" are the problem.

And I look back down, at my white baby boy.

Panic sets in, as my mind races with images of malicious strangers one day targeting my son for harm because of his skin color and gender.

And then...

The clarity.

Like that day on the subway.

Oh my God.

This...

I blink hard.

This is what black mothers feel.

Tears pool in my pale eyes.

This is what black mothers *have felt...* all this time.

They stream down my face without mercy now, as my mind races to shut off the feelings, to protect myself from the flood of unbearable fear breaking my very soul.

Tears pummel the cozy blanket our son is tucked under, as my eyes dart for a way out, and then...

The clarity, again.

FEEL IT, I feel instructed.

FEEL ALL OF THIS.

And so I sit.

With those very fears and feelings.

And I sob, silently, so as not to wake the baby.

And I wonder, how many black women over the course of our nation's life have been filled with a mother's love only to have these fears crash over them, drowning sweet moments with *their* babies.

Their black babies.

And I weep.

I weep for the fact that George Floyd called out for his "Mama" before he took his last breath.

A grown man, calling for his mommy.

And I picture *being* his mother... if that were *my* son being harmed...

The breath can barely enter and exit my lungs to keep me breathing, as I quietly heave with grief, with fear, with... *pure empathy.*

Finally.

I look down at my breathing boy.

And I say a prayer to God, like countless mothers before me, pleading to protect him.

And I wonder how many black mothers have said that very prayer in the quiet of a night over their dreaming babies, or during their afternoon naps after hearing news of a black man somewhere near them attacked.

Tears blind me now.

Oh God, please help me. Please remove this fear and remove anything in me that causes others to feel this fear.

I beg.

Oh God, please protect him. Please protect them all.

I am a mother praying for every child in the world.

God, be with the spirit of George Floyd and his family. And help me teach my son to be better than I am.

I stare down and recall the hate directed at gay teens because of what some believe "people like them represent" in our culture. I wonder the same, now, about white men.

And I can feel what the mothers of gay teens feel, too.

Empathy.

Compassion.

Fear.

The most primal urge to protect...

in a world that's too big for me to shield him from.

"God," I whisper, "I need You. My baby needs you. This *world* needs You. We all... need *You.*"

My husband is driving around our neighborhood with the baby while I take a bath and read.

He said he wants to make sure, now that I'm a mom, that I still have "me time."

As I climb into the tub, I am careful not to bump the wooden tray atop, which houses a burning lavender-scented candle, the book I've been working on since before the baby, and my cell phone which plays Christian music in the background.

As my body lowers itself into the sudsy water, I try to close my eyes, focus on the heat and turn off the humming to-do list in my mind.

I inhale slowly, having dropped my meditation practice almost completely after having the baby.

And then I exhale.

And then I inhale, guiding my mind back from the thought that I should have grabbed a bottle of water before getting in.

And then I exhale.

And then... *laughter.*

But not mine.

On our... *driveway?*

I can hear its general location through the walls.

Instantly, I pick up my cell phone and pull up live feeds from the cameras mounted on our garage.

It's two black people wearing medical masks, one leaning against an Amazon van and another, a woman, standing in front of a sleek Mercedes Benz.

Could she be my grocery delivery driver?

I blink hard.

Is it possible that a grocery delivery driver has such a nice car?

Maybe a boyfriend gave her the car...

I shake my head.

None of that is relevant.

Why are they hanging out on my driveway?

I glance around the area and it *does* appear that no one is home. No cars in the garage... no people milling about inside...

A full minute passes of me watching them chat and I grow increasingly annoyed.

If I weren't in the tub, I would open the door with a smile and ask if they "need anything."

A subtle nudge, I reason to myself.

They erupt into laughter again and my annoyance turns to anger.

My eyes squint at the screen.

Should I put on a robe and go to the door to make them leave?

Should I call the police?

As soon as the thought crosses my mind, I am snapped back into my soul.

They're talking.

They're *laughing*.

Moreover, they're *working*...

In such a difficult time, shouldn't I be bending over backward to support *all* of the above?

To support any shred of humanity still out there in this insane and unpredictable world?

My eyes soften toward them.

God, bless them. Bless them a hundred-fold over.

The same fear tightens my heart a bit that always does: "What if them having more abundance means I get less?"

And, as always, I pray through it and harder.

Help them and their families stay healthy and whole and together. Help give them the strength to work and compensation that supports them in abundance. Lord, give them abundance.

I watch them laugh, then each give a gentle wave to one another.

Maybe they were flirting, I think hopefully for them.

The man climbs into the van and drives away.

The woman grabs a package from her trunk and walks it to our front door.

God, please forgive my ignorance. Please forgive the racism still in my heart. Please continue to heal me.

She climbs into her car and drives off.

BLACK JOY.

The term dances across my mind.

I had seen it on a protestor's sign a few days prior on the news.

I remember the sign read: "Black joy is liberation."

I click into Safari on my phone and search the term.

My eyes scan the results, clicking into a few.

I nod, thinking about the two laughing people who were just on my driveway. And the laughing black boys on the LightRail all those years ago.

God, help me support more black joy in the world. Help me to stand with and support those who live joyfully despite their pain. And help me to not contribute to that pain anymore.

I think about how the thought of calling the police ran across my mind.

And I recall a video I once saw of an angry white woman calling a table of laughing, joyful black women **"that words"** trying to quiet them and steal their joy.

My thought to call the police on two black people laughing on my driveway comes from the same place.

I realize it with solemn gravity.

And God, thank You for making me conscious of the patterning in my mind. Help me to do my part— all I can— to break it, in myself and in this world.

I pick up my phone, doing a quick search, then donate to an organization helping essential workers.

Driving down our street a few days later, I see a black man running.

He has on a reflective vest and all the gear of somebody who runs *a lot.*

I've never seen him around before.

The only non-white people at our last Home Owners' Association meeting were a few Indian families. And it was an election meeting— nearly everyone was there.

I think of Ahmaud Arbery, the black man who was recently cornered and murdered by suspicious white residents of the neighborhood in which he was running.

Maybe he's new to the area.

Or maybe he's not from the area at all and he's simply running here.

As my car approaches him, I smile warmly and give him a wave.

He waves back.

No matter what the circumstance, I want him to feel welcome here.

He may receive dirty looks or, God forbid, somebody calling the police on him like I've seen on the news before and, regrettably, almost just did the other day.

God, protect him on his run. Help him to have a great run. Help him to feel welcomed, respected, and loved here in our community.

And I keep driving.

Later that night, I will be up with the baby and watch the documentary "Toni Morrison: The Pieces I Am."

That night, I'm on the phone with a friend from my new Bible Group.

"How crazy is everything going on?" Catherine asks, and I can feel her eyes widening from the other end of the phone.

"I know," I lament, "It's really gotten me thinking about a lot of stuff."

"For sure," she agrees.

"I feel like I've done a lot of work on myself over the years, but I'm not quite sure how to carry that out into the world now, you know?" I continue, "Like, I kind of know how to confront my own racism now, but how do I speak up when somebody else is being racist *around* me, especially, like, family?"

"You know," her tone lowers, "sometimes members of Nick's family say things that I don't agree with, like against certain groups."

I listen intently.

"And I know their hearts," she reassures me about her in-laws, characteristically looking on the bright side and giving the benefit of the doubt to others as she always does, "I know they're good, loving people. I know if they really thought about what they were saying, they wouldn't really believe those things. But sometimes they say things…"

452

"And what do you say?"

I don't ask Catherine *if* she speaks up. She's the kindest, most righteous woman I've ever met.

During the birth of her children, she didn't want any epidurals. She simply played praise music in the delivery room, because as she put it: 'Jesus is all I ever need.'

So I don't ask her *if* she speaks up. I know she speaks up.

"You know, I just say: that isn't kind. I don't like that, and we don't talk like that. That's not kind," she pauses, "I mean, that sums it up, right?"

"And what do they say?"

"They usually agree! And then, like, say sorry!"

I nod and take diligent mental notes.

I scroll my Instagram with one hand, though it is all black boxes.

"Aren't these black boxes on Instagram kind of counter-intuitive?" I turn to my husband.

The news plays in the background while he responds.

"From what I read, the whole purpose was for white people to be quiet and give the floor to black people to speak, so the algorithms can shift and highlight posts from black people," he shakes his head, "But then a bunch of white people started posting those black boxes, flooding all those hashtags with the black squares and negating the entire point."

I squint my eyes at my phone.

"Most people only post on Instagram once a day anyhow," I remark, "So the white people posting all these black boxes aren't *actually* being quiet and letting others speak. They're using the one post they would *already* make today to say: 'Hey, look at me. I'm being quiet. Here I am, being quiet!'"

I chuckle to myself with thinly veiled cynicism, as my husband nods.

"Pretty much," he replies, sorting through some mail.

My finger scrolls through a nearly completely blacked-out feed, then taps into one of the hashtags.

"It's literally all black squares!"

My husband shakes his head.

"That's why I've avoided Instagram all day."

I nod, swiping the app closed.

"Yeah."

Later that night, I will be up with the baby and watch Chris Rock's documentary "Bad Hair."

I will think about how I never truly took the time to listen to Reverend Al Sharpton before.

I will think of Becc and her beautiful Afro.

And I will think of— and pray for— the girl they called "Creatch."

The next night, I login to Zoom with a pit in my stomach.

I am this week's speaker for Group.

Even before the pandemic, I hadn't been to Group since we had moved.

Sam is the Group's organizer this quarter. Although she was a member while I was, I never knew her that well. And, although she hasn't explicitly said so, I'm sure she expects me to talk about my usual deliverance from alcohol.

I'm not.

Tonight I will be sharing about racism with the all-white virtual Zoom room.

My mind races.

What if somebody takes a screenshot and posts online that I'm racist or something?

What if they somehow record it, post it online, and try to cancel me or something?

Oh God.

Should I have spoken to my husband before doing this?

What if it reflects poorly on him?

What if it reflects poorly on me...?

Or my... family? ...Somehow?

Or...?

I sigh.

God, please give me the right words. Your words. Help me to replace my shame with hope and trust in You.

Please help me minister to somebody, to anybody who feels this issue pulling on their heart.

Help me to show them the hope and the help You always give.

People trickle onto the screen in their respective boxes.

I briefly wonder if I would have the courage to do what I am about to do if there were even one face belonging to a person of color.

I'll never know, because there isn't.

I see a couple familiar faces, and the pull of anxiety from the unfamiliar testimony I am about to deliver yanks at my heart and races my mind.

God, please settle my thoughts on You. And only You.

"Hi everybody! Thanks so much for logging on tonight," Sam greets the group, "Please welcome this week's speaker: Trisha Fenimore!"

I sigh, as I watch muted acquaintances and strangers clap.

"Hi guys, I'm Trisha." I feel my voice say.

I glance down at the wood top of the desk I'm sitting at, so as not to be distracted by a face on the screen, including my own.

"There's a few of you I know back from my day in Group and you guys are probably expecting me to talk tonight about how God delivered me from alcoholism, but I'm not going to."

I exhale, looking directly into the camera.

"Tonight I'm going to share how God is healing me of racism."

I take in a breath, stunned I'm actually doing this.

"A wise teacher once recounted to me the story about a slavetrader, on an old, wooden slaveship, coming back over from Africa, who looked up at the dark night sky after a storm and was struck by God's vastness and glory, contrasted against the ugliness he had been living in."

Dear God, help me to do Dr. Shepherd... and all my other teachers... justice.

457

Help me to honor them through honoring You.

"Similarly but, also, a *little* differently," I chuckle, "A few years ago, I was a normal person who was commuting to a normal job on a rickety metal subway car, looking at the dark, graffiti-filled space and was struck with a moment of clarity from God about the ugliness I, myself, had unknowingly been living in."

I suck in all the air in the room, then blow it out, thinking of the old, seated woman on the subway and wonder where she is now.

Then I look into the camera, begging them with my eyes to hold the trust I'm placing in them.

"God revealed to me that day that I was racist."

I pause.

"Like that old joke where a fish swims up to another and says 'Hey! Nice water today, right?' and the other fish responds with confusion 'What's water?' I didn't even *know* there was an undercurrent of racism in my soul, pulling my every thought and action out to sea, and, most dangerously, away from God. He revealed to me that day the racism that was living in me."

"Now," my blonde head shakes, "I've never been to a Klan rally..."

I think of my grandfather and his Catholic church.

"I don't belong to any racist groups online... and I've never committed a hate crime..."

I think about the black man in the green SUV who I witnessed being chased and screamed at, and wonder where he is now.

"But I've laughed at derogatory jokes," I confess, "and I've held prejudice in my heart. And I've locked the doors when people who don't look like me walk beside my car."

I look away, shaking my head.

"I've stayed silent in the face of others' racism. I've looked at different cultures' shortcomings, rather than their assets and strengths..."

I shrug honestly, alone in my office.

"And I've tried to find my worth within a hierarchy, *literally* based on the flesh, that I was subtly— and, at times, not-so-subtly— taught."

I think of the doll commercials I watched growing up.

"And I'm responsible for it now, because I've upheld this hierarchy into adulthood, because I had been satisfied with my place in it."

"I don't know about any of you, but when I forget that God is the source of my worth, I start looking for it out in the world for it, from other people, and from human-made systems, like racism."

I look down.

"And spoiler alert: it's never there."

I see a blonde girl I don't know silently nod in her square.

"Over the years, I've shared snippets of this battle with a few women who have been members of this Group. And all but one..."

Stacey.

"Always met it the same. They'd tell me: I'm not a racist. Those thoughts are 'just normal,' and I was not *'that bad.'*"

"And while I know they were trying to help as best they could, I know *now*, as Christians, we aren't called to be *not that bad*. We're called to be like Jesus. And there's not a single story in *my* Bible of Jesus clutching to his pearls as a black guy walks by."

I stare into the vacant black lens.

"Each moment I sacrifice to prejudice and false pride in an appearance or race, I sacrifice moments of bliss and connection with my God who loves all His children equally, and moments of fellowship and sincerity with His beautifully diverse children around me."

My head shakes itself, still in awe of all the ignorance I didn't even know was there.

"I miss out on so much in the moments my ego insists on being *better than*. How can I be better than somebody born in the image of God?"

I recall a piece I read a couple weeks ago from a black nun named Sister Gloria Purvis, in which she said that racism makes a liar out of God and His proclamation that we're all made in His image.

"Further, we are called to carry His message to others in the world."

Tears well, but I keep them at bay.

"How can I teach someone about God's love and mercy when under the lie that I'm somehow born *better than* them? And now, as a mother, I can ask: what kind of God would that *be* who would create some of His children as more valuable than others?"

My head shakes.

"That's not a God I'm willing to serve. That's not *my* God."

A sigh escapes me, wondering if any of this at all is making sense.

"Racism is so unbelievably hard to overcome," I confide to them, "I seek God *every day* for it. For those of you who know how God delivered me from my drinking, I can tell you: that was easy in many ways, by comparison. And for those of you who have, also, overcome addiction: you know that's saying *a lot*."

"Drinking was a physical action, something I could see myself doing, to know I'd screwed up and missed the mark. Racism— for the most part— occurs silently, between my ears, in my mind and in my heart, where it's much, *much* harder to catch."

I shake my head quickly.

"That's why meditation is so important. It's the only way I've ever been taught to *watch* my thoughts. And honestly, had I not learned how to do that: I still probably *would* believe I'm not racist. Because I wouldn't even be conscious of it! I wouldn't even *know* that those were my thoughts!"

"In my experience, sinning in our thoughts is so much harder than sinning in deeds, because deeds are much harder to do without noticing. Whereas *most* of our thoughts occur... without our noticing. But that day on the subway, I became conscious of it. And then I became conscious of more."

"Another way overcoming racism is harder than overcoming addiction is because my drinking was harming me, making me do things I didn't want to, and giving me shame and pain. But racism, *I thought,* was serving me. It made me feel *good... more capable...*"

I stare at them through the camera.

"But that's the lie. Because I'm not capable, only He is."

I see a guy nodding in his square.

"And while I *thought* that racism was helping me, I can see now that I don't need that help. I only need God."

"I sacrifice my own salvation whenever I believe it can come from any place other than Him. And if I've learned anything over the last few years, it's that pride and God cannot coexist."

My eyes meet with theirs through the lens.

"I believe that when I prayed that first day for God to relieve me of the sin of racism, He did. He changed my consciousness. He made me aware of things I'd never been aware of before. But, it's been a struggle to *live* and *act* out of that new consciousness, to now *do* what I now *know* is right. And now I feel something else when I feel racism swell up."

My head shakes.

"I don't feel better than or superior. I now feel humbled and fallible... every time... that it's still there... that I can still fall into it. And I often stumble, fall, and outright fail."

I press on.

"Do I permit hateful, racist language to be spoken around me? That sinking, sticking feeling I get whenever I do is the space between me and God in that moment."

My hands begin to fidget, as I try to align my spirit with Him once more.

"But I know if there's hope... and grace... for God to turn a *slavetrader* into an abolitionist... which He did... then I know God has enough mercy and grace to transform me, too. And although He isn't doing it as *fast* as I'd like," I emit a light laugh, "He *is* doing it. I just have to keep showing up, each day, to seek Him and choose the dignity of others over the sins of my ego."

"The next step of this journey for me, I know, is to stand up for love and acceptance in my home if someone brings in racism. The next step for me is having the strength of conviction to not allow anyone to speak their racism is my home. To *stop* them."

I think of Dr. Maya Angelou.

"And I don't know when I'll be able to have people in my home again," I break a final smile for the camera during this remarkably difficult time, "But I know He's going to give me the strength and the grace on the day, and in the moment, I need it. Because I'm called to carry out His love in this world, to everybody, and I want to do all I can to make the space between where I am and where He's calling me to be as small as possible."

"It sounds like you carried a strong, beautiful message," my husband tells me as I finish telling him about the meeting, "I'm proud of you."

I point at the TV.

"What's happening here?"

His voice turns low.

"More looting and rioting."

Martin Luther King Jr. once said: "A riot is the language of the unheard."

As I watch a masked young man scamper over broken glass while carrying an armful of red shoeboxes, something deep within me stirs and I wonder if this is what he meant.

And then, the memory of another quote by the late, great Reverend Doctor swells to my surface:

> "I must confess that over the last few years I have been gravely disappointed with the white moderate. I have almost reached the regrettable conclusion that the Negro's great stumbling block in the stride toward freedom is not the White Citizen's Council-er or the Ku Klux Klanner, but the white moderate who is more devoted to 'order' than to justice; who prefers a negative peace which is the absence of tension to a positive peace which is the presence of justice; who constantly says 'I agree with you in the goal you seek, but I can't agree with your methods of direct action...'"

Maybe judging a movement from the sidelines of a couch is the ultimate privilege.

I stare at a burning storefront on TV, then glance over at the tiny black and white screen of our sleeping son. He's swaddled, asleep, and breathing in his bassinet.

Some things are black and white.

But most are messy shades of grey.

465

Suddenly, my phone dings and lights up.

It's Olivia, a young woman in Group.

"Hey," her texts reads, "I was really moved by your share tonight. I struggle with the same thoughts and feelings. What are some things I can do to get rid of them?"

I blink hard, silently, and say a quick prayer.

Then I type back:
"I couldn't (and can't) heal the racism in me. Only God can. I could tell you steps I took, but those might not work for you. Only God knows what it will take to heal YOU."

Send.

"Ask Him for help, and then just follow where He leads you."

Send.

I think about Dr. Shepherd again and all the experiences I had in his class.

I think about the protest I took part in that night in New York City.

I think about how I have tried to increase the black people I follow on social media and the black musicians and movies I have listened to and watched over the years.

I think about Anthony Bourdain and how far I have left to go.

"Ask God for guidance. And go wherever He leads you. That's the only advice I have. That's the only thing I know for sure works."

Send.

But then...

"Oh wait, there's one more! The people you feel racist towards: you need to pray for them. Every day, pray for them."

Send.

A week later, I find myself on a rare phone call with my father.

Last summer, I paid him back in-full for all the money I owed him over the years. Plus interest.

True to form, he brings up the looting and the riots.

But then... something *shifts* in his tone.

"But, you know," he begins, "I saw that black landscaper in town yesterday."

My stomach tightens.

"Oh," horror runs through my voice.

"We got to talking about racism."

"Oh," my tone drops further with dread.

"He said a lot of things I'd never thought about before."

The tension in my eyebrows loosens, confused.

"You know, I didn't agree with all of it," my father's solemn voice recounts, "like we disagree about Al Sharpton. I don't like him."

I listen.

"But I listened to what he had to say, and I *did* learn a few things that I'd never thought about before," he confides in me, "It's really gotten your mother and I talking about things, and where, perhaps, we've been wrong and need to change."

As I hang up the phone, I think of Dr. Shepherd.

No one is too far gone for the grace of God... No one.

That night, I pray for my family.

I pray for people struggling with racism and for those who don't even *know* they're struggling with racism.

My ex-boyfriend, Oliver, flashes in my mind— he was never visibly racist toward black people, but he was vocally and *vehemently* racist against Indian people.

I think of the Indian girl behind the counter of the gas station all those years ago. I think of her kind smile.

I pray for everybody who holds racism anywhere in their heart and spirit, toward *any* racial group.

I think about all the people in this moment of history, who are waking up in the middle of a war for their soul they didn't know was taking place.

All the people struggling with the realization— the way I once did— that they, too, have work to do to heal this problem.

I think of how daunting, but necessary, it is to start at Day 1, like they'll be doing.

I think of the late Anthony Bourdain's quote. And I think of how far I still have yet to go.

I stare up at the dark ceiling in our bedroom, and I pray for them all.

My life cascades before me as my son sleeps in the bassinet beside me, and my husband, on my other side.

I reflect on Dr. Shepherd's prayer in class at NYTS, for those struggling with racism.

And I recall the black landscaper in my hometown who belongs to a church which prays for my father.

I continue to stare at the dark ceiling in our bedroom, and silent tears of exertion escape my pinched eyes, as I pray for them, too— those who have been on the spiritual frontlines of this battle long before I ever knew my soul was war-torn.

All the black individuals who have educated, prayed for, lovingly included, and been patient with those of us who are un-learning the invisible source of our souls' discontentment.

And I pray for them and their enduring strength.

I think of my Grandma GiGi. And of my father. And then I think of myself.

And I pray for everybody who passes down racism, knowingly or unknowingly, to innocent and impressionable children.

I think of those children.

Children, like the one I once was.

Children, like the one *he* once was. And *she* once was.

Who never asked to be handed this ideology, this strange... family *tradition*.

I think of Tabitha Brown... and Bishop T.D. Jakes, Dr. Myles Munroe, Eric Thomas, Les Brown, and Dr. Maya Angelou... and all the black mentors I've never met, but who are shepherding me into this new, loving consciousness.

I think about those who can't even expose themselves to the healing messages and works of black creators due to the friction it arises in their own souls, like that day, years ago, when I unfollowed everybody who was black.

I think about those white people who are in the middle of work and personal relationships that make this spiritual work to un-learn racism incredibly lonely, and who often feel misunderstood and confused, the way I did every time a friend reassured me that I'm not "actually racist."

I think about those friends who actually still believe that.

And I pray for them all.

I pray for *us* all.

The next afternoon, my husband emerges from another Zoom conference call in his home office during lockdown.

I am nursing our son on the couch, again with the news on in the background.

As I attempt to rectify the reckoning I am watching on TV, there is only one perspective I feel able to take as a mother.

My husband rustles behind me in the kitchen, making his afternoon coffee.

"We never base who we are friends with on what they look like," I look down and quietly instruct my suckling son, "or on the color of their skin, or how much money they have."

I continue, softly.

"We base it off of the kind of person they are. Do they have a good heart? Do they have good intentions? Do they want what's best for you?"

I pause.

"And we *always* pray for those who don't make our cut."

My husband speaks behind me, walking up to the back of the couch.

"And we never target the vulnerable," he adds, "We *always* defend them."

I nod, staring at our son.

My husband leans down and from over my shoulder, kisses my cheek.

"What if one day he comes home and tells us he heard a racial slur?" I look up at him, with pleading eyes.

"We tell him it's unacceptable. We tell him it's wrong."

I think of my Grandma GiGi. And then her son.

"What if it's a family member, like my father?"

My husband inhales, taking a sip of his coffee.

He continues in a measured tone.

"We tell him that your dad grew up in a different time, and that people had different ways of behaving back then, but that it's wrong."

I think of the confusion I felt that fateful day in our kitchen when my mother almost broke the syrup-coated plate she dropped.

Looking up at him, I add: "We have to tell him that it has *always* been wrong. Just because it was accepted as normal in the past didn't make it right back then, that it's *always* been wrong. It was wrong then, and it's wrong now."

My husband stares into my eyes and nods sincerely.

"Absolutely. Of course."

The first time I heard that word, I was six.

EPILOGUE

"What can be written in just a few pages may take
years for the Lord to accomplish."
Pastor Rob Reinow

Spring 2021
In honor of the three-fold "guilty" verdict reached in
the trial of the police officer
who killed George Floyd

One month before the historic verdict, it happened: a friend of mine made a racist remark at my home.

We were seated on opposite sides of a long outdoor patio table as she spoke the words...

"Why don't black people care about the violence in their *own* neighborhoods?"

My heart dropped.

Really?

For the briefest moment, I wished I'd simply shoved one of those cliche "Hate has no home here" signs into our yard. That way, people would just know not to say anything, and I wouldn't have to deal with it.

But that doesn't help heal the problem. It simply tells the problem where to avoid expressing itself. And, thus, pushes the problem deeper underground... where it can fester and grow.

A clarity overtook me. Compassion, even.

And I silently invited God into the conversation.

Now I will never say a bad word about Dr. Angelou, but I couldn't in good conscience ask my friend to leave...

To do so would have left her with her ignorance.

To do so wouldn't have fixed anything.

To do so wouldn't have helped her understand why what she was saying was wrong.

I looked at her, as my insides tightened, knowing that: *This is it. I have to say <u>something</u>.*

"Well, first of all, *of course* they do. And I've heard a couple personalities on the news say the same thing, but that feels like a racist argument to me," I remarked, intentionally not calling *her* racist.

When people used to call me "a drunk," I would deny it defiantly, storm off angrily, and— you guessed it— continue to drink maniacally.

To this day, I've never once seen an exchange wherein a white person calls another white person "a racist" and the white person expressing the racism insightfully responds with: "You know what, you're right! I've never thought of that. I'll change my ways for good!"

There's argument. There's denial. Because beneath it all, there's the belief— the same one I once had— that "I'm *not* a racist because to 'be a racist' means I do *x, y,* and *z*. And I don't do *those* things, so I'm not a racist."

But if I call their *words* racist, I disassociate it from who they believe themselves to be. And I instead offer them: "What you just said was racist and you don't want to be racist."

Because, as I explained earlier, no one *wants* to be racist. At least, no one reasonable.

And I knew my friend could be reasonable, if reason were presented. After all, if she couldn't, she wouldn't be my friend.

She leaned back in her chair, as I continued.

"It completely deflects from the original issue. The original issue is police brutality. To respond with: 'Well, what about the violence in their own communities?' seems like a cop-out, no pun intended. It seems like a dodge and a deflection from the original issue."

I kept my tone low, intentionally.

She looked surprised.

"I mean, I think trained police officers who wield deadly weapons should be held to *higher* standards of behavior than the civilian population. Don't you?"

She cocked her head, nodding and acquiescing.

And for the next forty-five minutes, we engaged in a conversation and emerged on the other side, still friends, and with her, on mine.

I don't judge Dr. Angelou for simply having asked her guests to leave.

I haven't fought this ignorance my whole life.

I'd been sitting on the bench and, on this day, was thrust into the game. I had fresh legs, energy, experience being on the other side, and, as a result of all of that, patience.

That is what I have to offer this fight: patience and the lived experience which now allows me to counter racist points with nuance and precision.

I could have yelled. I could have been self-righteous. I could have pointed my finger and wagged it at her.

But I remembered the white woman on the subway who denied me literature on Stop & Frisk while simultaneously trying to shame me.

None of that behavior helped me on my journey, so why would I believe I could help others that way?

Maybe that type of "holier-than-thou" behavior is the *ultimate* white privilege... behavior that doesn't seek to change anything in the world, but simply makes the white people engaging in it feel good about being "right" and others being "wrong," instead of fearing that a racist heart may have actually just been hardened rather than changed and, as a result, one more person's racism still exists in the world to wreak havoc.

Because to *those* white people, racism isn't a threat; it's an ego-trip.

The woman on the subway that day might have been right, but she wasn't helpful.

And I want to be helpful.

After all, I've been unhelpful long enough.

Lunch was winding down at my parents' house.

Our one year-old had woken up from his nap not long ago and in the process of lulling him back to sleep on the living room couch, my husband had dozed off with him.

As the rest of us stared at the uneaten scraps on our respective plates, the conversation about family history marched on.

Not long ago, we had a family member do an ancestral deep-dive and learned that among our ancestors— on the side of my beloved grandfather— was an incredibly vocal abolitionist, who actually served in Abraham Lincoln's Cabinet. His first Vice President, in fact.

Hannibal Hamlin was so vocal an abolitionist that Lincoln couldn't risk such a polarizing running-mate for his fateful second term. Tragically, he chose Andrew Johnson instead.

But I digress.

Around that same time, a photo surfaced of *another* ancestor, who smiled with other white faces beneath a banner containing a swastika. Upon its discovery, we tried to convince ourselves that maybe it wasn't what it seemed... that *our ancestor* wasn't what she seemed.

We sat with the photo's existence for some time, trying to rationalize to ourselves and one another that "the swastika used to mean something entirely different," attempting to abdicate ourselves from the shame that would, otherwise, course through our literal veins.

But after acknowledging that particular family branch's strong German lineage, as well as the fact that the photo was taken just after Hitler's failed coup attempt— while he sat in a German prison, penning *Mein Kampf*— we were slowly accepting the harsh reality.

We had an ancestor who was a Nazi.

And we had an ancestor who was a powerful abolitionist alongside Lincoln.

Closer on the timeline to *now*, I think of my grandparents.

I had a grandparent who used hate language.

And I had a grandparent who was the victim of a hate crime, at the hands of the KKK.

I sat, contemplating the insanely complicated and conflicting history of my family.

My ancestors include them all: the righteous, the wrong, and the wronged.

Perhaps my family history is a microcosm, of sorts, for our country.

Just then, my thoughts were interrupted by my father.

To his credit, I had not heard him say anything racist since our phone call in the aftermath of George Floyd's killing.

But, as I know well, a year of healing is only but a start.

My father began making rude remarks about the weight of a man in our hometown.

These types of comments were nothing new for me to hear, as "jokes" about people's weight and appearance were commonplace in the home I grew up in.

As he continued with snide laughter and disregard, I stared across the table at one of my nieces. She was only scarcely older than I was that fateful night at Grandma GiGi's, and she was not the only child at the table.

The story— and his cruelty— continued as though the little ones were not there at all.

My mind flashed to all the moments growing up, when I would sit silently at this very table, subjected to unkind comments about weight and race and other superficialities, feeling unable to speak up.

Unable to advocate for my own heart's discomfort.

Unable to upset the predetermined power structure of the traditional, father-centered "nuclear family."

Anxiety vibrated through every cell in my body, but I spoke.

"That isn't kind," my words stated clearly, recalling the strength Catherine had taught me.

Every muscle in my body, as well as the now-silent room, tightened.

"You have grandchildren who are listening."

I motioned to them, then mustered more strength as, now, the mother of one of them.

"That's very unkind to say, and it's incredibly inappropriate to be talking about," I stood up, carrying my porcelain plate to the sink, "How somebody else's body looks is none of our business."

I glanced over at the living room couch, trying to gain courage from my sleeping son and husband.

My father stayed silent.

"I think that should be the litmus test going forward for family conversations," I told the room of nearly ten people, "Is it kind? And is it appropriate?"

A voice spoke from my mother's direction.

"I agree with Trisha," she announced, standing up with a strange smile, "That's absolutely correct. Let's all focus on that going forward."

The conflicting morality of my family line, as well as my own life's humbling trajectory, has taught me much.

In the words of the Reverend Doctor Martin Luther King Jr.: "For evil to succeed, all it needs is for good men (or in my case, *women*) to do nothing."

And I have decided that in the face of *any* hate, I will no longer do nothing.

Later that night, on the way back to our hotel room, I told my husband about this notable first with my father and how proud of myself I felt.

He told me that he hadn't been fully asleep on the couch, had heard parts of the exchange, and was very proud of me, too.

I told him that, although I felt uncomfortable doing it, once the discomfort passed, I could see clearly: the person who makes the room awkward is never the one who speaks up. It is the person who spews hate— in any form— gambling that nobody will.

Back in college, before my drinking really took hold, I sat in a Philosophy course wherein we discussed what *actually* makes an action wrong: the motive or the outcome?

Our wise, young professor posited to the class: "If you lovingly baked peanut butter cookies for a friend who was in the hospital, but didn't realize they were allergic to peanuts, and those cookies *killed* your friend... was your action bad or good? Because you had good intentions, but it killed your friend, which is, obviously, a terrible outcome."

As we pondered his question, he continued.

"What if, on the other hand, you believed your friend in the hospital *did* have a peanut allergy and you baked them peanut butter cookies intentionally because you had a grudge against them and *wanted* to kill them? What if you brought them the cookies, they ate them, but they didn't die because you were wrong and they weren't actually allergic to peanuts at all... Was your action here bad or good? Because you had bad intentions, but you really just ended up bringing cookies to your friend in the hospital, which is rather thoughtful and nice."

I reflected on that lesson, as I finished reading Ebony Jones' gracious and loving response. The letter I had written to her two days prior accounted for my ignorance that day in the locker room, apologized for my inappropriate behavior, and told her some of the ways in which I'd been changing and working to do better.

The goal of the letter was to take accountability to someone whom I may have hurt and made uncomfortable and, hopefully, restore the dignity I might have taken from her that day by my thoughtless remark and gawking.

While motives matter most to God, I have found it doesn't excuse away my once hurtful "othering" behavior to His kids.

I didn't mean to hurt Ebony that day in the locker room, but if my actions *did* hurt her, it's my responsibility to acknowledge the hurt my actions caused and try to amend it, as best I can.

I glanced down at the Post-It note list on my desk.

The name Aliyah had a line through it. I had written to her last week.

Similarly to Ebony, Aliyah's response was filled with grace, love, and a bit of disbelief that I'd written her in the first place.

I picked up my pen and drew a line through Ebony's name.

I stared at the remaining names on the list: Jada, Jazmine, and Becc.

My husband and I had just watched a documentary on the notoriously brutal serial killer Ted Bundy.

I don't normally watch things like that, but we were barely emerging from the COVID pandemic and our TV pickings had grown painfully slim.

I'll never forget what the killer's eerie voice said in one of the production's obtained recordings.

Something along the lines of: Everyone thinks they'd be able to recognize a serial killer, as though it's some hideous, drooling monster of a man emerging from a dark alley or wooded lot. Nobody thinks that it's someone attractive, likeable, and... normal. The killers are among us and they're, otherwise, normal people.

Three days later, an inconspicuous-looking mom on the periphery of my social circle offered up a racist remark over an outdoor brunch.

She said: "I don't understand why black people refuse to teach white people once we ask for help. They say 'it's not our job' to educate us, but then how are we going to learn? Why are they refusing to help?"

I silently wondered how many times black people asked white people for help and didn't receive it.

There were four of us seated around the table, not counting the kids.

And I prayed.

God, this is it. I'm here. Please give me the words.

"Well black people aren't required to be our teachers," I volunteered in a tone of voice similar to the one I used with the police officer at the Eric Garner protest back in 2014, "Their purpose isn't to supply us with what we need. That burden shouldn't fall to them. I don't think that's their responsibility."

"I don't know," she shook her long, brunette hair, "It just seems like now they have a little bit of power, and they're being mean with it."

I tried not to blink as hard as that blinking blonde guy meme.

"Well," I began slowly, "what if you're the only black

person in a workplace of, like, fifty people? Are you now required to spend your time and energy becoming a part-time teacher to educate every white person who comes to you, availing yourself to every single request for information on race?"

"For free, too," one mom chimed in, offering.

I looked up, made eye contact with her, and we shared small smiles.

The original mom looked at me, as I chose to go on.

"I hear what you're saying because that can feel like the easiest course of action," I told her with genuine sympathy, "But just think if you were the only black person in a job and your white coworkers constantly thought you owed them your time to fix their ignorance. There's so much information out there these days. I don't think the burden to heal the crime, so to speak, falls to the people who have been being victimized by it."

I paused.

"That would be like asking survivors of rape to dedicate their time, for free," I gestured to the mom who volunteered that fact, "to help heal and fix rapists. Some of them do, and some of them feel called to do that, but do we need to add to their burdens of healing by piling on that expectation? Is that fair that they have to fix what's been hurting them?"

She looked down while scooting a cube of cantaloupe across her plate with a fork.

"So then what do we do?" she finally asked.

"Well, I think we first do the spiritual work within ourselves," I told the woman who knew nothing about my past, "and then, after that, we can try to help each other."

I could barely pick my jaw up off the floor.

Hate crimes?

Terrorist threats?!

As I continued editing this very book, I had decided to look up a few poignant people who mattered so much to me along the way.

On this particular day, I googled Wanda Lamb.

She had left her job in publishing and opened a little bookshop in Bayonne, New Jersey...

She and her bookshop had, also, been the target of hate crimes and death threats. They had found the man responsible— a Hoboken resident, as fate would have it.

I shook my head, wiped my tears and picked up my jaw long enough to share the story with my husband in our kitchen.

"Why don't you place a big online order?" he suggested, "And maybe one day we'll take a little family trip to Bayonne and stop in."

"She won't remember me," I smiled at him, "but I would love to see *her*."

"They probably packed the house full," my mother mockingly told the rest of the dinner table, "and the whole house probably smelled like curry."

She was telling everybody about the Indian family who recently rented out their beach house for a week.

I looked across the table at the children playing with their utensils so as to avoid eating more of their food.

I thought about Tiya Bhatt.

And the Indian girl who wished me well each time I bought alcohol.

And the beautiful, delicious Indian restaurants in New York and New Jersey that I'd frequented.

And all the wonderful, kind Indian people I'd had the privilege of meeting, working with, and befriending over the years.

"Have you ever eaten Indian food?" I asked my mother out loud in front of everybody, already knowing the answer.

Taken aback, she stammered and paused.

Then relented: "No."

"Has anybody?"

Everybody shook their heads, except my husband who had, in fact, eaten Indian food, but he stayed silent because he rightly suspected I was up to something.

"It's an incredible cuisine," I told the table.

"Isn't it all curry?" my mother asked in a pronounced tone, perhaps trying to salvage some pride.

"No," I looked at her and shook my head, "it's not."

Then I turned to the children, who I wagered were a better use of my time and efforts.

Gathering all the talents Dr. Shepherd had taught me, I weaved a story for them about the Indian restaurant on the Upper East Side of Manhattan that some girlfriends and I used to frequent. The beautiful, vibrant silk curtains... the heavy, decadent silver bowls... the soft, melodic Indian music... the delicious, warming spice blends... I watched their eyes light up with excitement and wonder.

And then I turned back to my mother, mustering all the love I could: "You should really try it sometime. It's incredible."

My eyes stared out the window at the Deep South that I'd never seen up until then.

A few days prior, my husband, son, and I had left the same beach house that an Indian family had rented a few months back, and I didn't know it at the time, but that would be the last time I would see my family of origin. (There were more reasons than the ones contained in this book.)

As the three of us drove from Birmingham, Alabama up to Memphis, Tennessee, I reflected on some of what I'd seen up to then on this unique trip we decided to take.

My mind kept taking me back to the 16th Street Baptist Church... the KKK had bombed it, killing four young black girls... I thought about my grandfather... and what he might have said at the site.

I thought about the water cannon display in the park adjacent to the church... how unbelievably scary it must have felt to have such weapons aimed at the Civil Rights protesters doing their Holy Work...

And I thought about how hate didn't win with the bombing of that church... in fact, it was dealt a crushing blow.

It was because of that very event, I learned, that Reverend Fred Shuttlesworth invited a young minister down to Birmingham whose efforts would help him desegregate the city, as well as thrust that young minister into the national spotlight.

That young minister was the Reverend Doctor Martin Luther King, Jr.

As the run-down shacks passed by one-by-one, I wondered what standing outside the Lorraine Motel in Memphis would be like. I wondered what it would feel like to stand at the place where the great Reverend Doctor King was assassinated. I wondered...

As I rubbed the side of my again-pregnant belly, I wondered what I would do if one of my children ever tried to make the other feel less loved, less worthy, or less valuable than the other.

I wondered what I would do if one of my children ever treated the other with disrespect, disdain or even malice.

I wondered what I would do if one of my children were being bullied and the other child didn't step in to help or, even worse, joined in.

I wondered what God thinks when we do any of that down here.

I wondered how I would find the courage to take whatever next steps God asks of me on this ongoing journey toward healing.

I wondered what would happen between me and my family of origin.

I wondered... and I prayed for them.

A drunk man continued to lambaste the worker behind the convenience store counter.

"You think taking sugar packets is a big damn deal?" he screamed, "It's not a big damn deal! You can go to hell!"

A man picking up some milk for his one-and-a-half-year-old glanced over at two young kids in the candy aisle. They must have been about twelve and seven years old, respectively.

They shouldn't be subjected to this, the man holding the milk thought.

He stepped slowly toward the counter to intercede.

"Why don't you just ride your camel back to Pakistan?!" the drunk man screamed at the employee, who appeared to be of Middle Eastern descent.

"HEY!" the man holding the milk shouted firmly, "That's enough."

The drunk man turned to him.

"What?"

The man with fresh stitches under his shirt held the half gallon of whole milk as he spoke: "It's bad enough you come in here cursing in front of kids..."

He gestured to the children in the aisle.

"But now you're going to try to spew hate and racism? Absolutely not."

The drunk man wobbled toward the door, muttering to himself.

"You know," the drunk turned slightly and slurred, "I'm Italian."

Wrong move.

494

"Hey," the man holding the milk stated with such force that the drunk man turned to face him fully.

For a moment, the man holding the milk wondered if he was about to get into a physical altercation while hiding dozens of fresh stitches on his torso.

His pregnant wife, in her third trimester, had agreed to let him go to 7/11 instead of the grocery store, as her raging hormones had her fearing all the mass shootings at grocery stores as of late.

He insisted on leaving the house.

She didn't want him in a grocery store.

7/11 was their compromise.

"I'm Italian, too," the man pointed to his chest with the hand not holding his child's milk, "And *we* don't act that way."

The drunk man took one step toward the milk, then turned and sheepishly slipped out the door, as the bell above him chimed.

"Thank you," the man behind the counter spoke up in a thick accent, "I'm new to America. That man was very rude."

"That's not what America is about. That's not who we are. *That guy* was an asshole."

Twenty minutes later, tears welled up in my eyes as I watched my husband put the milk away.

I never knew I could be proud and angry all at once.

"You haven't even been out of surgery for twenty-four hours," I shook my head, trying to compute it all but, deep down, knowing full well the man I married.

"I know you did what you needed to do," I finally relented, "and I know you were put there for a reason."

"I couldn't do nothing, Trisha. I wanted to step in with the swearing, but I *had* to step in when it turned racist."

I nodded.

"I know."

Staring at the father of my children, I thought of my own.

I thought of everything I grew up with and everything ours will grow up without.

I thought of my old friend Jenna and the husband she chose.

I thought of what her children are growing up with.

I thought about all of us in this hideous cycle. Those who choose to continue it. And those of us who choose to let it go.

I spent the last few months of working on this book steeped in dread.

"Uncomfortable" didn't even begin to explain how I had been feeling.

The prospect of placing my ignorance and hate on display for, theoretically, the *world* to see seemed daunting, at best, and arguably insane, at worst.

I knew many people wouldn't read the whole thing. I knew many people wouldn't read it at *all* (and simply associate my name, henceforth, with racism). I knew I would be told, perhaps all-too-eagerly, of the blind spots and gaps that, yep, *still* exist.

I knew this book might backfire in massive form, and the constant bombardment of imaginary scenarios refused to relent.

But on May 14th, all of that changed.

My husband and I had taken our two boys to a local tourist destination and while surrounded by people of every imaginable shade and background, I was more tempted to quit than ever before.

I didn't want to do it.

I didn't want people to know me as "the racist."

I didn't want any of it.

I had all but decided to quit when it happened.

As we sat outside a charming little ice cream shop, feeding our kids cold, dripping bites of vanilla-chocolate twist, our phones buzzed. There had been another mass shooting.

As we made the short trip home, foggy details were emerging.

A young white male.

A racially-motivated crime.

A livestream.

When I arrived home, I watched the news as my boys played on the floor at my feet.

With a hand over my mouth, I listened as they announced this young man had driven three hours, fired sixty bullets, and killed ten black people.

I stared at my young boys as they announced that this young man had been radicalized online.

I thought of the online hate I engaged in all those years ago, how easy it was to fall into and how easier, still, it had become to express...

A fear washed over me at the thought of my children falling prey to that same evil.

What if the soul this book helps is one of theirs?

498

And if not one of my children, I realized then, *is it not still <u>somebody's</u> child?*

Is it not still God's child?

I thought of the lives robbed from the victims by a perpetrator whose life had been robbed from him by hate.

As I watched two black women hold each other, one wearing the very same minimum wage grocery store clerk uniform that I used to wear...

The words overtook me.

> I've only heard God's voice a handful of times in my life.

> And, as anybody who has, you never mistake what it is when you do.

His words were, seemingly, a dare...

THE DEVIL ISN'T RETREATING.

SO WHY WOULD YOU?

I remembered the prayer I prayed years before this book ever revealed itself to me, promising God that I was ready to take new ground for His Kingdom.

Whether it be an inch, a foot, or a mile—I prayed—I wanted to contribute and enlarge His territory here.

And I'm going to quit?

And let the devil win?

I had spent so much time, in the latter parts of this book, pondering this idea of "white privilege," and I'm not proud to say that a part of me even somewhat enjoyed pointing the finger at the white woman on the subway for engaging in it.

But, true to His Biblical promise, pride really does go before the fall...

Because that day, God showed me that my temptation to quit was actually the embodiment of it.

Because the idea of my "comfort"—in the face of what is *actually* happening—is not only unimportant, but it's completely irrelevant.

There are so many stories I wanted to tell, but couldn't. (The book has to end *somewhere*, right?)

The end of this book finds me at a very different place than its beginning.

God has, indeed, brought me a long way.

I'd love to summarize it all in one poignant closing thought or some hauntingly poetic final line.

But, as I already warned, you won't find this story wrapped up in a neat, tidy bow.

This is a memoir, not a movie. *Remember?*

And I've finally accepted that while this story may, by necessity, have an ending, this journey never will.

It will never be over.

It is only to be continued...

Do not be conformed to this world,
but be transformed by the renewing of your mind,
that you may prove what is the good, and acceptable,
and perfect will of God.

Romans 12:2

AUTHOR'S NOTE

Sometimes human memory is flawed.

I wrote this book as honestly as I could, but nonetheless from a human memory.

I tried my best to be honest, no matter how uncomfortable it may make people (including myself). Some characters may remember events differently than I do.

The characters who were amalgamations were: Candice (who was a combination of two people), Sasha (who was a combination of two people), Steve (who was a combination of two people), Jenna (who was a combination of three people), and the pregnant cheerleader in my hometown (who was a combination of several). I, also, ascribed one story to Stacey which was actually a story involving another woman, but it made more sense to assign it to Stacey to facilitate the story's flow.

The party where I held hands with Terrell Jackson did not happen at a Kiwanis Club location, but at a small party rental space named "Schmid Hall," in our hometown's city park. I changed that part of the story because nobody outside of my small hometown would understand what "Schmid Hall" is and describing it would have merely distracted from the story.

I do not recall "Creatch," the young black woman in my old sorority, actually weighing in and saying anything about the black recruit named Holly. I added that portion of the book to depict both storylines (the one of "Creatch's" nickname and Holly being voted against) in a seamless way.

Additionally, on the evening I first came across the Christian Group in Hoboken—the night Oliver dumped me—I did not sit up at the pier at night, rather I sat watching the sunset in the lacrosse field bleachers at Stevens Institute of Technology. For this book, I changed the location to the pier overlooking the city to further ground the reader in the story's New York City backdrop.

Finally, there were many stories that didn't make it into the final draft of this book. Some were edited out, some memories were foggier than I felt comfortable committing to, and some—I assume— I don't even remember. I am confident that the stories which comprise this book accurately portray my journey and, hopefully, accomplish my ultimate aim.

I am very grateful for my past. (Yes, all of it.) It has taught me so much that I hope can be helpful to others.

A part of me, also, feels it's important to share with you that I do have some good memories of my childhood, too. After all, rarely is anything in life either all good or all bad. Those fond memories, however, were not relevant to this story or its topic of racism.

If you are feeling negatively toward anyone described in this story, I humbly encourage you to pray for them. I've found that taking such a tack may not change the person I'm praying for—though it sometimes does—but it *always* changes my understanding of them.

I've learned from experience that people who behave in ugly ways are living far away from God. And that is its own tragedy to be mourned. Please find hope in what Dr. Shepherd taught me all those years ago: "No one is too far gone for the grace of God. *No one.*"

And if it is *you* who is far away from God as you read this, please believe what I have found to be absolute truth in this world, that somehow—in an impossible twist of time and space and human understanding— when we are farthest from God, we are somehow actually the closest. You're not too far gone. Just look up.

Just look up.

I questioned more times than I can count whether I should write this book at all. I worried, among other things, how it would make me look and how it would make other people look. But, repeatedly, I was reminded that this isn't a story about me (or them).

It's a story about Him.

The only solution to every problem I've ever known.

To the women who showed up every Saturday night in Jersey City to participate in "Trisha's Teachings," while you are not described in this book, you are present in every scene wherein I demonstrate confidence and conviction. To those of you I've stayed in contact with, as well as the ever-rotating roster of women whose faces I could pick out of a crowd even if your names I can no longer remember: Thank you for entrusting me with your struggles and triumphs so that I could learn to minister to people. I will never forget those cozy, candlelit nights, eating poundcake and sipping on hot tea, all while talking about God and life. Preaching to you women taught me what it felt like to stand in my power and embody my giftings. From the very bottom of my heart, *thank you.*

Among all of the great spiritual teachers and mentors I've been blessed to know—both contained in this book and outside of it—I'd like to express my deepest gratitude to my husband. The Bible taught me that "love is patient" and "love is kind," but it was you who taught me that love is brave. Loving you is my greatest honor and being loved by you is my greatest privilege.

And to you, the reader: I have dreamed about you for so long. Thank you for reading my book. I grew and learned a lot from its writing. Thank you for the opportunity. I hope it was worth your time.

Stay hopeful, Trisha Fenimore

If you enjoyed this title, please connect with me on Instagram @trishafenimore

Also, please share this title with friends, social media followings and post a review on Amazon, Goodreads, Storygraph, or wherever else.

Other Titles by Trisha Fenimore

Barbed-Wire Sickness: A Short Story about Prison and the Time We All Serve

The Last Tomato on the Vine: A Short Story about Big Government and the Hunger for Freedom

RUN HIDE FIGHT: A Short Story about a School Shooter

STRANGE: A Short Story about Family Estrangement

Before You Leave: A Short Story about Interplanetary Consciousness Travel

Made in the USA
Middletown, DE
10 September 2024

60045134R00309